Whistleblower Law

Whistleblower Law

A Guide to Legal Protections for Corporate Employees

Stephen M. Kohn, Michael D. Kohn, and David K. Colapinto

Westport, Connecticut
London

Library of Congress Cataloging-in-Publication Data

Kohn, Stephen M. (Stephen Martin)
   Whistleblower law : a guide to legal protections for corporate employees /
  Stephen M. Kohn, Michael D. Kohn, and David K. Colapinto.
     p. cm.
   Includes bibliographical references and index.
   ISBN 0–275–98127–4 (alk. paper)
     1. Employees—Dismissal of—Law and legislation—United States.
   2. Discrimination in employment—Law and legislation—United States.
   3. Whistle blowing—Law and legislation—United States.   I. Kohn, Michael
  D. II. Colapinto, David K. III. Title.
  KF3471.K644   2004
  344.7301´2596—dc22   2004052154

British Library Cataloguing in Publication Data is available.

Library of Congress Catalog Card Number: 2004052154
ISBN: 0–275-98127–4

First published in 2004

Praeger Publishers, 88 Post Road West, Westport, CT 06881
An imprint of Greenwood Publishing Group, Inc.
www.praeger.com

Printed in the United States of America

The paper used in this book complies with the
Permanent Paper Standard issued by the National
Information Standards Organization (Z39.48-1984).

10 9 8 7 6 5 4 3 2 1

To Arthur, Max, and Nataleigh Kohn
and
In Memory of Daniel Colapinto

Contents

List of Abbreviations

AIR	Airline Safety Whistleblower Law ("AIR 21")
ALJ	Administrative Law Judge
APA	Administrative Procedure Act
ARB	Administrative Review Board
CAA	Clean Air Act
CERCLA	Comprehensive Environmental Response, Compensation and Liability Act (Superfund)
CFR	Code of Federal Regulations
CRA	Civil Rights Act
D&O	Decision and Order
DOL	Department of Labor
EEOC	Equal Employment Opportunity Commission
EPA	Environmental Protection Agency
ERA	Energy Reorganization Act
FCA	False Claims Act
FIRREA	Financial Institutions Reform, Recovery, and Enforcement Act
FRCP	Federal Rules of Civil Procedure
FRD	Federal Rules Decision
FLSA	Fair Labor Standards Act
FMSA	Federal Mine Safety Act
FOIA	Freedom of Information Act

FSMA	Federal Surface Mining Act
NLRA	National Labor Relations Act
NLRB	National Labor Relations Board
NRC	Nuclear Regulatory Commission
OSHA	Occupational Safety and Health Administration
RCRA	Resource Conservation and Recovery Act
RDO	Recommended Decision and Order
SDWA	Safe Drinking Water Act
SEC	Securities and Exchange Commission
SOL	Secretary of Labor
SOX	Sarbanes-Oxley corporate whistleblower provision
STAA	Surface Transportation Assistance Act
SWDA	Solid Waste Disposal Act
TSCA	Toxic Substances Control Act
USC	United States Code
WPA	Whistleblower Protection Act
WPCA	Water Pollution Control Act

Introduction

On July 30, 2002, as a direct result of the national and international corporate scandals that shocked the investor community and the general public, the Sarbanes-Oxley Act was enacted into law. When he signed the bill, President George Bush characterized the Sarbanes-Oxley Act as "the most far reaching reform of American business practices since the time of Franklin Delano Roosevelt." This sentiment was also echoed in Congress during the final debate on the Wall Street reform law. For example, Senator Mike Enzi (R-WY) described the reform law as "earthshaking" when he urged his follow members of Congress to support the law: "It had to be earthshaking because we are trying to counteract the tremors from the volcanic action of the mountaintop being blown off such companies as Enron, WorldCom, Global Crossing, and others."

The Act was one of the most comprehensive reforms of Wall Street investment practices ever passed by Congress. The law was a direct response to the financial collapse of two major multinational corporations, Enron and WorldCom, and a reaction to the "fraud and greed" that was blamed for these failures. Congress intended that the law would "play a crucial role in restoring trust in the financial markets" by ensuring that "corporate fraud and greed" would be "better detected, prevented and prosecuted."

The law contained numerous provisions increasing oversight of corporate conduct, enhancing criminal penalties for investment fraud, creating new professional responsibilities for corporate attorneys and accountants, and requiring the formation of "audit committees" at all publicly traded companies. The law is also a far-reaching corporate whistleblower law designed to protect employees in publicly traded companies.

When investigations commenced into the corporate misconduct and fraud that caused investors and pensioners to lose billions of dollars in scandal-plagued companies, the public soon learned that employees working in Enron and WorldCom had identified many of the fraudulent practices that ultimately brought down those companies. The public also learned that these employee-whistleblowers lacked legal protections, which contributed to a "corporate culture" of "silence" and caused many of the "tricks" and schemes used by these companies to hide their financial problems to escape any detection either from government regulators or from the investment community. For millions of people who lost money in the scandals, for the first time, the importance of protecting and encouraging whistleblowers became obvious. Public perceptions of whistleblowers would change, and instead of being labeled outsiders or troublemakers, *Time* named three whistleblowers its Persons of the Year for 2002. Two of the three, Cynthia Cooper and Sherron Watkins, were the very employees who had identified and attempted to correct the problems at Enron and WorldCom.

Given this change in the public perception of whistleblowers, it was not surprising that whistleblower protection would be a centerpiece in the Sarbanes-Oxley Act. In fact, the Sarbanes-Oxley Act contained four whistleblower provisions that, taken together, created the most systemic whistleblower protection framework enacted into federal law.

Unlike most whistleblower laws, the Sarbanes-Oxley Act's employee protection clauses were not limited to merely providing a legal remedy for wrongfully discharged employees. In addition to traditional employment discrimination protections, the law required publicly traded corporations to establish procedures to accept internal whistleblower complaints, confidentiality provisions, and provisions that required attorneys who practice before the Securities and Exchange Commission (SEC) to engage in mandatory whistleblowing. Moreover, the statute, for the first time, contained a criminal prohibition against whistleblower retaliation.

For the first time, Congress integrated into one statute a variety of diverse elements necessary for providing adequate whistleblower protection. The key protections contained in Sarbanes-Oxley are briefly described here.

Prohibition against employment discrimination: Section 806 of the Sarbanes-Oxley Act (SOX), 18 U.S.C. 1514A, protects employees of publicly traded companies from retaliation. This antiretaliation provision applies not just to publicly traded corporations, but also their contractors, subcontractors, and agents. SOX protects employees who report allegations of financial fraud or SEC violations. If employees prevail, they are entitled to a full "make whole" remedy and special damages, including reinstatement, back pay, attorney fees and litigation costs, compensatory damages, and interest.

Criminal penalties for discrimination against whistleblowers: SOX amended the obstruction of justice statute and criminalized retaliation against whistleblowers. Employers who retaliate against whistleblowers now face a 10-year prison sentence for intentionally "interfer[ing]" with the "lawful employment or livelihood of any person" who provides "truthful information" to a "law enforcement officer" "relating the commission or possible commission of any Federal offense."

Corporate responsibility to receive whistleblower complaints: For the first time, publicly traded corporations are required to establish internal programs to receive employee whistleblower complaints regarding "accounting" and "auditing matters." The audit committee or other internal program must have procedures protecting the confidentiality of employees who blow the whistle on "questionable accounting and auditing matters." Employees who blow the whistle to these committee/programs cannot be legally subjected to retaliation for making these disclosures.

Attorney whistleblowing: Section 307 of SOX established new rules of conduct for any attorney who appears or practices before the SEC. Under these rules, attorneys (this would include both in-house and outside counsel) are now *mandatory* whistleblowers. As a matter of federal law, Wall Street attorneys must report "evidence of a material violation of securities law" or "breach(es) of fiduciary dut(ies)" or "similar violation(s)" to a corporation's "chief legal counsel," "chief executive officer," or other entities mandated by the SEC.

By enacting these four provisions, Congress intended to fundamentally reform corporate culture. By law, Congress wanted to abolish the "corporate code of silence" that was identified as one of the primary causes of corporate greed and lawlessness.

This "corporate code of silence" not only hampers investigations but also creates a climate where ongoing wrongdoing can occur with virtual impunity. The consequences of this corporate code of silence for investors in publicly traded companies, in particular, and for the stock market, in general, are serious and adverse, and they must be remedied.

Just as Title VII of the Civil Rights Act of 1964 was intended to forever change workplace culture in order to ensure equal employment opportunity for all employees regardless of race, sex, religion, or national origin, the Sarbanes-Oxley Act was intended to alter the workplace culture facing employees in publicly traded companies. Congress wanted employees to serve the investor community in an honest manner, and created a legal framework that encourages whistleblowing. All four of the whistleblower provisions contained in Sarbanes-Oxley were intended to achieve this goal. First, by criminalizing retaliation in egregious cases, Congress intended to send a strong message that the mistreatment of employee whistleblowers was no longer acceptable conduct. Next, Congress mandated that an internal reporting structure be created, which permitted employees to anonymously report wrongdoing to an independent committee and required attorneys to make various whistleblower disclosures within their organization.

Third, Congress turned its eye toward the conduct of corporate attorneys, who often knew of the fraudulent schemes and practices. Congress altered the ethical and legal duties placed on attorneys who practiced law in SEC proceedings. These attorneys became obligated to actually report wrongdoing. The attorneys were obligated to "blow the whistle" on improper corporate practices.

Finally, the heart of these whistleblower protections was incorporated into section 806 of the Corporate and Criminal Fraud Accountability Act, Title VII of the Sarbanes-Oxley Act. This section, referred to throughout the book as the "SOX," created an administrative and civil remedy for whistleblowers. Unlike the criminal provisions of Sarbanes-Oxley, which require that a government prosecutor file a formal case, the SOX provisions are predicated on a private right of action. Specifically, the employee can initiate the SOX proceeding and have his or her case heard in a formal adjudicatory process. These civil and administrative remedies provide meaningful protections. For example, if an employee provides information to the "audit committee," that employee has engaged in protected activity under the SOX and, if retaliated against, can pursue a private claim for reinstatement or monetary damages. Similarly, the attorneys who now must report instances of fraud would be protected from discipline and discharge when they engage in the whistleblowing activity. In short, the SOX provisions tie together all of the diverse whistleblower protection clauses and mandate that the U.S. Department of Labor and the federal courts provide meaningful protection for corporate whistleblowers.

What makes the Sarbanes-Oxley Act so significant is not only its broad coverage (i.e., all publicly traded companies and their contractors and agents), but that it was Congress' first attempt to integrate into one law a meaningful systemic approach to corporate whistleblowing—an approach not only designed to protect employees who "blow the whistle," but designed to change and reform the corporate "code of silence." Congress's intent in passing corporate whistleblower protections was clear: "U.S. laws need to encourage and protect those who report fraudulent activity that can damage innocent investors in publicly traded companies." It is now up to the SEC, the Department of Labor, and the federal courts to ensure that Congress's intent is carried out.

The purpose of this book is to carefully review the judicial and administrative precedents and procedures that were enacted into law by the SOX. Only if employees, employers, and government regulators fully understand the dynamic case law and regulations that implement the SOX, can the law achieve its intended purposes. As set forth in this book, the SOX provisions were not written on a blank slate. There was a 30-year history of whistleblower protection laws in government and other areas of the economy. Congress took from these other laws certain critical elements and integrated them into the SOX. The authors have carefully reviewed this background, in light of the SOX's statutory language, legislative history, and administrative regulations, and fully explain how the law works and what rights are created and what obligations are placed on publicly traded companies and their employees.

Legislative History of SOX Whistleblower Protections

On May 6, 2002, the Senate Judiciary Committee unanimously reported its findings and proposed reform legislation regarding the Enron corporate corruption scandal. Less then three months later the Judiciary Committee's legislative proposal, which included a corporate whistleblower protection provision, was incorporated into the final version of the Sarbanes-Oxley Act, by a 97-0 vote in the U.S. Senate.[1] The Judiciary Committee's whistleblower provision was approved, verbatim, by the full U.S. Congress on July 25, 2002, and enacted into law by President George Bush on July 30, 2002.[2]

The Judiciary Committee's report on its corporate reform proposal found that "investors and pensioners" were being robbed by "highly educated professionals" who had spun an "intricate spider's web of deceit." These corporations "valued profit over honesty" and had "cook[ed] the books and trick[ed]" the public and federal regulators. The auditors hired by the companies were no better and "deceived the investing public and reaped millions for select few insiders." Together, Enron and its accountants from the Anderson accounting firm were able to take "advantage of a system that allowed them to behave" in a "fraudulent manner" and "engage in both the destruction of valuable evidence and retaliation against potential witnesses."[3]

Beyond just Enron's collapse, t he Judiciary Committee recognized that the entire system designed to ensure trust and honesty within the investment community had failed. "Instead of acting as gatekeepers who detect and deter fraud . . . accountants and lawyers brought all their skills and knowledge to bear in assisting the fraud to succeed and then in covering it up." There were major problems systemic to the corporate culture that encouraged greed and punished any employee who attempted to expose or correct the fraudulent activities. The regulatory system itself was broken:

> Many people and institutions contributed to the Enron debacle, including the corporate officers and directors whose actions led to Enron's failure, the well-paid professionals who helped create, carry out, and cover up the complicated corporate ruse when they should have been raising concerns, the regulators who did not protect the public or our public markets, and the Congress and the courts, which have thrown obstacles in the way of securities fraud victims. . . . Without discipline, professionalism, an effective legal structure, and the accountability, greed can run rampant, with devastating results.

The Committee found that a "corporate culture" existed that discouraged and prevented employees from acting honestly or reporting wrongdoing. The problems facing employees who uncovered fraud at firms such as Enron and Arthur Anderson were documented. For example, when one top executive at Enron, Sherron Watkins, "attempted to report or 'blow the whisle' on fraud," Enron's executives obtained legal advice on the "possible risks associated with discharging employees who report allegations of improper accounting practices." The lawyers told Enron that under current law, it could simply fire the whistleblower. Congress was outraged by this response: "In other words, after this high level employee at Enron reported improper accounting practices, Enron did not consider firing Anderson [the accounting company engaged in the fraud]; rather, the company sought advice on the legality of discharging the whistleblower."

In addition to the Watkins case, the Committee identified credible public reports of other corporate whistleblowers facing retaliation for exposing fraud and deceit. These cases included reports that a Paine Webber financial advisor was fired after recommending that Enron stocks be sold; a corporate risk assessment official complained that he was fired for "repeatedly warning" that Enron was engaging in "improprieties"; and an outside accountant lost a valuable account after expressing "reservations about [Arthur Anderson's] financial practices."

Congress recognized that "corporate whistleblowers are left unprotected under current law." This was considered a "significant deficiency" because whistleblowers were "insiders" and often were "firsthand witnesses to the fraud." Only whistleblowers were in the position to know "who knew what and when" or provide other crucial information needed in "all complex securities fraud investigations." The need to protect whistleblowers was obvious:

> These examples [i.e., of whistleblower discrimination] further expose a culture, supported by law, which discourages employees from reporting fraudulent behavior not only to the proper authorities, such as the FBI and the SEC, but even internally. This "corporate code of silence" not only hampers investigations, but also creates a climate where ongoing wrongdoing can occur with virtual impunity. The consequences of this corporate code of silence for investigators in publicly traded companies in particular, and for the stock market in general, are serious and adverse, and they must be remedied. . . .
>
> Although current law protects many government employees who act in the public interest by reporting wrongdoing, there is no similar protection for employees of publicly traded companies who blow the whistle on fraud and protect investors. . . . Unfortunately, as demonstrated in the tobacco industry litigation and the Enron case, efforts to quiet whistleblowers and retaliate against them for being "disloyal" or "litigation risks" transcend state lines. This corporate culture must change, and the law can lead the way. That is why [the Senate bill] is supported by public interest advocates, such as the National Whistleblower Center . . . who have called this bill "the single most effective measure possible to prevent recurrences of the Enron debacle and similar threats to the nation's financial markets."

Thus, whistleblower protection reforms became one of the centerpieces of the Wall Street corporate reform legislation that would pass Congress in July 2002: "The Enron debacle has arrived on our doorstep, and our job is to make sure that there are adequate doses of accountability in our legal system to prevent such occurrences in the future, and to offer a constructive remedy and decisive punishment should they occur. The time has come for Congress to rethink and reform our laws in order to prevent corporate deceit, to protect investors and to restore full confidence in the capital markets."

The SOX was originally drafted by the Senate Judiciary Committee as Section 806 of the Corporate and Criminal Fraud Accountability Act of 2002. The Committee's intent in drafting the law was unmistakable. It was concerned about "companies with a corporate culture that punishes whistleblowers." The law needed to be changed in order to "encourage and protect" employees who disclosed fraudulent activity:

> Section 806 of the Act would provide whistleblower protection to employees of publicly traded companies who report acts of fraud to federal officials with the authority to remedy the wrongdoing or to supervisors or appropriate individuals within their company. Although current law protects many government employees who act in the public interest by reporting wrongdoing, there is no similar protection for employees of publicly traded companies who blow the whistle on fraud and protect investors. With an unprecedented portion of the American public investing in these companies and depending upon their honesty, this distinction does not serve the public good.

The whistleblower provision, which was unanimously passed by the Judiciary Committee, was incorporated into the larger Sarbanes-Oxley Act as part of the Leahy-McCain amendment. The amendment was adopted by the Senate by a 97-0 vote during the summer of 2002.[4] Senator Patrick Leahy, the principal sponsor of the whistleblower law, explained its meaning on the floor of the Senate just prior to the Senate's passage of the final version of the Sarbanes-Oxley Act by a 99-0 vote:

> We include(ed) meaningful protections for corporate whistleblowers, as passed by the Senate. We learned from Sherron Watkins of Enron that these corporate insiders are the key witnesses that need to be encouraged to report fraud and help prove it in court. Enron wanted to silence her as a whistleblower because Texas law would allow them to do it. Look what they [Enron] were doing on this chart. There is no way we could have known about this without that kind of a whistleblower. . . . The provisions Senator Grassley and I worked out in Judiciary Committee make sure whistleblowers are protected.[5]

According to its legislative history, the SOX whistleblower law was directly modeled on prior Congressional attempts to protect whistleblowers. As noted by one DOL judge, "the whistleblower provision of Sarbanes-Oxley is similar to whistleblower provisions found in many other federal statutes. Since the Sarbanes-Oxley Act is relatively new, reference to case authority interpreting other whistleblowers statutes is appropriate."[6] Since 1972 Congress had granted jurisdiction to the U.S. Department of Labor (DOL) to adjudicate whistleblower claims under the Federal Water Pollution Control Act.[7] Thereafter, Congress utilized that model to provide whistleblower protection to employees under other environmental laws, the Energy Reorganization Act, the Surface Transportation Act, and the airline safety law. Under these precedents, the DOL had established a four-part mechanism for protecting whistleblowers. First, OSHA would conduct a preliminary investigation into the merits of a case and issue preliminary findings. Second, the parties would be entitled to a *de novo* review of their claims before a DOL Administrative Law Judge (ALJ). As part of this process, the parties would be afforded discovery and a full on-the-record public hearing. Third, ALJ's ruling was subject to an appeal within the DOL. Initially those appeals were heard directly by the Secretary of Labor, but in 1996 the Secretary established the Administrative Review Board (ARB) to adjudicate these appeals. Finally, any party could seek judicial review of a final order of the DOL in the U.S. Court of Appeals for the circuit in which the violation of the law occurred.

When Congress enacted the SOX, these DOL procedures were adopted verbatim. In fact, Congress incorporated by reference the administrative procedures contained in the airline safety law, the most recent of the various DOL-based corporate whistleblower laws enacted prior to the SOX.

In addition to procedurally copying its prior DOL-administered whistleblower procedures, Congress also intended that the substantive legal principles applicable to these other corporate whistleblower laws also be applicable to the SOX. In its report, the Senate Judiciary Committee summarized the scope of the new law and referenced its prior DOL enactments:

> This section would provide whistleblower protection to employees of publicly traded companies. It specifically protects them when they take lawful acts to disclose information or otherwise assist criminal investigators, federal regulators, Congress, supervisors (or other proper people within a corporation), or parties in a judicial

proceeding in detecting and stopping fraud. If the employer does take illegal action in retaliation for lawful and protected conduct, subsection (b) allows the employee to file a complaint with the Department of Labor, to be governed by the same procedures and burdens of proof now applicable in the whistleblower law in the aviation industry.

Congress also adopted the "reasonable belief" test used in the other DOL-administered whistleblower laws. Under this test, an employee-whistleblower would not have to prove that his or her allegations of misconduct were in fact correct. Congress cited directly to a Water Pollution Control Act decision issued by the U.S. Court of Appeals for the Third Circuit as guidance in interpreting the "reasonable belief" test under SOX. In that case the Court held that a whistleblower's subjective reason for exposing misconduct was not relevant to a proceeding. Instead, it was the employer's motive that was "under scrutiny," and the courts would protect employees even if their allegations were "ill-formed." The reasonable belief test was set forth as follows:

[A]n employee's non-frivolous complaint should not have to be guaranteed to withstand the scrutiny of in-house or external review in order to merit protection under [the whistleblower law] for the obvious reason that such a standard would chill employee initiatives in bringing to light perceived discrepancies in the workings of their agency.

Congress also looked to a key provision of the Whistleblower Protection Act of 1989 (WPA) in drafting the SOX. The WPA enacted whistleblower protections for most federal government employees. In its report on the SOX, the Judiciary Committee noted that most corporate whistleblowers were unprotected under federal law, whereas Congress had specifically provided remedies for federal employees. Congress wanted to cure this inadequacy:

Although current law protects many government employees who act in the public interest by reporting wrongdoing, there is no similar protection for employees of publicly traded companies who blow the whistle on fraud and protect investors. With an unprecedented portion of the American public investing in these companies and depending upon their honesty, this distinction does not serve the public good.

In drafting the SOX, Congress looked specifically at the legal standard of proof for demonstrating illegal retaliation first enacted into law in the WPA, and incorporated that standard directly into the SOX.

The WPA standard was crafted by Congress in 1989 and set forth a special burden of proof for evaluating whether employees should obtain protection under the WPA. Instead of ratifying the various burdens of proof established by the Supreme Court in traditional employment discrimination law, Congress created an entirely new procedure for whistleblower cases. This test significantly lowered the burden of proof for whistleblowers.

Under the WPA test, in order to obtain protection as a whistleblower, an employee only needed to establish that his or her protected activity was a "contributing factor" in an adverse action. Requirements set forth in prior judicial rulings requiring that employees demonstrate that discriminatory animus was a "motivating" or "significant" factor in an adverse action were specifically rejected. Instead of demonstrating that animus was the "motivating" factor, an employee would only have to prove that the animus was a "contributing" factor, regardless of how small the contribution.

Once an employee demonstrated that animus was a "contributing factor," the burden of proof to demonstrate that a legitimate business reason justified the adverse action was also changed. Employers would be required to demonstrate by "clear and convincing evidence" that they would have taken the same adverse action even if the employee had not blown the whistle.

Because the "contributing factor" test made it easier for employees to prove their discrimination cases, and more difficult for an employer to prove it did not retaliate, the new standard was initially challenged by the Executive Branch during the 1988-1989 debate over the WPA. The Department of Justice, which represented federal government employers, initially opposed the new standard of proof. However, after a compromise was reached on the WPA, the Justice Department dropped its opposition and Congress unanimously approved the "contributing factor test."

In its Joint Explanatory Statement regarding the WPA, the law's sponsors summarized the importance of the new "contributing factor" test applicable to whistleblower claims:

> By reducing the excessively heavy burden imposed on the employee under current case law, the legislation will send a strong, clear signal

to whistleblowers that Congress intends that they be protected from any retaliation related to their whistleblowing and an equally clear message to those who would discourage whistleblowers from coming forward that reprisals of any kind will not be tolerated. Whistleblowing should never be a factor that contributes in any way to an adverse personnel action. . . .

If an employee shows by a preponderance of the evidence that whistleblowing was a contributing factor in a personnel action, the agency action may be upheld only if the agency can demonstrate, by clear and convincing evidence, that it would have taken the same action in the absence of the whistleblowing. . . . "Clear and convincing evidence" is a high burden of proof for the Government to bear. It is intended as such.[8]

After 1989, Congress incorporated the "contributing factor" test into other whistleblower protection statutes, including the Energy Reorganization Act, banking whistleblower laws, and the airline safety whistleblower law. When Congress passed the SOX, it explicitly adopted the "contributing factor" test as the controlling legal analysis for adjudicating corporate whistleblower claims. Congress required that both the DOL and the federal courts apply this test in evaluating the merits of a SOX whistleblower case.[9]

The SOX employee protection provision contained two procedural changes not found in all the other DOL-administered laws. First, in order to ensure that wrongfully discharged employees would not be prejudiced by the delays often found in civil court proceedings, Congress authorized the DOL to immediately require the reinstatement of any employee it determined was wrongfully fired, even before the parties had their claims heard before a judge. This procedure was contained in the trucking and airline whistleblower laws, but not in the environmental and nuclear whistleblower laws.

The second procedural change was unique to the SOX. Under the prior DOL-administered laws, an employee was required to adjudicate his or her claim within the DOL, regardless of how long the administrative process lasted. Sometimes cases would languish within the DOL for years. To prevent this problem under the SOX, employees were provided a right to refile their claims in federal district court if they exhausted their administrative remedies within the DOL and if the DOL did not issue a final order within 180 days. Thus, provided that an employee initially filed within the DOL, litigated their case within the DOL for at least 180 days, and did not engage in any "bad faith" conduct to delay the DOL proceeding, the employee could directly file his or her case in federal court, if the DOL failed to issue a final order at the time of the federal court filing. Congress summarized this aspect of the law as follows:

> Under new protections provided by the Act, if the employer does take illegal action in retaliation for such lawful and protected conduct, subsection (b) allows the employee to elect to file an administrative complaint at the Department of Labor, as is the case for employees who provide assistance in aviation safety. Only if there is not final agency decision within 180 days of the complaint (and such delay is not shown to be due to the bad faith of the claimant) may he or she may bring a de novo case in federal court with a jury trial available (See United States Constitution, Amendment VII; Title 42 United States Code, Section 1983). Should such a case be brought in federal court, it is intended that the same burdens of proof which would have governed in the Department of Labor will continue to govern the action.

This provision of the law was intended to ensure that SOX whistleblower cases were adjudicated in a fair and timely manner. If the DOL process did not work, or did not provide employees with adequate due process rights to fully and fairly present their claims, employees were provided with a meaningful escape clause. Although free to remain within the DOL and have their cases heard before a DOL judge, employees were provided with the right to refile a case in federal court after the 180-day exhaustion requirement was satisfied.

Both in the Congressional history explaining the law and the actual language of the statute itself, Congress's intent to both protect and encourage whistleblowing was clear. Based on this history, both the DOL and the federal courts should broadly construe the language of the statute in order to effectuate remedial purposes.[10] It is well settled that a "narrow" or "hypertechnical" interpretation of whistleblower laws, such as the SOX, "will do little to effect" the statute's remedial purposes.[11] The courts recognize that whistleblowing "may expose not just private harms" but "hazards to the public."[12] In accordance with this underlying philosophy, the DOL has ruled that its obligation in whistleblower cases was "not simply provide a forum for private parties to litigate their private employment discrimination suits." The DOL also had an obligation to represent the "public interest."[13]

In a whistleblower case decided by the U.S. Court of Appeals for the 6th Circuit, the court noted that "under this anti-discrimination provision . . . the need for broad construction of the statutory purpose can well be characterized as 'necessary to prevent the [government's] channels of information from being dried up by employer intimidation.'"[14] This holding was also supported by a decision of the Third Circuit in *Passaic Valley Sewerage Commissioners v Department of Labor*. In that case, the Court noted that other courts of appeal had "consistently construed" the whistleblower statutes "to lend broad coverage."[15] The *Passaic Valley* case was favorably cited in the Senate Judiciary Committee report on the SOX.

Congress's intent behind the passage of the Sarbanes-Oxley Act was favorably cited by DOL judges in early SOX whistleblower cases. For example, DOL Judge Stuart A. Levin rejected a corporate request to dismiss a SOX whistleblower case on a narrow technicality by referencing the legislative history that gave rise to the corporate reform law:

> [S]hortly before, and contemporaneous with, its enactment, accounting scandals in some circles were causing painful economic dislocations among investors, lenders, and employees of several major firms and undermining investor confidence in the integrity of financial markets. Finding the status quo unacceptable, Congress set about to refashion the regulatory and private sector environments which had failed to detect or affirmatively allowed deception in reporting of corporate value and performance and permitted the types of shenanigans which brought several large concerns down in ruins and rocked others to their very foundations. To prevent the recurrence of such chicanery in the future, Congress examined the ethical standards and accounting and reporting systems flaws and failures which, in some instances, allowed fraud to flourish. Intent upon reforming the regulatory and private sector environments which allowed the fleecing to take place, Congress was determined to reassure the markets that effective preventive and exposure measures could be formulated, and it turned, among other remedies, to a valuable deterrent resource it had used in the past to help insure compliance with its mandates: employees within an organization who were willing to blow the whistle. Congress has long employed the inside whistleblower as a first line of defense against various types of abuses which it deems unacceptable. Moreover, it understands the risks it beckons the whistleblower to accept, and it endeavors to protect them. Under such circumstances, it does not serve the purposes or policies of the act to take too pinched a view of

the remedial statue when it comes to protecting those in an organization who can address the concerns Congress sought to correct.[16]

These DOL and court precedents broadly interpreting other whistleblower laws are well suited to protecting corporate whistleblowers who are covered by the SOX. By explaining in the SOX legislative history that the primary purpose of the law was to change corporate culture that resulted in widespread fraud and greed, Congress sent a strong message to Wall Street and corporate America. In order to achieve the goal of restoring investor confidence in corporate America, Congress took some of the stronger provisions of other whistleblower statutes to create effective civil remedies available to protect employees under the law.

SOX Complaints and Investigations

Under the Sarbanes-Oxley corporate whistleblower protection law (SOX), any employee[1] who alleges that he or she was retaliated against for "blowing the whistle" on SEC violations or shareholder fraud must file a written complaint with the U.S. Department of Labor (DOL) within 90 days of the alleged discriminatory conduct.[2] The Occupational Safety and Health Administration (OSHA) was delegated the responsibility for receiving employee complaints under SOX and investigating SOX claims and issued an interim rule governing these procedures on May 28, 2003.[3] This interim rule may be modified when the Department of Labor issues final regulations on the SOX. All DOL regulations related to the SOX may be found at http://www.whistleblowers.org/html/sarbanes-oxley.html. This includes the full text of the Sarbanes-Oxley law, the DOL adjudicatory regulations (which are not interim), and the interim procedural rules for filing claims with OSHA. When published, the final OSHA rules shall also be posted at this site. Both OSHA and the Department of Labor Office of Administrative Law Judges also sponsor Web sites that include postings of relevant DOL regulations.[4]

THE COMPLAINT

Unlike a civil action filed in federal court, an employee is under no obligation to serve his or her initial complaint on the employer.

Instead, after the complaint is filed, OSHA is required to serve a copy of the complaint or other information related to the filing of the complaint upon both the employer and the Securities and Exchange Commission (SEC).[5] The complaint is deemed filed when mailed, e-mailed, faxed, or filed in person at a DOL OSHA office.[6] The address for filing a complaint with the U.S. Department of Labor is

> Assistant Secretary for Occupational Safety and Health
> U.S. Department of Labor
> 200 Constitution Avenue, N.W.
> Washington, D.C. 20210

Under the regulations, the DOL encourages employees to file the complaint with their local OSHA office.[7] Addresses and telephone numbers for local OSHA offices may be found at the OSHA Web site: http://www.osha.gov. Once a complaint is filed, the employee should verify that the complaint was actually received by OSHA.

The complaint must be written, can be simple, and should include a full statement of the acts and omissions, with pertinent dates, that are believed to constitute the violation.[8] A Department of Labor whistleblower complaint need not set forth "every element of a legal cause of action."[9] In *Richter et al. v Baldwin Associates*,[10] the Secretary of Labor (SOL) held that such a complaint is "not a formal pleading setting forth every legal cause of action," but rather is an "informal complaint." After a complaint has been filed, it may be amended or supplemented to address events that occurred subsequent to the original filing.[11]

Although the initial complaint can be simple, an employee should fully augment or supplement the basis for the complaint during the OSHA investigatory process. Employers have relied upon limitations in the complaint as a basis for filing motions for dismissal once a case is docketed for a formal administrative adjudication.[12]

The traditional practice during the OSHA investigatory process is for an employee to supplement his or her complaint with a formal signed statement provided to the OSHA investigator. This practice is reflected under the DOL rules for SOX investigations. Under these rules, after a complaint is filed, the complaint may be "supplemented as appropriate by interviews of the complainant."[13] The final OSHA determination is not limited to the information contained in a complaint, but is based on "all of the relevant information collected during the investigation."[14]

THE FILING DEADLINE/STATUTE OF LIMITATIONS

A SOX case must be filed within 90 days of the alleged discriminatory action. The failure to comply with this deadline will result in the dismissal of a complaint, regardless of the underlying merits of the claim.[15] However, because a statute of limitations is "not jurisdictional" in nature, under limited circumstances an employee's deadline for filing a claim "may be extended when fairness requires."[16]

The regulations define the 90-day filing period as follows: "Within 90 days after an alleged violation of the Act occurs (i.e., when the discriminatory decision has been both made and communicated to the complainant), an employee who believes that he or she has been discriminated against in violation of the Act may file, or have filed by any person on the employee's behalf, a complaint alleging such discrimination."[17]

In determining the amount of time an employee has to file a complaint, the first issue concerns a determination on which day the 90-day period commences running—that is, the "date a complainant discovers he has been injured."[18] It is now well settled that a statute of limitations for filing a DOL whistleblower complaint commences running when an employee has "final and unequivocal notice" that a decision has in fact been made to take adverse action, not on the date the decision is implemented.[19] In other words, in counting the 90-day time period, the "filing period commences" to run on the date an employee is informed of a final adverse action, not on the date on which the impact of the adverse action is felt.[20] This rule was set forth in *Belt v United States Enrichment Corp.*:

> In whistleblower cases, statutes of limitation . . . run from the date an employee receives "final, definitive, and unequivocal notice" of an adverse employment decision. "Final" and "definitive" notice denotes communication that is decisive or conclusive, i.e. leaving no further chance for action, discussion, or change. "Unequivocal" notice means communication that is not ambiguous, i.e. free of misleading possibilities. . . . The date that an employer communicates to the employee its intent to implement an adverse employment decision marks the occurrence of a violation, rather than the date the employee experiences the consequences.[21]

Although the notification of adverse action and its negative impact often occur on the same day, employees must be aware of a number of circumstances in which a delay in implementing an adverse action can significantly impact on a filing deadline.

A common scenario that results in the inadvertent waiver of a claim occurs when management delays the negative impact of an adverse action. For example, when an employee is informed that he or she is being terminated, but is provided 60 days to find a new position within the company, the statute of limitations commences on the day the employee is informed of the termination, not after the 60-day time period for relocating is expired.[22] In a similar vein, an employee's utilization of an internal grievance or arbitration process does not extend a filing period.[23]

EXTENDING THE TIME PERIOD FOR FILING A COMPLAINT

If an employee fails to file a claim within the 90-day statute of limitations, there are a limited number of methods by which the filing deadline may be enlarged. But the grounds for extending a limitations period are "narrowly applied."[24] The basic theories used to enlarge a filing period are equitable tolling,[25] equitable estoppel,[26] fraudulent concealment,[27] or "continuing violation."[28]

In *School Dist. of Allentown v Marshall*[29] the court set forth the three basic fact patterns often used in justifying equitable tolling: (1) The defendant has actively misled the plaintiff respecting the cause of action; (2) the plaintiff has in some extraordinary way been prevented from asserting his rights; or (3) the plaintiff has raised the precise statutory claim in issue but has mistakenly done so in the wrong forum. Even if tolling is justified, an employee still must "bring suit within a reasonable time after he has obtained, or by due diligence could have obtained, the necessary information."[30]

In addition to various theories that may justify tolling a statute of limitations, the other major method used to enlarge a filing deadline is the continuing violation theory. The continuing violation theory cannot be applied to "discrete acts." Specifically, an employee must file a timely complaint when he or she suffers from a discrete act of discrimination, such as a "termination, failure to promote, denial of transfer, or refusal to hire."[31] In *National Railroad v Morgan* the Supreme Court clarified this rule:

[D]iscrete discriminatory acts are not actionable if time barred, even when they are related to acts alleged in timely filed charges. Each discrete discriminatory act starts a new clock for filing charges. . . . The existence of past acts and the employee's prior knowledge of their occurrence, however, does not bar employees from filing charges about related discrete acts. . . . Nor does the statute bar an employee from using the prior acts as background evidence in support of a timely claim.[32]

Hostile work environment claims are subject to the continuing violation theory.[33] The Supreme Court recognized that such claims are not predicated on "discrete acts," but occur over a period of "days or perhaps years" and constitute acts of harassment that may not be actionable standing alone.[34]

Although the Supreme Court did not address the issue in *National Railroad*,[35] the DOL and most courts apply the continuing violation theory in cases in which the discriminatory action is part of an ongoing policy or "pattern or practice" of retaliation. In a whistleblower case under a DOL-administered antiretaliation statute similar to the SOX, the U.S. Court of Appeals for the Second Circuit set forth the rule governing the continuing violation theory:

Under the continuing violation standard, a timely charge with respect to any incident of discrimination in furtherance of a policy of discrimination renders claims against other discriminatory actions taken pursuant to that policy timely, even if they would be untimely if standing alone. . . . Thus, in cases where a plaintiff proves i) an underlying discriminatory policy or practice, and ii) an action taken pursuant to that policy during the statutory period preceding the filing of the complaint, the continuing violation rule shelters claims for all other actions taken pursuant to the same policy from the limitations period.[36]

OSHA INVESTIGATION

After a complaint is filed, OSHA has 60 days to conduct an investigation into the merits of the charges.[37] Although OSHA investigatory findings are subject to *de novo* review, OSHA's findings are very significant. First, under the law, an employee is entitled to an order of preliminary reinstatement if they prevail during the OSHA investigation. This order is "effective immediately," and may not be subject to a stay or a delay in its implementation pending appeal.[38]

A preliminary order from OSHA reinstating an employee can be enforced, if necessary, in federal court.[39] Under such circumstances, the district courts have granted motions for preliminary injunctions requiring the immediate reinstatement of employees pending the final administrative adjudicatory results.

Second, the OSHA investigation provides an opportunity for the parties to obtain initial discovery. Although the investigation is *ex parte* in nature, the results of OSHA's investigation and its investigatory record are discoverable.[40] After the investigation is completed, the complainant can (and should) obtain a copy of the investigatory file through use of the Freedom of Information Act (FOIA) and Privacy Act.[41] If OSHA fails to release portions of its file pursuant to a FOIA exemption, the information provided to OSHA is discoverable directly from the party that provided the materials to OSHA. Although OSHA's legal findings are not admissible as evidence in an adjudicatory hearing, these findings are often very helpful in accessing potential weaknesses or strengths in a case. Witness statements and other materials contained in the investigatory file have been effectively used for examining witnesses during the formal hearing process.

For example, in one SOX case the employee introduced into evidence a letter the employer wrote to OSHA setting forth the company's position on the retaliation case. Although OSHA credited the letter and ruled against the employee, at the hearing the letter became a central piece of evidence *against* the employer. Specifically, at the hearing witnesses for the employer contradicted the explanation set forth in the employer's letter to OSHA. The ALJ found that the conflict created a "substantial inconsistency" that "harm[ed]" the employer's "credibility in general" and specifically impeached the employer's credibility on a critical factual dispute. Additionally, in the same case the DOJ judge admitted into evidence witness statements provided to the OSHA investigator.[42] Admission of such statements in SOX proceedings is appropriate inasmuch as the administrative hearing officer is not bound by the hearsay rule. 29 C.F.R. 1980.107(d) (formal rules of evidence do not apply in SOX proceedings).

Third, OSHA has discretion to intervene in the case if either party files a request for a fully adjudicatory hearing. The benefits of having OSHA participate on behalf of an employee during the hearing process are obvious. OSHA's support for a complaint can facilitate an expeditious resolution of a case.

OSHA will investigate SOX complaints on a priority basis, although an employer need not file a formal answer.[43] If OSHA fails to conduct an investigation or dismisses a complaint on improper grounds prior to the completion of an investigation, the administrative law judge (ALJ) or the Administrative Review Board have, from time to time, remanded the case to OSHA for an investigation.[44] However, such remands are the exception to the typical practice and are usually not permitted.[45]

If OSHA fails to complete its investigation in a timely manner, an employee may file a request for a hearing based on the constructive denial of the complaint. The Office of Administrative Law Judges will deny a constructive denial appeal if the complainant did not provide OSHA with a reasonable period of time, beyond the 60-day statutory time period for conducting investigations, to complete its review. An employee should make a "showing of prejudice" at the time he or she files a constructive appeal.[46] The failure of OSHA to adhere to the time constraints imposed under the SOX statute or regulations is not grounds for the dismissal of a complaint. Additionally, because of the *de novo* nature of the hearing process, "flaws" in the investigative process are not grounds for either remand or the reversal of an OSHA finding.[47]

INVESTIGATION PROCEDURES
FOR CORPORATE WHISTLEBLOWERS

After a complaint is filed, OSHA will typically assign the case to a field office investigator. The investigator will review the complaint and its supporting materials in order to ensure that the employee has alleged a prima facie case. If an employee cannot allege the elements of a cause of action, OSHA will terminate its investigation and issue a finding of dismissal.[48] Before dismissing a complaint, the OSHA investigator will contact the employee and determine whether the complaint can be supplemented by additional information in order to meet the prima facie case requirements. The OSHA investigator will review the materials submitted by the complainant (including the statement provided by the employee) and determine whether the following allegations were sufficiently pled:

1. The employee engaged in a protected activity or conduct;

2. The employer or the person named in the complaint knew or suspected, actually or constructively, that the employee engaged in the protected activity;
3. The employee suffered an unfavorable personnel action; and
4. The circumstances were sufficient to raise the inference that the protected activity was a contributing factor in the unfavorable action.[49]

Thus, when drafting an initial complaint and/or a formal statement by the complainant, it is important that these four items be addressed. If employee fails to make this "required showing," the employee will be notified that his complaint is being dismissed and no investigation will be conducted.[50]

After OSHA determines that an employee has set forth a prima facie case, the employer is notified and requested to set forth its position on the complainant's allegations. Under the regulations, "within 20 days of receipt of the notice of the filing of the complaint, the named person may submit to the Assistant Secretary [i.e., the OSHA investigator] a written statement and any affidavits or documents substantiating its position. Within the same 20 days, the named person may request a meeting with the Assistant Secretary to present its position."[51] If, on the basis of these filings, the employer can demonstrate, "by clear and convincing evidence that it would have taken the same unfavorable personnel action in the absence of the complainant's protected behavior or conduct," OSHA will not formally investigate the case and will issue a finding dismissing the complaint.[52]

If the employee can set forth a prima facie case, and if the employer cannot meet its burden of proof on the basis of its initial filings, OSHA will conduct a formal investigation of the complaint.[53] There are no formal rules for the OSHA investigation, but typically OSHA will conduct interviews of witnesses identified by either party. Normally, the identity of witnesses is not secret, but OSHA can grant witnesses confidentiality in accordance with DOL rule 29 C.F.R. Part 70.[54]

Because OSHA has the authority to order an employee reinstated prior to a hearing, an employer is entitled to additional due process rights. Before OSHA can issue a preliminary reinstatement order, OSHA is required to provide the employer an opportunity to learn the basis of OSHA's findings, and an opportunity to comment on those findings. Under the SOX administrative regulations, an employer is entitled to the following notification by OSHA:

Prior to the issuance of . . . a preliminary order . . . if the Assistant Secretary [i.e., OSHA] has reasonable cause, on the basis of information gathered under the procedures of this part, to believe that the named person [the employer] has violated the Act and that preliminary reinstatement is warranted, the Assistant Secretary will again contact the named person to give notice of the substance of the relevant evidence supporting the complainant's allegations as developed during the course of the investigation. This evidence includes any witness statements, which will be redacted to protect the identity of confidential informants where statements were given in confidence; if the statements cannot be redacted without revealing the identity of confidential informants, summaries of their contents will be provided. The named person will be given the opportunity to submit a written response, to meet with the investigators to present statements from witnesses in support of its position, and to present legal and factual arguments. The named person will be directed to present this evidence within ten business days of the Assistant Secretary's notification pursuant to this paragraph, or as soon afterwards as the Assistant Secretary and the named person can agree, if the interests of justice so require.[55]

INVESTIGATORY FINDINGS AND APPEAL

After 60 days, OSHA must issue written findings on the merits of the complaint.[56] The DOL is required to notify each party of its appeal rights.[57] If OSHA dismisses the complaint, it will notify the parties of this finding, usually by certified mail.[58] If OSHA determines that "reasonable cause" exists to support a finding that the employer violated the law, OSHA must issue a preliminary order granting relief to the employee.[59] If appealed, the preliminary order is automatically stayed, except that portion of the order that mandates that the employee be immediately reinstated. An employee is entitled to reinstatement based solely on the preliminary OSHA findings.[60] Employers' requests to obtain a stay of preliminary orders have been uniformly rejected.[61] Except in regard to a preliminary order of reinstatement, an OSHA finding is non-binding if either party appeals,[62] and "once a hearing has been requested, the investigated findings . . . carry no weight either before the ALJ or the Board [ARB]."[63]

In order to appeal the OSHA findings, a party must, "within thirty days of receipt" of the OSHA findings,[64] file written "objections and a request for a hearing on the record" to the DOL Chief

Administrative Law Judge in Washington, D.C.[65] The "objections" and "request for hearing" "must be in writing and state whether the objection is to the findings, the preliminary order, and/or whether there should be an award of attorneys' fees."[66] Failure to file a timely appeal can result in a party automatically losing his or her appeal.[67] If an appeal is not filed and received by the DOL within the 30-day period, the OSHA determination becomes the final decision of the SOL.[68] Moreover, unless an administrative appeal is filed, a party cannot seek judicial review of the OSHA determination.[69]

The 30-day filing deadline for the appeal is subject to equitable tolling.[70]

The address for filing the "objections and request for hearing" is

> Chief Administrative Law Judge
> U.S. Department of Labor
> 800 K Street, NW, Suite 400N
> Washington, D.C. 20210

The person filing the appeal must also be served notice of the appeal on the following persons:

- All parties of record
- The OSHA official who issued the findings and order
- The Associate Solicitor, Division of Fair Labor Standards, U.S. Department of Labor, Washington, D.C. 20210[71]

After objections and a request for a hearing are filed, the case is assigned a hearing officer or administrative law judge, who must "expeditiously set a hearing date." No party is required to file an answer to the request for a hearing.[72] The hearing is *de novo* and "on the record."

SOX Administrative Claims: Discovery and Hearings

After OSHA issues its determination letter or findings, any party to that proceeding may file an appeal with the Chief Administrative Law Judge of the U.S. Department of Labor (DOL) Office of Administrative Law Judges (ALJ). Once filed, the case is assigned to a judge and docketed for a trial on the merits. The appeal must be filed within thirty days' notice of the OSHA findings and consists of a formal request for a "hearing on the record" and the filing of "objections" to the OSHA findings.[1]

The hearing before an ALJ is the most significant phase of a DOL corporate whistleblower case. The case is heard *de novo*,[2] and the parties are permitted to have their claims adjudicated in a formal bench trial. ALJ procedures mirror those of the Federal Rules of Civil Procedure,[3] and parties are permitted to engage in pretrial discovery. At the hearing, each party is permitted to call and/or cross-examine witnesses and create a detailed factual record. Because the case is tried before a judge and not a jury, the federal rules of evidence do not apply, and the hearing procedures are less formal than a jury trial. Given the nature of a whistleblower case, in which a party's intent is at issue, hearings can often be long and complex. It is not uncommon for a trial to last well over two weeks and for hundreds of exhibits to be filed.

After the hearing, most ALJ's permit the parties to file detailed findings of fact and conclusions of law based on the full trial record. After the record closes, and the post-hearing findings are filed by the parties, the ALJ issues a recommended decision and order on the merits of the case. Unless appealed to the DOL Administrative Review Board,[4] this recommended decision constitutes the final order of the Department of Labor. Even if it is appealed, the ARB reviews the ALJ determination under a "substantial evidence" standard, and the factual record created before the ALJ becomes the formal agency record for purposes of any further appeals.[5]

Because the ALJ's adjudication of a whistleblower case is *de novo*, the parties are not bound by any of the factual or legal determinations issued during the OSHA investigation. The OSHA ruling does not constitute evidence, and under the case law, the OSHA determination does not constitute admissible evidence. Thus, the decision of OSHA to conduct an investigation, not to conduct an investigation, and/or to rule for or against an employee is rendered immaterial after the case is appealed to the Office of Administrative Law Judges.[6] The only action taken by OSHA that survives an appeal is the preliminary order of reinstatement.[7] That order is enforceable directly in federal court.[8] However, if after the hearing, the ALJ's ruling on reinstatement takes precedence over OSHA's, that ruling becomes enforceable in federal court.[9]

THE PARTIES TO THE HEARING

When a case is docketed before the Office of Administrative Law Judges, the DOL ALJ sits as a neutral hearing examiner. The employee and the employer are both parties to the proceeding.[10] If both the employee and the employer filed appeals to the OSHA finding, the case is automatically consolidated into one proceeding.[11] Often, an employee may file more than one complaint against the same employer regarding different adverse actions. Multiple complaints are generally consolidated into one hearing.[12]

Under the current rules, OSHA has the right to participate in the adjudicatory proceeding as a party and/or as an *amicus curiae*. OSHA's right to participate as a party is extremely broad:

> At the Assistant Secretary's discretion, the Assistant Secretary may participate as a party or may participate as *amicus curiae* at any time in the proceedings. This right to participate includes, but is not limited to, the right to petition for review of a decision of an administrative law judge, including a decision based on a settlement agreement

between complainant and the named person, to dismiss a complaint or to issue an order encompassing the terms of the settlement.[13]

Regardless of whether OSHA had decided to participate as a party in the adjudication, all the parties are required to serve OSHA with copies of all pleadings.[14] At the request of the Securities and Exchange Commission, the parties may also be required to serve the SEC with all pleadings.[15] In addition to the employee and employer, other "persons or organizations" that could be "directly and adversely" affected by a final decision have the right to intervene in the case within 15 days of learning of the proceeding or participate in the case as *amicus curiae*.[16] Government agencies have broad discretion, as a matter of right, to participate in the proceeding as *amicus curiae*.[17]

If an employee is participating in a case without an attorney, the DOL judges are required to liberally "construe his or her pleadings and the ALJs have" some responsibility for helping *pro se* litigants during the adjudication process. On the other hand, the necessary burdens of proof are the same, regardless of whether a person is represented by counsel, and a judge has a "duty of impartiality" and must "refrain from becoming an advocate" for a *pro se* litigant.[18]

PREHEARING PROCEDURES

Under the regulations, the ALJs are required to conduct corporate whistleblower hearings "expeditiously, except upon a showing of good cause or unless agreed to by the parties."[19] Because the regulations require expedited hearings, the initial hearing date should be set within 60 days of the filing of the notice of appeal with the Chief Administrative Law Judge. Consequently, if the complainant is willing to accept "limited discovery,"[20] an ALJ should set the hearing date no later than 60 days after the request for a hearing is filed with the Chief ALJ. Under 29 C.F.R. § 18.42, a party may specifically request that the ALJ schedule the hearing within the sixty-day time frame.

Time limits for responding to motions are short. All motions must be answered within 10 days (if the motion is mailed, 5 days are added to the answering period).[21] This includes all responsive motions, motions to quash discovery, and motions for protective orders.

Although time limits are short, the adjudication proceedings for DOL whistleblower cases are rarely conducted within these constraints. Under the whistleblower statutes on which the SOX law was modeled, the administrative law judges held that the short deadlines were designed to "assure [the] complainant of a speedy decision and may be waived."[22] Employers' attempts to have a case dismissed due to the Labor Department's failure to comply with various statutorily set deadlines have been uniformly rejected,[23] and numerous cases held that the failure of the DOL to comply with statutory time requirements did not strip the DOL of jurisdiction to render a final judgment.[24] As a matter of law, even though the time limits were set forth in the statutes or regulation, they were consistently "construed as directory, rather than mandatory or jurisdictional."[25] Consequently, it was common practice for parties to "waive" their right to an expeditious hearing to obtain more time for discovery and pretrial preparation.[26]

For example, the nuclear and environmental whistleblower laws had stricter time requirements than the SOX. The DOL was required to complete its full investigation and adjudication and issue a final order on the merits of a complaint within a statutory 90-day time frame. This time frame was rarely (if ever) met. Consistent with these precedents, the DOL held that it was erroneous for an administrative law judge to allow the statutory or regulatory time limits to "interfere with the full and fair presentation" of a case.[27] Parties must be provided adequate time for preparation, and "even an expedited process must be applied in a manner that is fundamentally fair and thus provides the parties an adequate opportunity for presentation of the case."[28]

Under the SOX, the ability of the parties to obtain continuances was liberalized. The grounds for a continuance under the environmental statutes was a "compelling reason" standard.[29] The SOX regulations lowered that standard to a "good cause" requirement, and specifically permitted the parties to stipulate to enlargements of time.[30]

A request for a continuance of a hearing date must normally be filed within 14 days of the hearing.[31]

As discussed earlier, even in cases heard under the "compelling reasons" standard, ALJs frequently granted requests for continuance.[32] Although administrative law judges have discretion on this issue, a "myopic insistence upon expeditiousness in the face of a justifiable request for delay" may violate due process.[33]

Although enlargements of time may be granted for both a hearing date and/or for other nonjurisdictional filing deadlines, it is very important for parties to meet all deadlines, as the failure to do so may result in the waiving of certain objections or claims.[34] Allowing a case to drag on can often harm a complainant, increase litigation costs, and provide time for employers to file questionable prehearing dispositive motions.[35]

Parties may file motions to dismiss and for summary dismissal. These motions must be filed at least 20 days prior to a hearing.[36] The DOL follows the case law under Federal Rule of Civil Procedure (FRCP) 12 when reviewing motions to dismiss[37] and FRCP 56 when reviewing a motion for summary dismissal.[38] Summary judgment motions are rarely granted in whistleblower proceedings because the central issue, causation, often requires consideration of a person's motive.[39] They may also be denied if discovery is still necessary.[40] However, the failure to file an affidavit or other supporting documentation on the record in opposing summary judgment or a motion to dismiss can be fatal to an employee's case: "Unadorned allegations argued by counsel are not sufficient."[41] The regulations explicitly permit parties to file prehearing briefs.[42] The failure to raise or preserve issues in this brief may result in a waiver of the issues.[43]

DISCOVERY PROCEDURE

Prehearing discovery is an integral element of the litigation process, enabling a complainant to obtain the evidence the employer will rely upon to prove its case and assisting the complainant in proving discriminatory motive and disparate treatment.[44] The ARB has noted that an "opportunity for extensive discovery is crucial" for "protecting employees and the public interest." Additionally, "discovery in a whistleblower proceeding may well uncover questionable employment practices" and "safety deficiencies."[45]

Most discovery issues are routinely heard by the presiding administrative law judge, whose rulings will be reversed only if they are "arbitrary or an abuse of discretion."[46] Parties are expected to attempt to informally resolve discovery disputes prior to filing motions to compel or requesting protective orders.[47]

The expedited nature of the Department of Labor proceedings affects prehearing discovery.[48] Unless the administrative law judge orders otherwise, a party has 30 days to respond to requests for documents, admissions, or written interrogatories. Depositions may be conducted with only 5 working days' notice,[49] if the notices are hand served, and may be videotaped.[50] Protective orders may be requested to keep information confidential or to otherwise limit or prohibit discovery.[51] In order to obtain answers to discovery in time for the hearing, discovery requests should be served on a person or party shortly after a request for hearing is filed. Although the discovery process may be expedited, the ARB has correctly noted that "requests to extend the time to respond to discovery" are "routinely" granted.[52]

The strict time limits set forth in many of the DOL-administered whistleblower provisions can be waived in order to permit broad discovery and provide the parties with an opportunity for the "full and fair presentation" of their cases.[53]

The DOL has not been granted explicit subpoena power in whistleblower cases. Although DOL subpoenas cannot be enforced in federal court, the DOL can order parties to produce witnesses under their control for testimony[54] and sanction parties for discovery abuses.[55] The failure of an employer to fully comply with discovery may lead to serious sanctions, adverse inferences, and default judgment.[56] Consequently, the vast majority of witnesses and documents either must be produced by a party who controls these persons/documents and/or are voluntarily produced by persons who support one side or the other.

In addition to formal discovery, parties often utilize the Freedom of Information Act (FOIA) and Privacy Act to obtain documents relevant to a case from governmental authorities. For example, it is common practice for parties to request OSHA's complete investigatory file under FOIA after the OSHA proceeding is closed and the case is appealed to the Chief ALJ. Likewise, a governmental regulatory agency may have files related to either the whistleblower and/or the concerns raised by the whistleblower. These files may be accessible under FOIA.[57]

THE SCOPE OF DISCOVERY

In whistleblower cases, the DOL follows the rule that broad discovery must be permitted in employment cases.[58] Broad discovery is essential in protecting the "public interest,"[59] and discovery is permitted on various subjects, including internal industry reports, contacts with regulatory agencies, OSHA witness statements, documentation related to the wrongdoing identified by the employee-whistleblower, and issues related to company-wide employment practices.[60] Jurisdictional discovery is also permitted.[61] Attempts to shield attorney work product have met with mixed results.[62] Attempts to file interlocutory appeals in order to block discovery have been firmly rejected.[63] Failure to permit broad discovery is an "abuse of discretion."[64] This is supported not only under case law applicable in employment cases, but due to the sweeping definition of "relevancy" applicable in DOL administrative whistleblower cases.[65] Liberal discovery is appropriate not only to prevent improper retaliation, but also to aid in uncovering "questionable employment practices" and "deficiencies about which the government should know."[66]

In the absence of a protective order, parties have a right to disseminate information obtained in discovery.[67]

THE HEARING

Department of Labor administrative hearings are conducted as formal adjudicatory proceedings according to the Administrative Procedure Act (APA).[68] The conduct of the hearings and the general rules of evidence are delineated in APA sections 5 U.S.C. § 556(d)[69] and 5 U.S.C. § 554.[70] It is extremely important for parties to create a full record at the hearing. The hearing record is the body of evidence upon which all future decisions will be made, and the ability of any party to introduce new evidence into the record after the close of a hearing is very limited.[71]

Although similar to courtroom trials, hearings are not as formal. For example, nonattorneys have the right to represent the parties, and telephonic testimony, where necessary, is permitted.[72] Further, there is never a jury, and one administrative law judge sits as the trier of law and fact. The administrative law judge has wide discretion in admitting testimony into evidence, and the Federal Rules of Evidence are neither binding nor applicable.[73] The basic rule for the admitting evidence in the proceeding is set forth in the rules as follows:

> Formal rules of evidence will not apply, but rules or principles designed to assure production of the most probative evidence will be applied. The administrative law judge may exclude evidence that is immaterial, irrelevant, or unduly repetitious.[74]

During the hearing process, the administrative law judge must ensure that each party has a "fair adjudication." Given the complex nature of a whistleblower case, this would include the "full presentation of a broad range of evidence that may prove, or disprove, retaliatory animus."[75]

The hearings are mechanically or stenographically reported and open to the general public.[76] In conducting the prehearing and hearing process, administrative law judges have "all powers necessary" to conduct a "fair and impartial" proceeding, including the powers to "compel the production of documents and appearance of witnesses in control of the parties," "issue decisions and orders," take any action authorized by the Administrative Procedure Act, and, "where applicable," take "appropriate action" authorized under the FRCP.[77]

The DOL applies three sets of rules governing whistleblower adjudications. First, 29 C.F.R. § 1980 controls the proceedings. When a situation is not controlled by Part 1980, the DOL applies the rule set forth under 29 C.F.R. § 18. If both sets of rules are silent on a particular situation, the DOL employs applicable provisions of the FRCP.[78] Moreover, administrative law judges have the discretion to modify the application of Part 18 or the FRCP if "no party will be prejudiced and the ends of justice will be served."[79] With proper notice, requirements under Part 1980 may also be waived or modified.[80]

The failure of an administrative law judge to follow basic due process rules,[81] or the hearing requirements of the Administrative Procedure Act, is grounds for reversible error.[82] The standard for procedural due process required in whistleblower cases was outlined by the SOL in *In the Matter of Charles A. Kent*:

> Due process in administrative proceedings of a judicial nature has been said generally to be conformity to fair practices of Anglo-Saxon jurisprudence, . . . which is usually equated with adequate notice and a fair hearing. . . . Although strict adherence to the common law rules of evidence at the hearing is not required . . . the parties must generally be allowed an opportunity to know the claims of the opposing party . . . to present evidence to support their contentions . . . and to cross-examine witnesses for the other side. . . . Thus it is not proper to admit *ex parte* evidence, given by witnesses not under oath and not subject to cross-examination by the opposing party.[83]

The administrative law judge is not bound by the formal rules of evidence but should exclude "immaterial, irrelevant, and unduly repetitious evidence."[84] An administrative law judge can commit error by failing to admit into evidence "probative" information.[85] The ARB explained that:

> a trial judge who, in the hearing of a non-jury case, attempts to make strict rulings on the admissibility of evidence, risks reversal by excluding evidence which is objected to, but which, on review, the appellate body believes should have been admitted. Thus, in a non-jury hearing, it is more efficient for the trier of fact to take under advisement questions regarding the admissibility of evidence than it is to consider arguments concerning the admissibility of evidence at the time that such questions are raised. He or she is then able to sift through that evidence after it has been received to determine what is admissible.[86]

Both parties have the right to call and cross-examine witnesses, introduce documents into evidence, and make opening and closing remarks.[87] Either before or at the commencement of the hearing, the parties must exchange all exhibits they seek to admit into evidence.[88] The parties usually file prehearing briefs, or other prehearing statements are required by the ALJ. Although the whistleblower statutes do not explicitly provide subpoena power to the DOL,[89] the failure of an administrative law judge to order a party to produce relevant witnesses under its control to testify in a proceeding is an abuse of discretion.[90]

There are specific administrative provisions for taking judicial notice,[91] exchanging and introducing exhibits into evidence,[92] determining the authenticity of documents,[93] obtaining *in camera* inspection of documents, and for protective orders for privileged or sensitive communications.[94] The following is a summary of other basic Department of Labor administrative rules of evidence

1. Grounds for objecting to evidence
   a. Privilege, 29 C.F.R. § 18.46
   b. Classified or sensitive, 29 C.F.R. § 18.46 (b)
   c. Improper use of deposition, 29 C.F.R. § 18.23
   d. Failure to have produced the information during discovery, 29 C.F.R. § 18.6(d)(2)(iii)
   e. Immaterial, 29 C.F.R. § 1980.107(d)

    f. Challenge to the authenticity of a document, 29 C.F.R. §§ 18.44(b) [revised, Department of Labor "Final Rule," 55 Fed. Reg. 13,216 (April 9, 1990)] and 18.50

    g. Failure to produce a true copy of a record from another criminal or civil proceeding, 29 C.F.R. § 18.48

    h. Irrelevant, 29 C.F.R. § 1980.107(d)

    i. Unduly repetitious, 29 C.F.R. § 1980.107(d)

2. Hearsay evidence may be admissible if there are circumstantial indicia of its truthfulness.[95]

3. Judicial notice is permitted.[96]

4. Admission of exhibits[97]

    a. All exhibits shall be numbered, marked, and a copy given to both the administrative law judge and the opposing party.

    b. Parties must exchange all exhibits, preferably before the hearing, but no later than the commencement of the hearing. Failure to exchange exhibits in a timely manner can result in the exclusion of the document.[98]

    c. All documents are presumed authentic unless objected to prior to the hearing. If a party has relevant information within his or her control, but fails to produce it (this includes both documentary evidence and answering to interrogatories and admissions), the administrative law judge may draw an inference that the evidence is unfavorable to that party.[99]

Depositions may be used at the hearing, but their use must conform to 29 C.F.R. § 18.23. Evidence may be admitted into the record after it is closed if such evidence is "new and material" and was not readily available prior to the closing of the record.[100] In a whistleblower case, evidence of management's attitude toward safety is highly relevant. An employer's attitude toward the raising of safety issues, such as past instances of "deliberate violations" of safety procedure, may provide evidence of "antagonism" toward environmental regulations and also "provide support" for raising an "inference of retaliatory intent" against the employee.[101]

THE HEARSAY RULE

Hearsay evidence is admissible if it bears "satisfactory indicia of reliability," it is "probative," and its use is "fundamentally fair."[102] There is no hard and fast rule that determines when hearsay is admissible.[103] Many factors must be considered by the administrative law judge, such as:

whether the statements are signed and sworn to as opposed to anonymous, oral, or unsworn, whether or not the statements are contradicted by direct testimony, whether or not the declarant is available to testify and, if so, whether or not the party objecting to the hearsay statements subpoenas the declarant, or whether the declarant is unavailable and no other evidence is available, the credibility of the declarant if a witness, or of the witness testifying to the hearsay, and finally, whether or not the hearsay is corroborated [citations omitted].[104]

Thus, hearsay evidence cannot be excluded on the grounds that it is an out-of-court statement made to prove the truth of the matter asserted. Hearsay is admissible up to the point of relevancy.[105] An administrative law judge may base his or her final decision on hearsay evidence, although "uncorroborated hearsay or rumor" does *not*, unto itself, constitute substantial evidence and cannot be the sole basis for a decision.[106]

Generally, the admissibility of evidence is within the discretion of the administrative law judge.[107] Improper exclusion of evidence by the administrative law judge can provide grounds for reversal and remand of an agency decision by the court of appeals.[108]

RECOMMENDED DECISION

After the hearing, the parties may file posthearing briefs, including detailed findings of fact and conclusions of law.[109] Absent an order from the ALJ, posthearing briefs may be filed within 20 days of receipt of the hearing transcript. Posthearing briefs must refer to the "portions of the record and to all authorities relied upon for each proposal" set forth in the brief.[110] After the filing of posthearing briefs, the administrative law judge will issue a recommended decision. The recommended decision must be based on the record as a whole and include findings of law and fact (including, where appropriate, determinations of the witnesses' credibility).[111] Pursuant to 29 C.F.R. § 1980.109, the following must be contained in an ALJ's recommended decision issued under the SOX:

The decision of the administrative law judge will contain appropriate findings, conclusions, and an order pertaining to the remedies. . . . A determination that a violation has occurred may only be made if the complainant has demonstrated that protected behavior or conduct was a contributing factor in the unfavorable personnel action alleged in the complaint. Relief may not be ordered if the named person demonstrates by clear and convincing evidence that it would have taken the same unfavorable personnel action in the absence of any protected behavior. . . . If the administrative law judge concludes that the party charged has violated the law, the order will provide all relief necessary to make the employee whole, including reinstatement of the complainant to that person's former position with the seniority status that the complainant would have had but for the discrimination, back pay with interest, and compensation for any special damages sustained as a result of the discrimination, including litigation costs, expert witness fees, and reasonable attorney's fees.

The recommended decision is subject to review by the DOL Administrative Review Board (ARB), if an appeal is filed by any party (or by OSHA) within 10 business days from the date of the ALJ order.[112] The 10-day deadline is subject to tolling.[113] If an appeal is not filed within the 10-day period of time, the ALJ's order becomes the final order of the Department of Labor and is not reviewable in any court.[114] Even if an appeal of the ALJ's order is filed, an ALJ order of reinstatement is subject to immediate enforcement. All other aspects of the ALJ's order are stayed, pending the final decision of the DOL ARB.[115]

SANCTIONS AND INVOLUNTARY DISMISSALS

The Department of Labor and the SOX have special rules and procedures related to sanctions and involuntary dismissals. These procedures are not the same as Federal Rule of Civil Procedure 11. Under the SOX, if an employee is found to have filed a "frivolous" or "bad faith" complaint, the maximum sanction permitted under law is a $1,000 fee. Moreover, the employee has the right to contest this sanction and have a hearing on the validity of this sanction.[116]

All persons who appear in a DOL proceeding must "act with integrity and in an ethical manner."[117] Specific provisions exist for the disqualification of counsel[118] and the disqualification of an administrative law judge.[119] Attorneys who have engaged in unethical behavior or "contemptuous misconduct" have been disqualified from appearing in specific proceedings.[120] Disqualification orders may be appealed to the Chief ALJ.[121]

An administrative law judge has the power and responsibility to police the conduct of the parties and sanction parties for misconduct.[122] He or she may dismiss a complaint if a party fails to comply with a lawful order or engages in other misconduct.[123] However, before a complaint may be dismissed, the administrative law judge must issue an order to show cause why dismissal should not be granted.[124] A dismissal with prejudice is a "severe sanction," which must be "tempered by a careful exercise of judicial discretion."[125] Absent "willful or contumacious" misconduct or other aggravated circumstances, a default judgment for misconduct by either party will rarely be justified.[126]

Claims have been dismissed against parties for failure to comply with discovery orders,[127] for disrupting a proceeding,[128] abandonment,[129] failure to adhere to a prehearing order,[130] and for failure to comply with an order from an administrative law judge.[131] Simply put, a party is not permitted to "thwart" or "retard" an adjudication by violating an administrative law judge's orders or engaging in misconduct.[132] Attorneys have also been sanctioned for misconduct. Such attorneys have been ordered disqualified and have been subject to nonmonetary sanctions.[133] An ALJ may also be recused or disqualified from hearing a case.[134]

The DOL has held that a complainant may not be sanctioned under Rule 11 of the FRCP.[135] The SOL ruled that the sanction available for "conduct which is dilatory, unethical, unreasonable, and in bad faith" is the disqualification of counsel pursuant to DOL rule 29 C.F.R. § 18.36, not FRCP Rule 11 sanctions.[136] Unlike matters tried in federal courts, monetary sanctions under FRCP 11 are not available in DOL whistleblower actions.[137]

In *Rex v EBASCO Services, Inc.*, the SOL overturned a $77,000 sanction against a complainant's attorney.[138] The SOL ruled that only an employer can be required to pay attorney fees and costs.[139] Further, the SOL held that 29 C.F.R. § 18.36(b) governed the type of sanction available for "dilatory, unethical, unreasonable or bad faith conduct."[140] But an attorney who engages in sanctionable conduct may be subject to disqualification:

> The Department of Labor is not entirely without recourse where an attorney or the representative of a party abuses the procedures for administrative adjudication of disputes. It is clear that the Secretary has the authority to regulate the admission to practice of those who represent parties in cases arising under the ERA, and to discipline those whose conduct interferes with the carrying out of his responsibilities under the Act.[141]

Other sanctions available to an administrative law judge or the DOL include the refusal to permit a party to testify, taking certain facts to be established, and dismissal of a matter.[142] However, the DOL cannot punish a party for contempt or utilize other sanctions contained in the Federal Rules of Civil Procedure that are not also authorized by the whistleblower laws or administrative regulations.[143]

Although deliberate misconduct by a party may result in the dismissal of a claim,[144] a complainant/employee who provides misleading or false testimony is not automatically barred from obtaining relief under the laws.[145]

The only monetary sanction available against a complainant under the SOX is a maximum $1,000 for attorney fees incurred by the respondent-employer. In order to obtain this sanction, an employer must allege that the "complaint was frivolous or was brought in bad faith." This allegation should be made during the OSHA investigation.[146] Any findings on this allegation are subject to *de novo* review before the ALJ, in the same manner as the ALJ reviews other aspects of the case.[147] An ALJ determination on the $1,000 sanction is thereafter reviewable before the Administrative Review Board and would also be subject to judicial review at the Court of Appeals.[148] Both the burden of proof and the procedural difficulties in obtaining a monetary sanction are extremely high. Since this provision was first incorporated into another whistleblower law in 2000, there are no reported cases in which a sanction was awarded or sustained.

DISMISSALS AND DISMISSALS WITHOUT PREJUDICE

An employee may seek to have his or her claim dismissed by the Department of Labor at any time during the administrative proceeding. Dismissals can be with or without prejudice. The procedure for requesting such dismissals is set forth in 29 C.F.R. § 1980.111(a):

> At any time prior to the filing of objections to the findings or preliminary order, a complainant may withdraw his or her complaint under the Act by filing a written withdrawal with the Assistant Secretary [i.e., OSHA]. The Assistant Secretary will then determine whether the withdrawal will be approved. The Assistant Secretary

will notify the named person of the approval of any withdrawal. If the complaint is withdrawn because of settlement, the settlement will be approved in accordance with paragraph (d) of this section. § 1980.111(b) The Assistant Secretary may withdraw his or her findings or a preliminary order at any time before the expiration of the 30-day objection period described in § 1980.106, provided that no objection has yet been filed, and substitute new findings or preliminary order. The date of the receipt of the substituted findings or order will begin a new 30-day objection period. § 1980.111(c) At any time before the findings or order become final, a party may withdraw his or her objections to the findings or order by filing a written withdrawal with the administrative law judge or, if the case is on review, with the Board.

Under the DOL whistleblower statutes on which the SOX was modeled, employees often obtain voluntary dismissals without prejudice. Such dismissals are sought for a variety of reasons. Most notably, due to the short statute of limitations, it is often prudent to file a complaint first and conduct the type of factual review that often precedes the filing of a formal complaint during the OSHA investigation process.

Regardless of the motive behind seeking a voluntary dismissal, the DOL has applied the rule of law outlined in Federal Rule of Civil Procedure 41 in reviewing voluntary dismissals.[149] A complainant should be entitled to unilateral and unconditional dismissal of his or her whistleblower complaint if a respondent has not filed the functional equivalent of either an answer to the complaint or a motion for summary judgment.[150] The filing of a request for a hearing constitutes the functional equivalent of an answer.[151]

If the litigation is in an advanced stage and the respondent has expended considerable time and money defending a complaint, an employee is still entitled to a dismissal without prejudice if the respondent was not the party who appealed the determination of the ALJ or if the respondent failed to file a motion for summary judgment.[152] Even if a respondent did file a telegram appeal or a motion to dismiss, a complainant is still generally entitled to a conditional dismissal without prejudice.[153] In *Brown v Holmes & Narver*, the SOL ruled:

> The ALJ correctly stated the law governing a decision maker's discretion to impose conditions on the grant of a request for dismissal without prejudice. I agree with the ALJ's analysis that to avoid legal

harm or prejudice to a respondent as the result of a dismissal without prejudice, a complainant needs pay only for items that will not
be useful to respondent in defending an anticipated litigation in
another forum.[154]

The Chief ALJ's recommended decision in *Brown*, which was
explicitly adopted by the SOL, explained the policy reasons behind
allowing complainants to withdraw complaints without prejudice:

> Alleged whistleblowers should not be discouraged from reporting
> health and safety hazards or from filing discrimination complaints,
> and it follows that complainants not be discouraged from pursuing
> their issues before the Department merely because it may appear at
> some later date that an action before a state court is an alternative.
> While this public policy concern is not dispositive of whether attor-
> ney's fees should be attached to a given dismissal order, this valid
> concern does affect the manner in which the parties' arguments have
> been considered.[155]

Dismissals without prejudice have been granted while a case is
on appeal before the ARB.[156]

A dismissal without prejudice allows a complainant to withdraw a
DOL complaint and file a new action under other laws without fear
that a nonfinal determination of the DOL will prejudice that case:

> Respondent accuses complainant of attempting to avoid the conse-
> quences of orders that had been previously entered by the ALJ, fol-
> lowing a great expenditure of time and money. . . . Procedural tactics
> employed by the party are not determinative of the legal questions
> posed here. . . . The effect of Complainant's notice of voluntary dis-
> missal without prejudice was to render the proceeding a nullity and
> leave the parties as if the action had never been brought.[157]

If a party desires to pursue a DOL whistleblower claim in an alternative forum, a voluntary dismissal is also important to ensure that
any ruling of the DOL is not afforded *res judicata* effect or acts to otherwise preclude a party from litigating the claim in another forum.[158]

DISTRICT COURT JURISDICTION
OF DISCRIMINATION COMPLAINTS

The SOX statute permits employees to file their SOX claims in
federal district court, if they have exhausted their remedies in the

Department of Labor, and DOL has not issued a final order within 180 days from the filing of the initial complaint. If an employee seeks to have his or her case heard in federal court, DOL regulations require the employee to provide the DOL with 15 days' notice that they will be bringing their SOX claim in federal court.

The DOL regulation on this matter, set forth in 29 C.F.R. § 1980.114, states as follows:

> If the Board has not issued a final decision within 180 days of the filing of the complaint, and there is no showing that there has been delay due to the bad faith of the complainant, the complainant may bring an action at law or equity for *de novo* review in the appropriate district court of the United States, which will have jurisdiction over such an action without regard to the amount in controversy.
>
> Fifteen days in advance of filing a complaint in Federal court, a complainant must file with the administrative law judge or the Board, depending upon where the proceeding is pending, a notice of his or her intention to file such a complaint. The notice must be served upon all parties to the proceeding. If the Assistant Secretary is not a party, a copy of the notice must be served on the Assistant Secretary, Occupational Safety and Health Administration, and on the Associate Solicitor, Division of Fair Labor Standards, U.S. Department of Labor, Washington, DC 20210.

Once a claim is filed in federal court, the Department of Labor procedural rules are no longer applicable, and the proceeding is governed under the Federal Rules of Civil Procedure and the Federal Rules of Evidence. Although the procedural rules governing the judicial vers. Administrative proceedings would be very different, both tribunals should follow the same substantive legal analysis when weighing the merits of a SOX case. In this regard, Congress, by statute, mandated that the federal courts apply the same burden of proof as applied by the DOL when deciding SOX cases.

SOX Appeals

The Sarbanes-Oxley corporate whistleblower law (SOX) has two stages of appellate review. The first is within the Department of Labor (DOL) and the second is within the federal courts. The basic steps for appeal are these:

- A DOL administrative law judge's (ALJ) Recommended Decision and Order (RDO) on the merits of a case will become the final decision of the DOL unless a petition for review of that decision is filed with the DOL Administrative Review Board (ARB) within 10 days of the decision's issuance.[1]
- If appealed, the ARB is vested with jurisdiction to issue the final decision of the DOL. In order to seek judicial view of a DOL order, a party must exhaust his or her administrative remedies by filing a petition for review with the ARB.[2]
- Within 60 days of a final decision by the ARB, any party may seek judicial review of the final DOL order in the U.S. Court of Appeals for the circuit in which the violation of the SOX allegedly occurred. Decisions of the appeals court are subject to review by the U.S. Supreme Court.[3]
- A decision by either OSHA or an ALJ to reinstate an employee is immediately enforceable in U.S. District Court. Other relief ordered by the DOL, including back pay and attorney fees, are

subject to judicial enforcement only after either the ALJ or ARB issues a final order.[4]

- The ARB has "inherent authority" to hear motions for reconsideration filed by a party within a "reasonable time after the first decision" is rendered.[5]

REQUIREMENTS OF THE ADMINISTRATIVE
LAW JUDGE'S DECISION

The recommended decision of the administrative law judge becomes part of the official record. These factual findings of the ALJ are given substantial weight by the reviewing authorities.[6] Under the DOL regulations, the ARB reviews ALJ factual findings under a "substantial evidence" standard. Legal conclusions are viewed *de novo*.[7]

The administrative law judge is the initial trier of fact and must weigh contradictory evidence, judge the credibility of witnesses, and reach ultimate conclusions as to the facts of the case.[8] The ALJ must clearly set forth the rationale for his or her findings. Failure to do so can result in remand of the case by an appellate court.[9] In *Director, Office of Workers' Comp. v Congleton*, the court stated, "An administrative law judge's conclusory opinion, which does not encompass a discussion of the evidence contrary to his findings, does not warrant affirmance."[10]

The recommended decision must be based upon an analysis of all relevant evidence and should indicate explicitly which evidence has been weighed by the ALJ and the weight or credibility he or she assigns to it.[11]

REVIEW BY THE ADMINISTRATIVE
REVIEW BOARD (ARB)

Under the provisions of the SOX whistleblower regulations, the ARB has the responsibility to issue a final order if an administrative law judge's decision is appealed.[12] The specific procedures for seeking review before the ARB are as follows:

- Within 10 business days of the date of the ALJ decision, any party seeking review before the ARB must file a petition for review. The failure to file a timely petition for review can result in the dismissal of the appeal.[13]

- The petition for review must identify "findings, conclusions or orders to which exception is taken." The failure to identify such issues will "ordinarily" result in the waiver of such issues.
- If a petition is filed, the ARB must decide whether to take jurisdiction over the appeal within 30 days of the filing of the petition. If the ARB does not take jurisdiction over the appeal, the Recommended Decision and Order of the ALJ becomes the final decision of the DOL. If the ARB takes jurisdiction over the appeal, the decision of the ALJ (except an order of reinstatement) becomes "inoperative" until the ARB issues the final DOL decision.
- The ARB is mandated to issue its final order within 120 days of the "conclusion" of proceedings before the ALJ.
- If the ARB remands a case to an ALJ for new proceedings, that decision is not subject to immediate appeal to the Court of Appeals, and the ALJ's remand jurisdiction is limited to the issues identified by the ARB.[14]

The regulations governing the appeal of an ALJ decision to the ARB are subject to change by the U.S. Department of Labor. The current interim DOL rule governing SOX procedures is codifed at 29 C.F.R. Part 1980 and may be found at http://www.whistleblowers. org/html/sarbanes-oxley.html. If the interim rule is changed, the new rule will also be published at this Web site.[15]

A petition for review must be filed and received by the ARB within 10 business days of the date of the ALJ's Recommended Decision.[16] The petition must be served upon all parties, the Chief ALJ, the Assistant Secretary (OSHA), and the Assistant Secretary (Division of Fair Labor Standards) at the "time it is filed with the Board."[17] The address for the ARB is

Administrative Review Board
U.S. Department of Labor, Rm. S-4309
200 Constitution Ave., NW
Washington, D.C. 20210

A petition for review may be "filed" with the ARB by mail, facsimile, e-mail, or by hand service. The date of the postmark/transmittal date will be deemed the date the petition is filed.

The ARB is not bound by the legal conclusions or findings of the administrative law judge, *Hobby v Georgia Power*, 90-ERA-30, Order Denying Stay (April 20, 2001), and has "all the powers" the SOL "would have in making the initial decision."[18] However, under the regulations, the ARB reviews the "factual determinations" of the ALJ "under the substantial evidence standard."[19] An order granting summary decision is reviewed *de novo*.[20]

Although the ARB can rule *de novo* on issues of law, it cannot declare an act of Congress unconstitutional.[21] In addition, the ARB will not normally consider new evidence that was not put into the record established by the administrative law judge, even if the new evidence is "material" to the issues adjudicated.[22] Newly discovered evidence will only be admitted if a party was "excusably ignorant" and had acted with "reasonable diligence" to discover the material prior to trial.[23] For example, the record may be supplemented if a party had attempted to obtain certain documents prior to the hearing but the documents only became available after the hearing record closed,[24] or when new evidence was obtained concerning a witness who was ordered to testify but failed to testify.[25] Impeachment evidence usually will not be admitted after the hearing record is closed.[26]

Once a petition for review is filed, and the ARB accepts the case for review, the ARB sets a briefing schedule in which the parties set forth their respective positions.[27] Briefs filed before the ARB must be served on all parties and the Assistant Secretary (OSHA) and Associate Solicitor, Division of Fair Labor Standards. After the ARB issues a final order, both parties have 60 days to file a petition for review to the appropriate U.S. Court of Appeals.[28] If either party is dissatisfied with the result of the court of appeals, it may file a petition for a writ of *certiorari* to the U.S. Supreme Court.

The scope of the ARB's review of the administrative law judge's initial Recommended Decision is broad and is controlled by 5 U.S.C. § 557 and 29 C.F.R. § 1980.101(b). Briefly, the SOL has "the authority to conduct a *de novo* review of all issues raised in [the] proceeding,"[29] but factual findings are reviewed under the substantial evidence test.[30] The ARB has this hybrid standard as follows:

> [T]he ARB is bound by the factual findings of the ALJ if those findings are supported by substantial evidence on the record conspired as a whole. Substantial evidence is that which is "more than a mere scintilla. It means such relevant evidence as a reasonable mind might accept as adequate to support a conclusion. In reviewing the ALJ's conclusions of law, the Board, as the designee of the Secretary, acts with "all the powers [the Secretary of Labor] would have in making

the initial decision. . . ." Therefore, the Board reviews the ALJ's conclusions of law *de novo*.[31]

The failure of the ARB to review an ALJ's factual finding under the "substantial evidence" standard can constitute reversible error.[32] Regardless of the "substantial evidence" requirement, the ARB is free to accept specific factual findings of an ALJ, but to disagree with the ALJ's legal conclusions or "quasi-legal" conclusions drawn from a factual finding, noting that the ARB could agree with an ALJ's finding "yet still reach a contrary legal conclusion."[33] Moreover, in whistleblower cases, findings related to the existence of a retaliatory motive are considered conclusions of law, not findings of fact.[34]

The courts of appeals will give weight to the administrative law judge's opinion on issues of credibility of witnesses.[35] In *Pogue v United States Department of Labor*,[36] the Court of Appeals reversed an order of the SOL in which the SOL had failed to appropriately evaluate an administrative law judge's credibility determinations: "[w]eight is given the [ALJ's] determinations of credibility for the obvious reason that he or she 'sees the witnesses and hears them testify.'"[37] The SOL may reject an administrative law judge's credibility determination if the record does not support the determination,[38] especially if the credibility findings are based on the "substance" of the testimony, rather than the "demeanor" of the witness.[39] As a general rule, the ARB has deferred to the administrative law judge's credibility determinations.[40] But the ARB has rejected such credibility determinations that were not supported by substantial evidence.[41]

The ARB can also reject an administrative law judge's findings as to "actual motive." Even if the administrative law judge does not find discriminatory motive, the ARB may rely on other evidence, "reasonable and supported by substantial evidence on the record as a whole," and conclude that there was discriminatory motive. The ARB has the discretion to differ with an administrative law judge on the proper inference that can be drawn from the record and the "proper application of the statute."[42]

After a Final Order has been issued, the ARB has infrequently granted a motion to reconsider. Although there is authority that suggests that the ARB does not have jurisdiction to grant such a motion,[43] the ARB and one Court of Appeals has upheld its power to grant reconsideration.[44] The filing for a petition for review in the court of appeals can divest the DOL of jurisdiction.[45]

INTERLOCUTORY APPEALS FROM
THE ADMINISTRATIVE LAW JUDGE
TO THE SECRETARY OF LABOR

The Department of Labor regulations contain no provision for interlocutory appeals to the ARB of preliminary orders or rulings from the administrative law judges. The ARB has repeatedly refused to accept jurisdiction over interlocutory appeals and has held that such appeals are "disfavored."[46] Likewise, the U.S. courts of appeals have refused to take jurisdiction over interlocutory disputes.[47] Absent an administrative law judge certifying a question for interlocutory review under 28 U.S.C. § 1292(b),[48] it is highly unlikely that the ARB would accept any issue for interlocutory review. In deciding motions for interlocutory review,[49] the ARB has applied the collateral order review doctrine.[50]

APPEAL TO THE U.S. CIRCUIT COURTS
OF APPEALS

An appeal of a final order[51] of the ARB must be filed within 60 days of the date of the ARB order.[52] Appellate review of a final decision of the ARB is controlled by 5 U.S.C. §§ 701-706.[53] These sections of the Administrative Procedure Act cover a petitioner's right to review, the actions that are reviewable, methods of obtaining relief pending review, and the scope of review. Judicial review of SOX decisions conforms to the basic rules of law that govern review of administrative orders. A final order of the SOL may only be reviewed by the U.S. Court of Appeals for the circuit "in which the violation, with respect to which the order was issued, allegedly occurred."[54] This is usually limited to a review of the record on which the Department of Labor's decision was based.[55]

The general rule of appellate review in Department of Labor whistleblower cases was summarized by the 9th Circuit in *Mackowiak v University Nuclear Systems, Inc.*: "We review the Secretary's decision under the Administrative Procedure Act, 5 U.S.C. § 706. We will set aside the agency decision if it is "unsupported by substantial evidence" or "arbitrary, capricious, an abuse of discretion, or otherwise not in accordance with the law."[56] This is the same standard of review the circuit courts use when reviewing a decision of the National Labor Relations Board.[57] In its relevant parts, Section 706 states:

To the extent necessary to a decision and when presented, the reviewing court shall decide all relevant questions of law, interpret constitutional and statutory provisions, and determine the meaning or applicability of the terms of an agency action. The reviewing court shall—

(1) compel agency action unlawfully withheld or unreasonably delayed; and

(2) hold unlawful and set aside agency action, findings, and conclusions found to be—

    (A) arbitrary, capricious, an abuse of discretion, or otherwise not in accordance with law;

    (B) contrary to constitutional right, power, privilege, or immunity;

    (C) in excess of statutory jurisdiction, authority, or limitations, or short of statutory right;

    (D) without observance of procedure required by law;

    (E) unsupported by substantial evidence.[58]

In regard to the standard of review for questions of law, the U.S. Court of Appeals for the 3rd Circuit described it as follows:

We exercise plenary review over legal questions concerning the construction of statutes which an agency administers where Congress has unambiguously addressed the question at issue. Federal Administrative Procedures Act, 5 U.S.C. §§ 704, 706. Here, however, we find the facial language of the Clean Water Act's whistleblower protection provision to admit of more than one interpretation, and hence we are compelled to uphold the Secretary's interpretation if it is "based on a permissible construction of the statute."[59]

An argument may be preserved for review even if it was not "forcefully raised" before the DOL.[60] However, an argument is waived if not presented to DOL.[61]

REVIEW OF A LEGAL CONCLUSION OR AN INTERPRETATION OF LAW

Although courts may substitute their own judgment when determining questions of law, they usually defer to an agency's interpretation of its own enabling statute.[62] Under the Supreme Court's formulation in *Chevron v Natural Resources Defense Council*[63] a court must "keep in mind the deference" they must pay to an administrative agency's construction of statutes Congress has "charged" them with administering.[64] In *Udall v Tallman*, the Supreme Court stated:

> When faced with a problem of statutory construction, this Court shows great deference to the interpretation given the statute by the . . . agency charged with its administration. . . . Particularly is this respect due when the administration of a statute by the men charged with the responsibility of making the parts work efficiently . . . while they are yet untried and new [citations omitted].[65]

Applications of law to fact are reviewed under the substantial evidence test.[66]

The failure of the SOL to follow past secretarial precedent may be grounds for reversal. It is a basic tenet of administrative law that "an agency must either conform to its own precedents or explain its departure from them."[67] When appellate courts review an agency's interpretation of its own regulation, rather than an enabling statute, the agency's construction is given "controlling weight unless it is plainly erroneous or inconsistent with the regulation."[68]

If a final order of the SOL is not based upon "substantial evidence," it will be vacated and remanded by the court of appeals.[69] Substantial evidence is a difficult term to define. In a landmark labor case, the Supreme Court interpreted substantial evidence as:

> more than a scintilla. It means such relevant evidence as a reasonable mind might accept as adequate to support a conclusion. [Accordingly, it] must do more than create a suspicion of the existence of the fact to be established . . . it must be enough to justify, if the trial were to a jury, a refusal to direct a verdict when the conclusion sought to be drawn from it is one of fact for the jury [citations omitted].[70]

In its review, the U.S. Court of Appeals must consider the entire record including evidence that detracts from the Secretary's decision, as well as that which upholds it.[71]

The ARB must also review all relevant information in his or her written decision and generally must "indicate explicitly" what "evidence has been weighed and its weight."[72] In *Arnold v Secretary of H.E.W.*, the 4th Circuit held: "Unless the Secretary has analyzed all evidence and has sufficiently explained the weight he has given to obviously probative exhibits, to say that his decision is supported by substantial evidence approaches an abdication of the court's 'duty to scrutinize the record as a whole to determine whether the conclusions reached are rational.'"[73]

Thus, under 5 U.S.C. § 706, the appeals court will analyze the SOL's decision and determine whether, based on the record as a whole, the decision of the Secretary was reasonable. The court should not substitute its own judgment for that of the Secretary: "In reviewing an agency's decision for substantial evidence, a court may not displace the agency's 'choice between two fairly conflicting views, even though the court would justifiably have made a different choice had the matter been before it *de novo*'" (citations omitted).[74]

The court begins with the Secretary's findings and then determines if the evidence makes those findings reasonable.[75]

A decision or order of the SOL can be reversed if it is "arbitrary and capricious" or an "abuse of discretion." Under both of these standards the scope of review is narrow. Generally, a decision is not arbitrary and capricious if it is "rational," is "based on consideration of relevant factors," and does not "deviate from the ascertainable legislative intent." In the process of determining these factors, the court of appeals should "engage in a substantial inquiry into the facts," and need not be just a "rubber stamp."[76]

Findings of abuse of discretion are based on an even stricter standard of review. The Secretary can be reversed for abuse of discretion if he or she fails "to apply the appropriate equitable and legal principles to the established or conceded facts and circumstances."[77]

RELIEF PENDING REVIEW—STAYS OF DOL FINAL ORDER

After the ARB issues a Final Order, an aggrieved party can file for a stay of the DOL's decision directly with the ARB.[78] If an appeal is filed to the appeals court, the filing of the appeal does not automatically stay a final order of the ARB.[79]

Rule 18 of the Federal Rules of Appellate Procedure provides that the application for stay "shall ordinarily be made in the first instance to the agency" (i.e., the ARB). The ARB will only grant a stay if the petitioner demonstrates four factors: (1) that petitioner will prevail on appeal; (2) that there has been irreparable injury; (3) that a stay will not cause substantial harm to the other interested person; and (4) that a stay would not interfere with the public interest.[80] Merely having to pay a complainant money damages and pay attorney fees pending appeal are not grounds for a stay.[81] If the SOL denies the request or refuses to act upon the request, the aggrieved party may then file for relief pending review with the appropriate U.S. court of appeals. A stay of an agency order is an exercise of judicial discretion, and the propriety of its issue depends on the circumstances of the particular case. There is no procedural or statutory right to a stay.[82]

The court of appeals can issue a stay "to prevent irreparable injury."[83] It has been found that retaliatory discrimination or other retaliatory activity may cause a chilling effect that can constitute such irreparable harm.[84] Financial injury alone does not constitute irreparable injury.[85]

The courts consider injunctive relief pending review to be an extraordinary exercise of their authority; as such, the petitioner carries a heavy burden of proof, and there is a strong presumption in favor of an agency decision. In a decision under the nuclear whistleblower law, the Seventh Circuit denied an employer's petition for a stay, holding that the employer "had not persuaded us that it would suffer irreparable harm from being forced to continue one weld inspector in its employ for a few months while its petition for review is under consideration by this court."[86]

Thus, an aggrieved party is not entitled, as a matter of right, to a stay of a Department of Labor order pending review of the Secretary's decision. In order to receive such a stay, the aggrieved party must meet the stringent tests put forward in 5 U.S.C. § 705, Rule 18 of the Federal Rules of Appellate Procedure and *Commonwealth-Lord Joint Venture v Donovan.*[87]

The SOL has repeatedly denied employers' requests for a stay pending the review of a SOL order issued on behalf of an employee[88] and has required employers to pay monetary damages to employees while a case is in appellate review.[89]

ENFORCEMENT PROCEEDINGS

If any person fails to comply with a preliminary order of reinstatement, or a final order by the DOL, the person on whose behalf the order was issued can file a claim for enforcement in federal district court.[90] On its own initiative, or at the request of an employee,[91] the Solicitor of Labor can also seek enforcement of DOL orders in federal court.[92]

When an enforcement action is filed, the district court is not empowered to retry the merits of the case, but must simply perform a "ministerial" role in enforcing the order.[93] In such cases, the federal district court is empowered to grant all appropriate relief, including injunctive relief, compensatory damages, punitive damages, and reasonable attorney fees and litigation costs.[94] In order to ensure compliance with preliminary orders of reinstatement, federal district courts have issued enforcement orders, and have granted preliminary injunctions requiring an employer to immediately reinstate an employee.[95]

Federal Court Actions

Congress provided employees who file a Sarbanes-Oxley corporate whistleblower case (SOX) a unique procedural right. The SOX permits employees who exhaust their administrative remedies within the DOL to withdraw their DOL cases and refile their case, *de novo,* in federal district court.[1] This election may only be utilized by employees. Corporate employers must defend SOX cases in the forum chosen by the employee. No other DOL-administered whistleblower law contains this election procedure.

In drafting this clause, Congress intended federal courts to hear SOX cases in the same manner they hear other federal civil rights cases. The Senate Judiciary Committee report clarified that SOX cases filed in federal court should be heard by the court as a "normal case in law or equity, with no amount in controversy requirement."[2] A "jury trial" would be "available" to the parties in federal court, and the case was likened to a Civil Rights Act claim filed in accordance with 42 U.S.C. 1983. However, federal courts would be required to follow the "contributing factor" test in adjudicating liability. As explained in the Judiciary Committee report: "[The claimant] may bring a de novo case in federal court with a jury trial available (See United States Constitution, Amendment VII; Title 42 United States Code Section 1983). Should such a case be brought in federal court, it is intended that the same burdens of proof which would have governed in the Department of Labor will continue to govern the action."[3]

An employee's right to file in federal court was qualified. All SOX claims must be initially filed with the DOL, and the DOL must be given an opportunity to issue a final enforceable order within 180 days of filing. Only if the DOL does not comply with that statutory time requirement can an employee exercise his or her election rights. After the 180-day time requirement is exhausted, an employee can continue to have his or her claim adjudicated by the DOL, or can refile the case in federal court.

The SOX law sets forth an employee's right to file in federal court:

> A person who alleges discharge or other discrimination by any person in violation of [the SOX] may seek relief . . . by filing a complaint with the Secretary of Labor; or if the Secretary has not issued a final decision within 180 days of the filing of the complaint and there is no showing that such delay is due to the bad faith of the claimant, bringing an action at law or equity for de novo review in the appropriate district court of the United States, which shall have jurisdiction over such an action without regard to the amount in controversy.[4]

The implementing regulations mirror this provision, but require an employee who elects to file in federal court to provide the DOL and the parties to the SOX administrative proceeding 15 days' advance written notice of "his or her intention to file such a complaint." The notice must be served on all the parties and the Assistant Secretary of Labor for OSHA and the Associate Solicitor of the Division of Fair Labor Standards.[5]

In order to exercise this right, an employee must do the following:[6]

- File their initial complaint in the Department of Labor (DOL) in accordance to the rules and regulations of the DOL.
- Participate in the DOL proceedings. If the employee engages, in "bad faith" conduct that could delay the DOL proceedings, the employee's right to file in federal court could be compromised or delayed.
- After participating in the DOL proceedings for 180 days, the employee may withdraw his or her proceeding from the DOL and file a claim in federal district court under the SOX.
- The current DOL regulations require that an employee provide the DOL and the parties to the proceeding at least 15 days'

notice of an intent to withdraw a claim from the DOL in order to file a federal court action.

- If the DOL issues a final order within the 180-day time period, an employee may not file the federal court action.
- Only an employee can elect to withdraw his or her claim from the DOL; the employer is required to defend the claim in the forum chosen by the employee.
- Once a SOX claim is filed in federal court, the court must hear the case *de novo*. In other words, any preliminary or recommended decisions issued by OSHA or an ALJ are nonbinding in federal court.

A case filed in federal court is heard *de novo*, and consequently the federal court is not bound by any interlocutory order of the DOL (i.e., a decision by OSHA or an Administrative Law Judge), provided that the Administrative Review Board has not issued a final order.

Once filed in federal court, the court will hear the claim under its federal question jurisdiction, and should have the authority to award any remedy normally applied by a federal court.[7]

Regardless of whether the claim is heard before the DOL or a federal court, most of the substantive case law applicable in DOL proceedings should be equally applicable in federal court proceedings. Thus, regardless of which court hears the case, the same definitions of employee, employer, adverse action, protected activity, and discriminatory conduct should apply. Moreover, the courts are required to apply the same "contributing factor" test in evaluating evidence of discrimination as is applied by the DOL.[8]

Although the substantive law applicable in federal court will be similar to that applied by the DOL, procedurally the two forums are very different. In federal court, the Federal Rules of Civil Procedure and the Federal Rules of Evidence are applicable. These rules are not applicable in the DOL. Although the statute is silent on the question, the legislative history of the SOX clearly states that cases heard in federal court under this provision may be tried before a jury. DOL cases are heard before an Administrative Law Judge. Also, the applicability of punitive damages in a federal court action is an open question. Punitive damages are available in civil actions filed in federal court, and they are available in Section 1983 actions.

A decision whether to file a claim in federal court must be balanced against a number of factors. The DOL offers an employee a

number of favorable options. First, the DOL adjudicatory procedures are less complex and costly than those in federal court. The
informality of the hearings, combined with the traditional willingness of ALJs to provide whistleblowers with a full opportunity to
present their case, weigh heavily in favor of pursuing a case within
the labor department, even after the 180-day time period has
expired.

Second, the DOL has a 20-year record of deciding whistleblower
cases. Many of the major legal precedents have been established,
and most DOL judges have experience in the corporate whistleblower laws on which the SOX was modeled. Many complex legal
questions heard initially in district court may relate directly to
issues which were thoroughly litigated within the DOL. Having the
case heard in federal court could result in relitigating many of these
issues, some of which are very favorable to whistleblowers.

Based on their experience hearing whistleblower cases, some
DOL judges have recognized that whistleblowers often are "brave,
dedicated and conscientious public-spirited citizens" who have
become a "vital part of American society."[9]

Third, most litigators who have appeared before the DOL have
found its adjudication process to be fair and reasonable. For example, in the mid-1980s a controversy arose regarding whether a DOL
corporate whistleblower law covering the nuclear power industry
(one law on which the SOX administrative procedures were modeled) preempted state wrongful discharge law. Industry vigorously
argued that if the courts did not find preemption, employees would
abandon the federal statutory remedies, and flock to the state courts
in which they could obtain jury trials and punitive damages.

In 1990, the Supreme Court rejected industry's preemption arguments, and found that employees could pursue state tort causes of
action as well as a DOL administrative procedure.[10] Thereafter,
most nuclear whistleblowers continued to pursue their cases
within the DOL, and of the hundreds of nuclear whistleblower
cases filed after 1990, the overwhelming majority have been filed
within the DOL. The reason for employee reliance upon the DOL is
fairly simple. The DOL established a reputation of fairly treating
employees and providing employees with a less complex and less
costly forum in which they could present their claims. Damages
awarded by the DOL were comparable to other forums. For example, in one nuclear whistleblower case the employee was awarded
approximately $5 million in damages.

On the other hand, there may be very compelling reasons to file in federal court after the expiration of the 180-day period. Beyond the obvious forum-shopping issues that would arise under any circumstances, the following concerns would need to be weighed:

- *Subpoena power.* The DOL lacks formal subpoena power over witnesses not in the control of a party. If such a witness is essential for a case, an employee may decide to file in federal court, where subpoena power exists.
- *Pendent state and federal causes of action.* Many states provide tort remedies for wrongfully terminated whistleblowers.[11] Also, the banking laws, Title VII of the Civil Rights Act, and the False Claims Act permit employees to file discrimination law suits in federal court.[12] If an employee decides on combining a SOX case together with a state whistleblower case and/or a federal employment discrimination case, the employee should remove his or her SOX case from the DOL after the 180-day time period, and refile the case in federal court. On the other hand, the employee could decide to separately pursue the causes of action.[13]
- *Pendent DOL causes of action.* The DOL has exclusive jurisdiction over a number of specialty corporate whistleblower laws, such as the nuclear safety law, the airline safety law, and the environmental safety laws.[14] None of these DOL-administered laws permits employees to file a private cause of action in federal court. Thus, if an employee seeks to pursue cases under the SOX and one or more of these other specialty laws, the employee may want to have all of the cases heard together within the DOL.
- *Costs and sanctions.* The DOL procedures are less complex and costly than federal court procedures. Moreover, in the DOL the maximum sanction which can be applied to an employee for engaging in "bad faith" litigation is $1,000.00, and the DOL has ruled that Federal Rule of Civil Procedure 11 (which permits sanctions to be awarded against any party in a federal court action with no limitation) is not applicable in DOL proceedings. On the other hand, in federal court an employee could face sanctions under Federal Rule of Civil Procedure 11 and other federal rules which permit a court to sanction parties for misconduct.

Ultimately, the decision to file in federal court must be made on a case-by-case basis, weighing a number of factors, many of which may be unique to a specific case. Regardless, it would be a mistake for employees to withdraw from the DOL process in a knee-jerk manner.

Proof of Discrimination: The Contributing Factor Test

In 1989, Congress statutorily created a new standard of proof applicable in whistleblower cases, commonly referred to as the "contributing factor" test.[1] This standard was directly incorporated into the Sarbanes-Oxley corporate whistleblower law (SOX). The test was designed by Congress to make it easier for whistleblowers to win their cases.[2]

The standard of proof set by Congress or the courts can be extremely significant. As the U.S. Supreme Court recognized, the standard "instruct(s) the factfinder" regarding the "degree of confidence our society thinks" needs to be established concerning the "correctness of factual conclusions." In other words, the standard "serves to allocate the risk of error between the litigants and to indicate the relative importance attached to the ultimate decision."[3]

Most civil cases are adjudicated on the "preponderance of the evidence" standard, in which litigants "share the risk of error in roughly equal fashion."[4] In SOX cases, the traditional "preponderance of evidence" standard was modified in order to make it easier for whistleblowers to prove their cases, reflecting the "society's" interest in ensuring adequate protection for employees who risk significant adverse action for having the courage to blow the whistle.

When Congress first developed the "contributing factor" test, its intent to modify the traditional burdens of proof in employment cases was crystal clear. Congress wanted to make it "easier for an individual to prove that a whistleblower reprisal has taken place." This intent was spelled out in Congress's Joint Explanatory Statement setting forth its understanding of the new "contributing factor" test:

> The bill makes it easier for an individual (or the Special Counsel on the individual's behalf) to prove that a whistleblower reprisal has taken place. To establish a prima facie case, an individual must prove that the whistleblowing was a factor in the personnel action. This supersedes the existing requirement that the whistleblowing was a substantial, motivating or predominant factor in the personnel action. One of many possible ways to show that the whistleblowing was a factor in the personnel action is to show that the official taking the action knew (or had constructive knowledge) of the disclosure and acted within such a period of time that a reasonable person could conclude that the disclosure was a factor in the personnel action. The bill establishes an affirmative defense for an agency. Once the prima facie case has been established, corrective action would not be ordered if the agency demonstrates by clear and convincing evidence that it would have taken the same personnel action in the absence of the disclosure. Clear and convincing evidence is a higher standard of proof than the preponderance of the evidence standard now used.[5]

The "contributing factor" test sets forth a statutory mechanism governing the burdens of proof in whistleblower cases. The often conflicting or confusing burdens of proof set forth in numerous judicial decisions under other employment discrimination laws were replaced by a statutory formula.[6] Under this formula, an employee has the burden of proof to establish the following:

1. That she or he is an employee covered under the SOX;
2. That she or he engaged in activities protected under the SOX;
3. That the employer was aware of this protected activity;
4. That the protected activity was a "contributing factor" in an adverse action taken by the employer.[7]
5. Once the employee demonstrates a "contributing factor," the burden of proof shifts to the defendant to establish, by "clear and convincing evidence," that the employer would have taken the same adverse action even if the employee never engaged in protected activity.[8]

The DOL Administrative Review Board summarized the "contributing factor" test applied by the ARB and the DOL judges as follows:

> If a complainant demonstrates, i.e. proves by a preponderance of the evidence, that protected activity was a contributing factor that motivated a respondent to take adverse action against him, then the complainant has established a violation [of the Act]. Preponderance of the evidence is the greater weight of the evidence, superior evidentiary weight that, though not sufficient to free the mind wholly from all reasonable doubt, is still sufficient to include a fair and impartial mind to one side of the issue rather than the other. Assuming a complainant establishes a violation of the Act, he nonetheless may not be entitled to relief if the respondent demonstrates by clear and convincing evidence that it would have taken the same adverse action in any event. Clear and convincing evidence is evidence indicating that the thing to be proved is highly probable or reasonably certain.[9]

CONTRIBUTING FACTOR

To be a "contributing factor," the animus does not have to be the primary reason for the adverse action. Instead, the animus need only play a part in the overall motivation:

> The words "a contributing factor" . . . mean any factor which, alone or in connection with other factors, tends to affect in any way the outcome of the decision. This test is specifically intended to overrule existing case law, which requires a whistleblower to prove that his protected conduct was a "significant," "motivating," "substantial," or "predominant" factor in a personnel action.[10]

In order to meet the "contributing factor" test, an employee's burden was "ease(d)." As explained by the U.S. Court of Appeals for the Federal Circuit in a case under the WPA:

> Even though evidence of retaliatory motive would still suffice to establish a violation of the employee's rights . . . a whistleblower need not demonstrate the existence of retaliatory motive on the part of the employer taking the alleged prohibited personnel action in order to establish that her disclosure was a contributing factor to the prohibited action.[11]

The DOL has also accepted this view of an employee's burden to establish a "contributing factor." In *Kester v Carolina Power and Light Company*, the DOL recognized that Congress's use of the term "contributing factor" was designed to lower the standard of proof required of employees under other employment laws. Under prior cases, the employee was "required to prove that protected activity was a 'motivating factor' in the employer's decision. Congress adopted the less onerous 'contributing factor' standard in 'in order to facilitate relief for employees.'"[12] This standard is followed by DOL administrative judges.[13]

CLEAR AND CONVINCING EVIDENCE OF THE EMPLOYER'S DEFENSE

Once an employee demonstrates that discriminatory animus was a "contributing factor" to an adverse action,[14] the burden of proof shifts to the employer to demonstrate, by "clear and convincing evidence," that the employer would have taken the same adverse action even if the employee had not engaged in whistleblowing activity.[15] The "clear and convincing evidence" test is "tough standard" for employers. Congress intended that employers "face a difficult time defending themselves" in whistleblower cases.[16]

In order to meet the "clear and convincing" standard, an employer must establish its defense by evidence stronger than a mere "preponderance" of the evidence. The level of proof needed to meet this standard is usually explained as "highly probable."[17] The U.S. Court of Appeals for the Federal Circuit explained the standard as follows: "Clear and convincing evidence has been discredited as evidence which produces in the mind of the trier of fact an abiding conviction that the truth of the factual contention is 'highly probable.'"[18] One court articulated three factors that need to be evaluated in order to determine if an employer is able to prove by "clear and convincing" evidence that it would have taken the adverse action even in the absence of protected activity:

1. The strength of the agency's evidence in support of its personnel action.
2. The existence and strength of any motive to retaliate on the part of the agency officials who were involved in the decision.

3. Any evidence that the agency takes similar action against employees who are not whistleblowers but who are otherwise similarly situated.[19]

Although the contributing factor test is distinct from the burden of proof standard required under most other employment laws, the DOL "routinely" applies "the framework of burdens developed" under Title VII as guidance in reviewing evidence.[20]

PROOF OF DISCRIMINATION

The heart of a SOX whistleblower case rests in demonstrating that protected activity was a "contributing factor" in an adverse action.[21] A "contributing factor" may be demonstrated through direct or circumstantial evidence.[22] It is well settled and established that employers will rarely, if ever, directly admit that protected activity contributed in any manner whatsoever to an adverse action. The typical case scenario requires a court or jury to weigh various subtle facts or admissions and determine whether these circumstances demonstrate that discrimination "contributed" to an adverse decision.[23] A "contributing factor" may be proven by either direct or circumstantial evidence. Likewise, direct evidence of retaliatory motive is not needed in either a "pretext" or a "mixed motive" case.[24]

Direct Evidence

Exactly what constitutes "direct evidence" of animus has been the subject of a number of differing definitions.[25] It is commonly defined as evidence that, if believed, "proves the existence" of a disputed fact "without inference or presumption."[26] Put another way, "direct evidence" is "evidence that directly reflects the use of an illegitimate criterion in the challenged decision" or "actions or remarks" that tend to "reflect a discriminatory attitude" and are related to the "decisional process."[27]

Obtaining such evidence in an employment case is very difficult. Most employers do not admit to discriminating against employees, and "smoking gun" documents exist only in rare cases.[28] Consequently, as a matter of law, it is "improper to require plaintiffs to produce direct evidence of discriminatory intent in order to prevail at trial" in a whistleblower case.[29] Not only is direct evidence of discrimination not required, the Supreme Court has recognized that circumstantial evidence "is not only sufficient" to prove a case but, in some instances, may be even more "persuasive than direct evidence."[30]

Circumstantial Evidence

In the majority of cases, employees rely upon circumstantial evidence to demonstrate discriminatory motive[31] or evidence that protected activity was a "contributing factor" for the adverse action.[32] Circumstantial evidence is "often the only means available to prove retaliation claims.[33] In *Ellis Fischel State Cancer Hospital v Marshall*,[34] the court held that "[t]he presence or absence of retaliatory motive is a legal conclusion and is provable by circumstantial evidence even if there is testimony to the contrary by witnesses who perceived lack of such improper motive."[35] This process requires "careful evaluation of all evidence pertinent to the mind-set of the employer and its agents regarding the protected activity and the adverse action taken."[36] Moreover, evidence that an employer's justification for an adverse action is untrue may itself constitute "persuasive" circumstantial evidence of "intentional discrimination."[37]

These general principles of legal analysis are applied to SOX whistleblower cases. For example, in a 2004 SOX decision, the DOL Administrative Law Judge noted that employee was unable to produce any "direct evidence" of retaliatory "intent." The judge analyzed the record and found that a variety of circumstantial evidence supported a finding of retaliation. This included temporal proximity, an employer's lack of evidence that the employee had "poor performance" prior to the whistleblower incident, evidence that the employer's accusations against the employee were "unsupported," the employer's "dishonesty regarding" a number of "key issues," and discrepancies in the reason given for the discipline.[38]

Some of the factors that have been used successfully to establish circumstantial evidence of discriminatory motive in whistleblower cases are:

1. *Work Performance:* high work-performance rating prior to engaging in protected activity, and low rating or problems thereafter;[39] absence of previous complaints against employee.[40]

2. *Timing:* The timing of an adverse action (i.e., discipline or termination shortly after the employee engaged in protected activity).[41]
3. *Disparate Treatment:* Treating a whistleblower differently from a nonwhistleblower.[42]
4. *Deviation from Procedures:* Deviation from routine procedure;[43] manner in which the employee was informed of adverse action or the inadequate investigation or review of a disciplinary decision;[44] absence of warning before termination or transfer;[45] pay increase shortly before termination;[46] a pattern of "suspicious circumstances" or a "suspicious sequence of events" surrounding the discipline of an employee.[47]
5. *Attitude:* Attitude of supervisors toward whistleblowers;[48] charges of "disloyalty" or other derogatory remarks concerning protected activity;[49] low regard for corporate oversight personnel.[50]
6. *Pretext:* Failure of the company to prove allegations;[51] contradictions or shifting explanations in an employer's explanation of the purported reasons for the adverse action;[52] proof that the purported reason for taking an adverse action is not true or believable;[53] the magnitude of the alleged offense.[54]
7. *Antagonism to Protected Activity:* Reference to an employee engaged in protected activity as a "troublemaker"[55] or an otherwise "unfavorable attitude" toward employees who reported violations;[56] antagonism toward a "regulatory scheme;"[57] anger, antagonism, or hostility toward complainant's protected conduct;[58] a pattern of antagonism.[59]
8. *What an Employee Exposed:* Evidence that the whistleblower's concerns were correct and the potential magnitude of the problem identified by the employee.[60]
9. *Dishonesty:* Dishonesty regarding a "material fact."[61]

This list of factors is not exhaustive.[62] Many cases follow established patterns, but the circumstances that may potentially give rise to an inference of retaliatory intent are as diverse as the labor force.

The following factors have been used in a large amount of cases either to establish a contributing factor or to rebut an employer's defense concerning the legitimacy of the disciplinary action.

Timing

One of the most common factors used to establish motive is timing: "Adverse action closely following protected activity is itself evidence of an illicit motive."[63] The fact that an employer takes disciplinary action shortly after an employee engages in protected activity is, unto itself, usually "sufficient to raise an inference of causation" and establish that element of the *prima facie* case.[64] Timing can be relevant not only as support for a *prima facie* case but also as evidence supporting an ultimate finding of discrimination: "Disbelief of the reasons proffered by a respondent [for an adverse action] together with temporal proximity may be sufficient to establish the ultimate fact of discrimination."[65]

Pretext

Proving that the reason given by an employer for taking adverse action was false (or a pretext) can be critical evidence demonstrating discrimination. As the Supreme Court set forth in *St. Mary's Honor Center v Hicks:*

> The fact finder's disbelief of the reasons put forward by the defendant (particularly if disbelief is accompanied by a suspicion of mendacity) may, together with the elements of the prima facie case, suffice to show intentional discrimination. Thus, rejection of the defendant's proffered reasons will permit the trier of fact to infer the ultimate fact of intentional discrimination.[66]

Moreover, if an employee can demonstrate that the purported reason justifying an adverse action is a "lie," that finding constitutes "even stronger evidence of discrimination." In other words, "a lie is evidence of consciousness of guilt."[67]

Unquestionably, demonstrating that the reason an employer gave for an adverse action is not believable can be compelling evidence, both of the fact that an employer had a discriminatory motive and that the employer cannot meet its burden of proof. Common sense would dictate this result. If an employee is a whistleblower, and the employer lies about the reason for an adverse action, the employee will almost always win the case. Citing directly to controlling cases of the U.S. Supreme Court, the weight given proof of pretext was explained by the DOL:

Rejection of the [employer's] proffered reasons [for the adverse action] will permit the trier of fact to infer the ultimate fact of intentional discrimination. Indeed, proof that an explanation is incredible constitutes a piece of indirect evidence, which becomes part of (and often considerably assists) the greater enterprise of proving that the real reason was intentional discrimination. Once the employer's justification has been eliminated, discrimination may well be the most likely alternative explanation. Thus, a plaintiff's prima facie case, combined with sufficient evidence to find that the employer's asserted justification is false, may permit the trier of fact to conclude that the employer unlawfully discriminated.[68]

Disparate Treatment

Evidence of "disparate treatment" is also "highly probative evidence of retaliatory intent."[69] Disparate treatment simply means that an employee who engages in protected activity was treated differently, or disciplined more harshly, than an employee who committed a similar infraction and did not engage in protected activity.[70] For example, in the context of the National Labor Relations Act, in which a union organizer and another employee were both caught drinking on the job and the company fired only the union organizer, the court found disparate treatment.[71] Although an employee need not demonstrate "disparate treatment" in order to prevail on the merits,[72] the "essence of discrimination . . . is treating like cases differently."[73]

Where a disciplinary response clearly does not fit with the type of infraction at issue, an inference of discrimination may be demonstrated.[74] Likewise, evidence that the employer "orchestrated" justifications for a termination is evidence of discrimination.[75] However, absent proof of discriminatory motive, courts "do not sit as a super-personnel department" and second-guess employment decisions.[76] Corrective action is warranted only if an employee can demonstrate that discriminatory animus played a role in the decision, regardless of how "medieval" a firm's practices or "mistaken" a manager's decision.[77]

Employers and Employees under the SOX

The Sarbanes-Oxley corporate whistleblower law (SOX) contains a definition of employees and employers covered under the SOX:

> *No company with a class of securities registered under section 12 of the Securities Exchange Act of 1934 (15 U.S.C. 78l), or that is required to file reports under section 15(d) of the Securities Exchange Act of 1934 (15 U.S.C. 78o(d), or any officer, employee, contractor, subcontractor, or agent of such company,* may discharge, demote, suspend, threaten, harass, or in any other manner discriminate against *an employee....*
>
> *A person* who alleges discharge or other discrimination *by any person* in violation of subsection (a) may seek relief....[1]

As can be seen from the wording of the statute, the scope of coverage under the SOX is broad. Not only are most publicly traded companies covered,[2] but "any officer, employee, contractor, subcontractor, or agent" of a publicly traded corporation is also covered. Consequently, nonpublicly traded companies, which serve as contractors, subcontractors, or agents of Wall Street traded firms would also be covered under the SOX. Also, individual "officers," "employees," and other "persons" who work for or control the conduct of publicly traded companies may also be liable under the act. Given the broad statutory definition of "employer," it may be advantageous for employees to name specific persons and/or contractors and agents in their complaint, along with the publicly traded corporation that may own and/or control such persons or agents.

Permitting nonpublicly traded corporations that have a contractual or agency relationship with publicly traded corporations to be liable under the SOX is consistent with the case law developed under other whistleblower laws. For example, under the nuclear whistleblower law, a corporation that was not licensed by the Nuclear Regulatory Commission (NRC) objected to an NRC subpoena filed in a whistleblower investigation. The company argued that it was not subject to the employee protection regulations because the corporation was not a licensee of the NRC. However, the Court of Appeals rejected this argument, and found the fact that the company in question had a contract with an NRC-licensed established jurisdiction. Under the nuclear whistleblower act, non–NRC-licensed companies that act as suppliers or vendors for NRC-licensed projects have been found to be employers under the ERA.[3]

In other whistleblower statutes, including those upon which the SOX was modeled, the terms "employer" and "employee" have been construed broadly by the responsible administrative agencies and the courts.[4] For example, the U.S. Department of Labor (DOL), in an environmental whistleblower case, reasoned that:

> The term "employee" as used in this Act must be given a most liberal interpretation, particularly in view of the evils the Act was designed to prevent. It is obvious the Act is intended to prevent employers from engaging in acts of discrimination, whether it takes the form of termination of employment or simple intimidation. In light of these statutory objectives, the overriding policy considerations involved would compel that the term employee be as inclusive as is rationally possible.[5]

This holding is consistent with the Supreme Court's decision in a Title VII case, finding that former employees were fully protected under that law's antiretaliation provisions:

> According to the EEOC, exclusion of former employees from the protection of [the antiretaliation provision] would undermine the effectiveness of Title VII by allowing the threat of post-employment retaliation to deter victims of discrimination from complaining to EEOC, and would provide a perverse incentive for employers to fire employees who might bring Title VII claims. . . . Those arguments

carry persuasive force given their coherence and their consistency with a primary purpose of antiretaliation provisions: Maintaining unfettered access to statutory remedial mechanisms.[6]

Consistent with these precedents, separate business entities have been found liable as employers where the interrelation between the company actually employing the worker and the independent corporation was sufficient to qualify the parent company as a "joint employer."[7] The joint employer doctrine is applicable to the SOX.[8]

Hiring employees as independent contractors also will not automatically insulate employers from liability.[9]

The issue of subsidiary liability under the SOX has not been fully resolved.[10] However, in the handful of cases in which the issue of subsidiary liability has been raised, one of the key factors in upholding an employee's claim has rested on naming the parent corporation in the initial complaint. Once a parent corporation has been named as a respondent, there are a number of theories upon which liability of the parent can be sustained. However, if the parent corporation is not initially listed as a respondent, employers have opposed attempts to amend a complaint to name the parent corporation.[11]

In a SOX case, the DOL judge rejected a motion to dismiss filed by a nonpublicly traded subsidiary of a publicly traded company. The judge held as follows:

> A finding that Respondent is not covered under the Act merely because it is a subsidiary of a parent company would arguably allow the parent company to exploit circumstances peculiarly afforded it the capability of discriminatorily interfering with employment opportunities available to employees of its subsidiaries that are not publicly traded, while it could not do so with respect to employment in its own service under the Act.[12]

In another SOX case, *Morefield v Exelon Services, Inc.*, the DOJ judge also rejected an employer's attempt to escape liability because an employee worked for a subsidiary of a publicly traded company: "A publicly traded corporation is, for Sarbanes-Oxley purposes, the sum of its constituent units; and Congress insisted upon accuracy and integrity in financial reporting at all levels of the corporate structure, including the non-publicly traded subsidiaries. In this context, the law recognizes as an obstacle no internal corporate barriers to the remedies Congress deemed necessary. It imposed reforms upon the publicly traded company, and through it, to its entire corporate organization."[13] However, the DOJ judge also indicated that an employee should name both the publicly traded company and the subsidiary in his or her complaint in order to ensure that the claim is not dismissed on a technicality.

Employers may also be prohibited from discriminating against employees who do not directly work for them.[14] Regardless of the "proximate relation of the employer and employee," an employer named in a complaint may be "prohibited from engaging in discriminatory conduct against any employee, prospective employee, former employee or an employee seeking employment or working for another employer."[15] The Secretary of Labor, citing established U.S. Supreme Court and U.S. Courts of Appeals precedent under other employment discrimination laws, held that an employer "may violate" the whistleblower laws "with respect to employees other than his own":

> For example, a bank which owned a fifty-story office building told picketers outside a restaurant, occupying leased space on the 46th floor, to leave the building and threatened them with arrest. The Ninth circuit held that the bank was an employer and had committed an unfair labor practice . . . even though it was not the employer of the picketers.[16]

The SOX does not limit the definition of "employer" to corporations or formal business entities. Congress specifically included individuals who work on behalf of the publicly traded company, including corporate "officers, employees" and "agents" as potential respondents under the Act. Congress also permitted the Department of Labor or the federal court to order that relief be paid directly by "any person," not necessarily the formal corporate employer. The inclusion of individuals in the definition of "employer," and in the definition of who is responsible in a SOX "enforcement action," would permit complainants to name individuals as responsible parties in a SOX case.[17] Thus, were an officer for a publicly traded corporation to be responsible for an adverse action taken against an employee of nonpublicly traded corporation, that officer should be listed as a named respondent in a SOX case.

The term "employee" is also not limited to "employees of a particular employer." The law's protection may encompass disputes in which there is no "proximate relation" between the employer and employee.[18] An employee should be protected from discrimination or harassment from any publicly traded corporation (or agent/contractor, etc.)—not just the employer for whom the worker is presently employed or for whom he or she formerly worked.[19] In the context of other whistleblower laws administered by the DOL, the Secretary of Labor made this point: "A broad interpretation of 'employee' is necessary in order to carry out the statutory purpose. . . . Protecting the reporting employee against retaliation only while that employee is in the employ of the violator has a 'chilling effect' and discourages, rather than encourages, the reporting of . . . violations."[20]

"Employee" has been defined to include former employees, contract workers, and probationary or temporary employees;[21] independent contractors;[22] applicants for employment, former employees, and prospective employees;[23] contract job shoppers;[24] and temporary workers.[25] The laws generally protect workers "regardless of their function."[26]

Protected Activity and the SOX Reasonable Belief Standard

When the Senate Judiciary Committee drafted the Sarbanes-Oxley corporate whistleblower law (SOX), they intended the law to "encourage and protect" employees who "report fraudulent activity" that could "damage innocent investors in publicly traded companies."[1] The Judiciary Committee's evaluation of the causes behind the Wall Street scandals of 2001–2002 demonstrated that had employee whistleblowing been legally protected and culturally accepted, the financial implosions that caused millions of Americans to lose their investments and retirements could have been avoided or significantly mitigated.

The need for broad whistleblower protections was obvious. One Department of Labor judge described the social recognition given to whistleblowers (including two leading corporate whistleblowers):

> Whistleblowers, a vital part of American society, have been acknowledged by *Time* which recognized PERSONS OF THE YEAR FOR 2002 Sherron Watkins (a vice-president at Enron Corp.), Cynthia Cooper (an executive at WorldCom) . . . for exposing malfeasance and nonfeasance that eroded public confidence in their institutions. . . . [Whistleblowers are] brave, dedicated and conscientious public-spirited citizens.[2]

In order to encourage employee whistleblowing, Congress defined protected activity with a very broad brush:

> This bill would create a new provision protecting employees when they take lawful acts to disclose information or otherwise assist criminal investigators, federal regulators, Congress, their supervisors (or other proper people within a corporation), or parties in a judicial proceeding in detecting and stopping actions which they reasonably believe to be fraudulent.[3]

The statutory language in the SOX reflects Congress's intent. First, the law broadly defines the scope of potentially fraudulent conduct that is reportable under the SOX. Second, the law protects employee disclosures to numerous persons and entities, ranging from law enforcement officers to supervisors within the company. Third, the allegation of misconduct or fraud need not be proven; it only has to be "truthful" and have a "reasonable" basis in fact.

REPORTABLE VIOLATIONS

The types of misconduct reportable under the SOX include any violations of rules or regulations of the Securities and Exchange Commission (SEC), allegations of violations of criminal and civil laws protecting investors, and also includes allegations of fraud under any federal law that may harm shareholders. The statute sets forth the framework of reportable misconduct as follows:

> to provide information, cause information to be provided, or otherwise assist in an investigation regarding any conduct which the employee reasonably believes constitutes a violation of section 1341, 1343, 1344, or 1348, any rule or regulation of the Securities and Exchange Commission, or any provision of Federal law relating to fraud against shareholders.[4]

Under the statute, a wide variety of disclosures are protected. The securities laws "broadly prohibit fraudulent activities of any kind in connection with the offer, purchase, or sale of securities." They require that investors receive truthful information about a company's financial condition and other material aspects concerning a corporation. These laws also govern management activities of publicly traded companies; the requirements of audit committees; ethical and reporting duties related to accountants, auditors, corporate attorneys, and chief executive officers, the rights of shareholders; the voting and disclosure requirements at shareholder meetings; the use and counting of proxy votes; "the contents of materials filed with the SEC or with shareholders, and the requirement to disclose all important facts concerning the issues on which holders are asked to vote." Additionally, various market activities are regulated or prohibited, such as insider trading, efforts to purchase over 5 percent of a company's stock (e.g., a potential corporate takeover), prohibited conflicts of interest, the activities of certain investment advisors, and the enhanced criminal prohibitions and corporate responsibility requirements set forth in the Sarbanes-Oxley Act itself.

In addition to the criminal statutes referenced directly in the SOX definition of protected activity, employees who blow the whistle on any SEC rule or regulation or any potential violation of "any provision of federal law relating to fraud against shareholders," are fully protected.

Reportable violations under the SOX include the following:

- Employee allegations regarding violations of the federal criminal fraud laws, such as sections 1341, 1343, 1344, and 1348 of Title 18.
- Employee allegations of possible violations of the numerous federal civil laws related to fraud against shareholders, including the Securities Act of 1933, the Securities Exchange Act of 1934, the Public Utility Holding Company Act of 1935, the Trust Indenture Act of 1940, the Investment Company Act of 1940, the Investment Advisors Act of 1940, and the Sarbanes-Oxley Act of 2002.
- Employee allegations regarding any employer violation or noncompliance with the numerous and detailed requirements set forth in the rules and regulations of the SEC, including those rules published at Title 17 of the Code of Federal Regulations and the numerous laws administered by the SEC. Many of the laws, rules, and regulations incorporated into this provision of the SOX are published by the SEC on its Internet site located at http://www.sec.gov.
- All laws related to fraud against shareholders. This provision potentially encompasses all of the laws, rules, and regulations just referenced, and any other law, rule, or regulation that could be reasonably argued protect investors from fraud. This would clearly include those portions of the Securities Act of 1933 that permit shareholders to file civil actions concerning

corporate deceit, misrepresentations, and other fraud in the sale of securities. The broad scope of this provision is reflected in the numerous class action lawsuits filed by investors related to fraud against shareholders or other violations of SEC rules and regulations.

The SOX "participation clause" protects employees who "file, cause to be filed, testify, participate in, or otherwise assist in a proceeding filed or about to be filed (with any knowledge of the employer) relating to an alleged violation of section 1341, 1343, 1344, or 1348 [of Title 18], any rule or regulation of the Securities and Exchange Commission, or any provision of Federal law relating to fraud against shareholders."[5] Case law interpreting "participation clause" provisions protect a wide range of conduct, including direct participation in SEC proceedings and other securities-related proceedings.

Among the proceedings for which employees could participate are civil lawsuits filed by or on behalf of shareholders. Between 1992 and 2002 almost 2,500 class action lawsuits were filed by investors. These suits cover a broad range of deceptive investment practices, including conduct that could artificially inflate stock prices or an initial offering; false or misleading statements filed with the SEC; activities not in compliance with "generally accepted accounting principles"; overstatement of earnings by a subsidiary; "misrepresentation" of material facts that could create a "substantial likelihood" that a "reasonable investor" could inappropriately rely upon the false information; inflating revenue; and "manipulative or deceptive" trade or investment practices.[6]

Information about investor class action lawsuits is available on the Internet from the Stanford Law School Securities Class Action Clearinghouse, posted at http://securities.stanford.edu. The Clearinghouse contains copies of class action complaints and the court files related to those complaints, decisions issued in the cases, and settlement agreements.

PROTECTED ACTIVITIES

Not every disclosure to any person regarding SEC violations is protected activity. The statute sets forth four categories of persons or organizations upon which an employee is permitted to "blow the whistle." These encompass the following: reports to government officials, internal reports, reports to Congress, and conduct that initiates a "proceeding" under the securities laws. On the face of the statute itself, and in light of the court precedents interpreting similar laws, the scope of protected activities is extremely broad.

As a matter of judicial and administrative interpretation, whistleblower laws that contain even more restrictive language than that included in the SOX have been broadly construed.[7] In the leading case under Section 8(a)(4) of the National Labor Relations Act (NLRA), the Supreme Court[8] held that antiretaliation provisions, such as the SOX law, need to protect the flow of employee information to government regulators and thus must be broadly construed:

> This complete freedom is necessary, it has been said, "to prevent the Board's channels of information from being dried up by employer intimidation of prospective complainants and witnesses.". . . Which employees receive statutory protection should not turn on the vagaries of the selection process or on other events that have no relation to the need for protection.[9]

Similar employee protection provisions in the Occupational Safety and Health Act, the Fair Labor Standards Act, the Surface Transportation Assistance Act, the False Claims Act, the Federal Mine Safety Act, the Energy Reorganization Act, and the environmental whistleblower laws have all, for the most part, received similarly broad and liberal interpretations.[10] Because the SOX law was directly modeled on these other precedents, its definition of protected activity also must be broadly constructed.

The U.S. Department of Labor (DOL), following judicial precedent, has continuously given a broad interpretation to the scope of protected activity under the whistleblower laws it administers. The DOL has protected a broad range of employee conduct, including internal complaints to management,[11] contact with citizen intervener groups,[12] safety-related complaints made by employees who perform supervisory or managerial functions,[13] refusal to perform unsafe work,[14] complaints to union representatives,[15] and refusal to perform work in violation of federal safety standards.[16]

Under the SOX and the established case law interpreting similar laws, the following conduct is protected as described next.

CONTACTS WITH THE SEC AND
OTHER FEDERAL GOVERNMENT AGENCIES

The ability of an employee to communicate directly with federal law enforcement or regulatory authority is a critical component to employee whistleblowing and is explicitly protected under the SOX.[17] Under the law, direct contact with government agencies, federal courts, and Congress is protected.[18] The SOX statute explicitly protects employees who blow the whistle to a "federal regulatory or law enforcement agency." This provision speaks for itself, and would cover employees who make protected disclosures to the SEC, a U.S. Attorney's office, the U.S. Department of Justice, and other government agencies involved in any manner in regulating publicly traded companies, such as the Public Company Accounting Oversight Board. Disclosures to any federal regulatory agency or law enforcement office, even those not directly tied to the securities industry, should also be fully protected, if the contents of the disclosure relate to fraud against shareholders or violations of the laws or rules referenced in the SOX.

The SEC will accept complaints from any person. Complaint forms can be obtained online from the SEC and filed at enforcement@sec.gov. The address for mailing or faxing a complaint is:

> SEC Center for Complaints and Enforcement Tips
> 450 Fifth Street, NW
> Washington, D.C. 20549
> Fax 202-942-9634

Although complaints regarding the potential violation of securities law and/or SEC rules and regulations can be filed with the SEC, whistleblower retaliation complaints must be filed with the U.S. Department of Labor. The Labor Department will forward a copy of the complaint to the SEC, but only the Labor Department has jurisdiction over the merits of a SOX whistleblower employment discrimination case.

Any prohibition on permitting employees to contact federal law enforcement agencies also would constitute an illegal obstruction of justice under the Sarbanes-Oxley amendment to the Obstruction of Justice statute. Under 18 U.S.C. § 1513(e) it is a criminal violation of federal law to "knowingly, with the intent to retaliate" take "any action harmful to any person, including interference with the lawful employment or livelihood of any person, for providing to a law enforcing officer any truthful information relating to the commission or possible commission of any Federal offense."

Contacts with Congress

The SOX explicitly protects employee contact with "any Member of Congress or any committee of Congress."[19] Even without explicit protection for these contacts, communications with Congress are fully protected under other whistleblower laws, as core-protected activities.[20]

This statutory language is directly modeled on other whistleblower laws. FN 42 U.S.C. 5851(a).[21]

INTERNAL PROTECTED ACTIVITY

The SOX explicitly protects internal employee complaints to management officials who exercise "supervisory authority" over the whistleblower. It also protects whistleblower disclosures to any "person working for the employer who has authority to investigate, discover or terminate misconduct."[22] This is a very broad definition of internal protected activity, and clearly establishes that reports to supervisors or managers, without direct contact with government regulators, is fully protected activity. In addition to a supervisor, disclosures to the following persons should be fully protected:

- Audit committee and auditors
- Office of General Counsel
- Chief Executive Officer of the company
- Company-instituted "employee concerns" programs

Significantly, even without this explicit statutory grant of authority, the DOL-administered whistleblowers laws upon which the SOX was based have been interpreted to fully protect internal whistleblowing since the landmark case *Phillips v Interior Board of Mine Operators*.[23] In that case, although the statute was silent on the issue, Justice Wilkey of the U.S. Court of Appeals for the District of Columbia Circuit held that internal whistleblowing was protected. The court looked at the underlying purpose of the act and the "practicalities" that confront employees, management, and government in attempting to enforce health and safety regulations.[24]

Simply put, it is realistic to assume that an employee who discovers a potential problem will first report it to management and that such a disclosure could result in discrimination or possible termination.[25] The *Phillips* holding has been widely followed by other courts,[26] and was congressionally endorsed.[27]

In numerous whistleblower cases, the DOL reaffirmed its long-standing doctrine that internal whistleblowing is fully protected.[28]

The DOL has also upheld the mirror opposite of internal whistle-blowing. In one case, the DOL directly addressed the tension between an employee's expectation of loyalty to management and an employee's right not to inform potential wrongdoers of facts related to a whistleblower concern: "[D]isciplining an employee for refusing to reveal safety concerns to management when he is about to report his concerns to the [appropriate governmental body] is a violation of the [whistleblower laws]."[29]

AGGRESSIVE AUDITING/OVERSIGHT

It is now well settled that "self-auditing work," and the "compliance" concerns it generates, constitutes protected activity. Specifically, "employees whose assigned job is to discover and report instances of noncompliance so that the employer may correct them" engage in protected activity when they identify potential violations. This would include the "initial statement of the employee" that "points out a violation," as well as the additional statements that employee may make if the concern is eventually reported to the government.[30]

An employee's proper performance of his or her quality control, quality assurance, or auditing functions may be fully protected activity.[31] For example, in the context of providing protection for auditors in the nuclear safety area, the DOL ruled: "The protection afforded whistleblowers by the ERA extends to employees who, in the course of their work, must make recommendations regarding how best to serve the interest of nuclear safety, even when they do not allege that the *status quo* is in violation of any specific statutory or regulatory standard."[32] Federal courts have upheld these holdings and have fully protected inspectors who, in the performance of their job, disclosed violations or misconduct.[33]

Given the importance the Sarbanes-Oxley Act attached to the competent and honest auditing of publicly traded corporations, these precedents, which were clearly established under the laws upon which the SOX was based, should be fully applicable to corporate accountants, auditors, and in-house counsel who do their job and internally report wrongdoing.

FAILURE TO FOLLOW THE CHAIN OF COMMAND WHEN RAISING CONCERNS

A necessary component of protecting internal whistleblowing is fully protecting employees who make disclosures outside of their chain of command. Once internal whistleblowing is protected, this rule is not only logical but necessary to protect the integrity of internal disclosures. Thus, regardless of a company's policy, an employee's ability to choose the internal component of a company to which he or she desires to make a whistleblower disclosure is extremely significant. On the one hand, an employee may feel comfortable discussing his or her concerns with a supervisor. However, the employee may want to remain confidential, and may raise a disclosure directly to the audit committee. Moreover, when an auditor conducts a review of a department or program, the employee would need to be protected when he or she provided the auditor truthful information regarding potential misconduct.

The DOL has adopted a firm rule in whistleblower cases that employees may circumvent the chain of command when reporting allegations of wrongdoing protected under various whistleblower laws. "[A]n employer may not, with impunity, discipline an employee for failing to follow the chain-of-command, failing to conform to established channels, or circumventing a superior, when the employee raises an environmental health or safety issue."[34] As a matter of law, it is "not permissible to find fault with an employee for failing to observe established channels when making safety complaints."[35] Consequently, taking "adverse action" against an employee merely because the employee "circumvented the chain of command" would constitute a violation of the whistleblower protection statutes.[36] Similarly, an employee cannot be disciplined by management merely for refusing to inform management of the allegations he or she filed with government regulators.[37]

In this vein, employees are protected even if they go "around established channels" in bringing forward a "safety complaint,"[38]

go "over" their "supervisor's head" in raising a concern,[39] violate
or fail to follow the workforce "chain of command" or normal procedure,[40] or refuse to disclose information they confidentially told
regulators.[41]

Accusing an employee of not being a "team player" due to his or
her raising concerns is direct evidence of improper motive.[42]

Although employees can ignore a mandatory "chain of command" reporting requirement under a number of federal laws, they
are not free to participate in protected activities in any manner they
so choose. Reasonable restrictions on employee conduct will be
sustained, even if the restrictions may impact otherwise protected
activities.[43] Thus, an employee who engages in protected activity
still may be discharged for "insubordinate behavior, work refusal,
and disruption."[44]

PARTICIPATING IN, ASSISTING IN, AND
INITIATING ENFORCEMENT PROCEEDINGS

Under the SOX, employees who "participate" in legal or administrative proceedings related to adjudicating a whistleblower case
or an SEC enforcement proceeding are entitled to "exceptionally
broad protection."[45] The SOX contains a sweeping "participation
clause" provision, which protects employees who file charges, testify, or participate in any SEC proceedings or proceedings related to
"any provision of Federal law relating to fraud against shareholders."[46] The statute's participation clause, which is modeled directly
from similar clauses in other whistleblower laws, states:

> to file, cause to be filed, testify, participate in, or otherwise assist in a
> proceeding filed or about to be filed (with any knowledge of the
> employer) relating to an alleged violation of section 1341, 1343, 1344,
> or 1348 [of Title 18], any rule or regulation of the Securities and
> Exchange Commission, or any provision of Federal law relating to
> fraud against shareholders.[47]

Given the broad protection courts and the Labor Department
have afforded employees under such participation clauses, the
scope of this section of the law is highly significant.[48]

For example, in similar "participation" clauses employees who
file charges are protected even if management maintains that the
allegations are purely "fabricated."[49] The "participation" clauses

also protect witnesses who assist in antidiscrimination proceedings, even if these witnesses are "reluctant" or are compelled to testify "involuntarily."[50] Coverage under the "participation" clauses "does not turn on the substance of an employee's testimony," and retaliatory actions are prohibited "regardless of how unreasonable" an employer finds the "testimony."[51]

Filing a whistleblower complaint with the U.S. DOL is, unto itself, protected activity.[52] Protected activity also includes meeting with DOL investigators or testifying in a DOL whistleblower proceeding.[53]

THREATENING OR STATING AN INTENTION TO DISCLOSE VIOLATIONS TO THE GOVERNMENT

The SOX statute, like other whistleblower statutes, makes explicit reference to protecting employees who are "about to" testify or file a claim against an employer.[54] This language has been interpreted as explicitly protecting employees who threaten to file complaints with federal authorities, despite the fact that the employee has not actually filed a formal charge.[55]

Under the DOL-administered whistleblower laws, the Secretary of Labor has broadly interpreted the "about to" provisions of these laws.[56] To be protected, an employee does not have to directly inform management of his or her intention to report disclosures to the government. Instead, circumstantial evidence indicating this intention, including internal complaints to management and the circumstances surrounding the whistleblowing, can indicate an intention to report the violation to the government.[57] The DOL has protected employee activities that may cause an employer to fear that an employee is going to report an alleged violation to the government: "An employer who receives an internal complaint may fear that the complainant is about to cause trouble with the government or cause other employees to create such trouble and act to silence the complainant for those reasons. Employees should be protected against such discrimination."[58]

TAPING

Whistleblowers often engage in "one-party" taping of conversations in an attempt to document wrongdoing or retaliation.[59]

Under federal law,[60] one-party taping motivated by a desire to "preserve evidence"[61] or to "protect" oneself and to prevent "later distortions" of a conversation is legal.[62] Even before the passage of the federal wiretapping laws, former Chief Justice Earl Warren, while recognizing the "great danger to the privacy of the individual" arising from the misuse of electronic recording devices, upheld the legality of one-party taping in the context of protecting the "credibility" and "reputation" of a government employee who needed to document wrongdoing. Chief Justice Warren found "nothing unfair in this procedure" because an honest employee would otherwise be "defenseless against [the] outright denials" of a wrongdoer.[63] The contents of such tapes are usually admissible evidence.[64]

In the context of employment law, a number of cases have raised the issue as to whether one-party surreptitious taping in a state that allows such activity is protected activity. In *Heller v Champion International Corp.*,[65] the U.S. Court of Appeals for the 2nd Circuit, in a 2-1 decision, rejected the argument that employee taping constituted "disloyalty" for which discharge was warranted. The court rejected claims that an employee could "never be justified in tape-recording" on the job and noted that a "range of factors" could justify taping, including the "gathering" of "evidence" to document a "possible claim" of "discrimination."[66] The dissent in *Heller* would have upheld discharging an employee for one-party taping.[67]

Under the DOL-administered whistleblower laws, the Secretary of Labor held that taping can constitute protected evidence-gathering activity. For example, the DOL upheld the legality of one-party surreptitious taping when the taping was conducted at the request of a government investigator.[68] In *Mosbaugh v Georgia Power Co.*, the SOL held that an employee's "making lawful tape recordings," on his or her own initiative, was protected activity:

> I find that [the employee] engaged in protected activity under the ERA by making lawful tape recordings that constituted evidence gathering in support of a nuclear safety complaint. [The employee's] tape recording is analogous to other evidence gathering activities that are protected under employee protection provisions, such as making notes and taking photographs that document environmental or safety complaints.[69]

Additionally, under DOL regulations, taped conversations may be admitted into evidence as "non-hearsay admissions of a party-opponent."[70]

CONTACTS WITH THE MEDIA, TRADE UNIONS, OR CITIZEN ENVIRONMENTAL ORGANIZATIONS

Whistleblower disclosures to nongovernmental agencies and the news media have been protected by the DOL under whistleblower laws that are virtually identical to the SOX. Often employee protected activities include a combination of speech-related activities, all directed at calling attention to allegations of misconduct and attempting to apply pressure on regulatory agencies to do their job. For example, in one case in which the DOL found protected activity, the employee had engaged in extensive activities to "publicly reveal information" about his misconduct allegations. In addition to contacting members of Congress, the employee had communicated with a public interest organization and reporters. He was quoted in "three prominent" newspapers. All these activities were protected.[71]

Under OSHA, courts have protected communications with the press because it was "clear" that an "employee's communication with the media" could result in the initiation of regulatory proceedings.[72] This holding has been regularly followed by the DOL.[73]

Numerous cases have also held that federal whistleblower laws fully protect employee disclosures to other nongovernmental bodies, such as trade unions, attorneys,[74] and public interest organizations. In one of the first cases to weigh protecting employees who contacted the news media or public interest groups, *Wedderspoon v City of Cedar Rapids, Iowa*,[75] the administrative law judge wrote:

> Complainant's contribution to the institution of these investigations is twofold: (1) to bring the sludge discharge information to the attention of a friend who was an "environmental activist" and could be expected to act on the information as, indeed, he did; (2) to state the information which he had together with his views and charges against the City to a reporter of the *Des Moines Register* (the state's premier newspaper) whom he could expect to publish them (as the Register did over the reporter's by-line) and to bring about a full public airing of the matter. While complainant did not himself ask

either the cognizant federal authorities or DEQ (Iowa Dept. of Environment Quality) for an investigation, the causal nexus between what he in fact did and the official action which resulted is so close as to compel the conclusion that complainant "caused to be . . . initiated [a] proceeding under this chapter" [i.e., the Water Pollution Control Act].[76]

The DOL has treated the following types of conduct as protected under the whistleblower laws it administers: threat to file a public interest–related lawsuit,[77] contacting a union representative,[78] contacting a newspaper reporter,[79] threatening to contact the press,[80] causing "negative publicity" in the press,[81] and participating in a television report.[82] However, merely discussing misconduct allegations with a member of the "general public," without putting forth evidence that the employee is "about to file a complaint" or participate in a proceeding, is "too remote" to be considered protected activity.[83]

REPORTING CONCERNS TO CO-EMPLOYEES

Whistleblower disclosures made directly to co-employees have been protected under state and federal law.[84] Under the nuclear whistleblower law, the DOL held that a "complaint to a coworker may be the first step" in reporting a violation.[85]

MISTAKEN BELIEF OR "SUSPICION" THAT AN EMPLOYEE ENGAGED IN PROTECTED ACTIVITY

Under established case law, the DOL-administered whistleblower laws prohibit employers from discharging employees even if they only "suspect" that the employee engaged in protected conduct.[86] The laws also protect employees who are not personally engaged in protected activity but are believed to be so engaged by their supervisors. The focus of the inquiry is on an employer's perception that an employee engaged in protected activity and whether the employer was motivated by its belief that the employee had engaged in such conduct.[87]

THE MANNER OF ENGAGING IN PROTECTED ACTIVITY

If the manner in which an employee engages in whistleblowing is completely outrageous or improper, the conduct may lose its status as protected activity. Outrageous activity by employees constitutes an independent justification for discipline. Courts have held that where otherwise-protected protest activities unjustifiably interfere with an employee's job performance, discipline against such an employee may be proper.[88]

In analyzing whether the manner in which an employee engages in protected activity is so outrageous as to lose protection, the U.S. Supreme Court has drawn a distinction between protected activity that involves speech versus protected activity that involves conduct. Alleged misconduct based solely on the content of employee speech is subject to stricter scrutiny than cases in which employee conduct is at issue.

Under federal law, if an employee files a charge or complaint against an employer with a government regulatory body, the employee cannot be disciplined, even if the content of the charge is libelous.[89] Internal protected speech, whether written or oral, should be protected even if it is "vehement, caustic" or "unpleasantly sharp."[90] In *Linn v United Plant Guard, Workers of America*, the U.S. Supreme Court applied the *New York Times v Sullivan* rule to speech issues arising under the NLRA:

> The enactment of the NLRA manifests a Congressional intent to encourage free debate on issues dividing labor and management. And, as we stated in another context, cases involving speech are to be considered against the backdrop of a profound . . . commitment to the principle that debate . . . should be uninhibited, robust, and wide-open, and that it may well include vehement, caustic, and sometimes unpleasantly sharp attacks.[91]

Under the *Linn* analysis, speech was protected so long as it did not contain "deliberate or reckless" untruths,[92] was not "grossly disproportionate" to the goal sought,[93] and did not constitute flagrant misconduct.[94] Case law under Title VII's "participation clause" is also consistent with the *Linn* rule. For example, employee testimony is protected, even if management views it as "unreasonable" or potentially "fabricated."[95]

Employers may place some restrictions on employee speech. For example, employers may prohibit employee speech that improperly portrays a whistleblower's criticism as an "official" agency position.[96]

Employee conduct is subject to stricter scrutiny than speech. An employee who "behaves inappropriately" is not immunized from discipline merely because the "behavior relates to a legitimate safety concern."[97] Alleged protected activity may lose protection if the conduct is indefensible or unduly disruptive.[98] The courts, on a case-by-case basis, consider whether the employer's interest in the "smooth functioning of his business" is outweighed by the employee's interest in internally resolving the discrimination dispute.[99] Under this balancing test, unprotected conduct included dissemination of false and derogatory accounts of an employer's management practices to nongovernmental sources,[100] the interference of a company's business relationship with a customer,[101] misuse of a company telephone to call one's attorney,[102] and other conduct that interfered with the employee's job performance or disrupted the workplace.[103]

The SOL has recognized that "intemperate language," "impulsive behavior," and even alleged "insubordination" often are associated with protected activity.

In general, employees engaged in statutorily protected activity may not be disciplined for insubordination so long as "the activity (claimed to be insubordinate) is lawful and the character of the conduct is not indefensible in its context."[104] The issue of whether an employee's actions are indefensible under the circumstances turns on the distinctive facts of the case.[105]

Given the very nature of whistleblowing, employee whistleblowers are often accused of personality problems, criticized for not being able to "get along with" "co-workers,"[106] or attacked for "disloyalty" and for not being a "team player."[107] Relying upon these types of criticisms to justify adverse actions, employers often build a defense on the grounds that they have discretion to set a "wide range of requirements on employees," even if such requirements may be "arbitrary" or "ridiculous." However, courts have rejected employer reliance upon so-called personality problems when such problems arose as a result or manifestation of protected activity.[108] For example, when criticisms of an employee's "communication style" arose as a result of "auditing work," such conduct is not "indicative of behavior that would negate protection" under whistleblower laws.[109]

Likewise, a loss of "trust" arising from protected activity does not justify adverse action.[110] In *Hadley v Quality Equipment Company*,[111] the SOL declined to protect employee conduct that was "beyond the bounds of behavior appropriate to the work place." However, in another case, an employee's "attitude" was not sufficient justification for including an employee in a Reduction-in-Force (RIF).[112]

Employees may investigate or file complaints regarding matters that are "outside the course and scope" of their employment. In *Helmstetter v Pacific Gas & Electric Company*,[113] the SOL reasoned that limiting coverage under the whistleblower provisions only to employees who made disclosures related to their "official duties" would "hobble the intended broad protection" afforded employees under the acts. But an employee does not have "carte blanche" authority to "choose the time, place and/or manner" of engaging in protected activity.[114] An employee's on-the-job disobedience in refusing to stop investigating potential wrongdoing on matters that fell outside of his job duties was not protected.[115]

Theft of company documents will almost certainly be found unprotected.[116] The SOX only protects "lawful" activities. Similarly, employees who have rummaged through a supervisor's desk attempting to obtain and copy "confidential documents" and show those documents to coworkers have lost protection.[117] But under the appropriate set of circumstances, obtaining documents from work is protected conduct. For example, in *Kempcke v Monsanto Co.*,[118] the U.S. Court of Appeals for the 8th Circuit protected the conduct of an employee who provided company documents to his attorney. The documents at issue had been "innocently acquired" and were not "misused."[119]

WORK REFUSALS

An employee's refusal to perform work is generally not protected. There are, however, exceptions to this rule. First, under a number of antiretaliation laws, employees can refuse to perform work that they believe, in good faith, would be unsafe or unhealthful.[120] Second, a number of cases protect employees who have refused to perform illegal work or commit an illegal act.[121] Work refusals are usually "no longer protected" if the underlying cause of the refusal is "properly investigated, found wanting, and adequately explained."[122]

In the context of the SOX, a DOL ALJ found that an employee's refusal to change the rating of a stock during an internal management meeting was fully protected activity.[123] In this case, the judge relied upon the case law mandating that courts broadly interpret the anti-fraud provisions of the securities laws and held that a stock research analyst was protected when she refused to change the rating of a stock:

> The testimony indicates that a stock rating is a predictor of the future value of the stock, and that a "strong buy" is essentially a precondition that a stock's value will increase in the future and that it is therefore a good investment. Respondent attempted to misrepresent the value of Chyolestech's stock because it attempted to rate it at a level higher than its own expert, Complainant, deemed accurate. . . . The action of pressuring Complainant to give the stock a higher rating was therefore attempted fraud because it represents the dissemination of false information into the market. . . .
>
> * * *
>
> The requirements of the [whistleblower] Act are therefore satisfied in that Complainant refused to change her rating and thereby refused to engage in the illegal activity suggested by her managers.[124]

In *Diaz-Robainas v Florida Power & Light Company*, an employee was discharged after he refused to submit to a psychological "fitness for duty" examination.[125] The SOL reversed the discharge, reasoning that the employee "did not refuse to perform a particular job function or activity" and that the requirement to be examined by a psychologist was "outside the scope of his normal work requirements." The Secretary cautioned employees that his ruling was based on a finding that the referral to the psychologist was itself discriminatory. Had the Secretary found that the employer's referral was nondiscriminatory, Mr. Diaz-Robainas's refusal would have been "at his peril," and Florida Power & Light's decision to discharge him would have been upheld.[126]

THE "REASONABLE BELIEF STANDARD" AND THE GOOD FAITH REQUIREMENT FOR ALLEGATIONS

Under the SOX, an employee is under no obligation to demonstrate the validity of his or her substantive allegations.[127] The concern that resulted in the initial whistleblower disclosure need only be based on a "reasonable belief" that an actual violation occurred.[128] This "reasonable belief" must be based on "reasonably perceived violations" of the applicable law or regulations.[129] The "standard for determining" whether an employee's "belief is reasonable involves an objective assessment" of the employee's concerns.[130] In a SOX whistleblower case a DOL judge explained this standard as follows:

> A belief that an activity was illegal may be reasonable even when subsequent investigation proves a complainant was entirely wrong. The accuracy or falsity of the allegations is immaterial; the plain language of the regulations only requires an objectively reasonable belief that shareholders were being defrauded to trigger the Act's protections.[131]

Employees are under no duty to demonstrate the underlying veracity or accuracy of their allegations.[132] In this vein, allegations remain protected even if facts later demonstrate that the concern was "corrected," that the regulatory agency was "already aware" of the problem,[133] or even if the regulatory authority later rules that the concern was not correct.[134] Even a potentially libelous complaint may be protected.[135]

The rationale for not requiring employees to prove the veracity of their complaints was explained in *DeFord v Secretary of Labor*, a nuclear whistleblower case.[136] The *DeFord* court expressly rejected any requirement that an employee show "that he disclosed unique evidence." Citing from the Supreme Court case of *NLRB v Schrivener*,[137] the court stated that one of the purposes of the law was to "prevent employers from discouraging cooperation with NRC investigators, and not merely to prevent employers from inhibiting disclosure of particular facts or types of information."[138] The legislative history of the SOX clearly supports these precedents. Congress specifically cited to one of the leading cases upholding protection for whistleblowers based on a reasonable belief standard:

> A reasonableness test is also provided . . . which is intended to impose the normal reasonable person standard used and interpreted in a wide variety of legal contexts (See generally *Passaic Valley Sewerage Commissioners v Department of Labor*, 992 F.2d 474, 478).[139]

An employee's motivation for filing a complaint is, in most jurisdictions, irrelevant, and even if an employer believes that the safety allegations are "trivial," an employee may still be protected.[140] In

Guttman v Passaic Valley Sewerage Commissioners,[141] the underlying
case that the Third Circuit affirmed in *Passaic Valley Sewage Commis-*
sioners v Department of Labor, an administrative law judge initially
rejected an environmental whistleblower claim, finding that the
employee's motivation for blowing the whistle was "job and ego,
rather than public pollution protection."[142]

The SOL completely rejected this finding, holding that "it is not
complainant's underlying motive" for "reporting violations" that
"must be established or considered."[143] The whistleblower law
protects an employee's conduct "notwithstanding his motives" for
blowing the whistle.[144] The SOL held that it was "Respondent's
motivation" that must be placed "under scrutiny," not the motivation of the employee. This holding was affirmed by the U.S. Court
of Appeals for the 3rd Circuit. In *Passaic Valley Sewerage Commis-*
sioners v United States Department of Labor,[145] the court affirmed the
SOL's protection of an employee who had filed an "ill-formed"
complaint due to being "misguided" or "insufficiently informed."
The court explained some of the policy considerations underlying
this judgment: "Moreover, an employee's non-frivolous complaint
should not have to be guaranteed to withstand the scrutiny of in-
house or external review in order to merit protection under § 507(a)
for the obvious reason that such a standard would chill employee
initiatives in bringing to light perceived discrepancies in the workings of their agency."[146]

However, if an employee's concern is not "grounded in conditions" for which violations of environmental laws could be "reasonably perceived," the employee's allegations may not be protected.[147]

Usually, courts should not adjudicate the merits of an underlying
disclosure and should refrain from even making findings on these
matters. For example, the DOL has reasoned that under various
employee-protection laws they lack jurisdiction over substantive
safety issues: "[I]t is clear that this office does not have jurisdiction
to decide any issues relative to the quality of the construction work
in question. Those questions are within the province of other federal regulatory agencies. Therefore, any references to quality in this
Decision and Order are not to be construed in any manner as finding in that regard."[148]

Although complaints need only be based on a "good faith" belief
that an employer engaged in wrongdoing, proof of the underlying
wrongdoing may be highly relevant in evaluating *employer* motive
and credibility.[149] For example, demonstrating management

"antagonism" toward safety regulations or proving a supervisor disregarded safety procedures is highly relevant evidence of motive.[150]

Many whistleblower or antiretaliation statutes contain a "participation clause" that even further protects employee speech. When engaging in activities protected under a "participation clause," such as testifying in a proceeding or providing information to a government investigator, the scope of employee protections is "exceptionally broad."[151] Under this clause, "it is not necessary" for an employee to "prove" that the underlying allegations were accurate.[152] When engaging in whistleblower speech in the context of participating in a protected proceeding, the public interest in "maintaining unfettered access to statutory remedial mechanisms" is extremely strong,[153] and Congress intended to "carve out" a "safe harbor from employer retaliation."[154] Thus, even an employee who is forced, not in good faith, but against his will, to "participate" in a covered proceeding is protected from retaliation on the basis of the content of the testimony.[155]

KNOWLEDGE OF PROTECTED ACTIVITY

In order to establish a *prima facie* case, an employee must not only demonstrate that he or she engaged in protected activity but must also demonstrate that the employer or respondent knew of this protected conduct.[156] Simply put, there can be no discriminatory motivation without prior knowledge that an employee engaged in protected activity.[157] Consequently, unless an employee can demonstrate that the "officials who made the challenged decision" knew of the employee's protected activities,[158] the case will be dismissed.

Knowledge of protected activity may be established by either direct or circumstantial evidence.[159] This can include proof that managers suspected the employee of having engaged in protected activity.[160] But regardless of the method used to prove this element, an employee bears the ultimate burden of persuasion on this issue: "Although knowledge of the protected activity can be shown by circumstantial evidence, that evidence must show that an employee of Respondent with authority to take the complained of action, or an employee with substantial input in that decision, had knowledge of the protected activity."[161]

An employer cannot insulate itself from liability by creating "lay-
ers of bureaucratic 'ignorance' " between a whistleblower's direct
line management and the final decision maker.[162] "Constructive
knowledge"[163] of the protected activity can be attributed to the
employer's final decision maker.[164] In U.S. Department of Labor
(DOL)–administered whistleblower cases, the Secretary of Labor
reasoned that "the purpose" of the whistleblower statutes [would]
be undercut were the discharging official able to hide behind the
shield of a lack of actual knowledge where the discharge had, in
fact, been effected by a subordinate because of the employee's protected conduct."[165]

Likewise, employer knowledge of protected activity can be
inferred from other circumstances, such as the size of the workplace.[166] Also, a deciding official who is "suspicious" that an
employee engaged in protected activity is "sufficient to show" an
employer's knowledge.[167]

If an employee with knowledge of the protected activity "contributed heavily" to the decision to take an adverse action against
an employee, knowledge on the part of the employer will be
inferred, even if the actual decision maker had no knowledge.[168]
An employer cannot defend this element of a case by alleging that
its "managers did not know" that a concern implicated a potential
violation of law, if the employee's allegations "reasonably" should
have been "perceived" as communicating such a violation.[169]

9

Adverse Action

The SOX broadly prohibits adverse action in retaliation for an employee's engaging in protected activity. The statute includes numerous types of discriminatory conduct in its definition of adverse action, and is not limited to prohibitions against wrongful discharge. The law states that no employer may "discharge, demote, suspend, threaten, harass, or in any other manner discriminate against an employee in the terms and conditions of employment" based on the employee's "lawful" protected activity.[1]

This definition is similar to the prohibition that is included in other whistleblower laws. The Department of Labor's SOX regulations reflect this broad statutory mandate, and the DOL defines adverse action under the SOX to prohibit employer conduct that "intimidates, threatens, restrains" or "blacklists" employees who engage in protected activity.[2]

The case law interpreting discriminatory conduct under the laws upon which the SOX was modeled reflects the broad definition of adverse action, and includes disciplinary actions, "even if no loss of salary is involved."[3]

Adverse action falls into three general categories, which are relevant to this proceeding. The first category concerns "tangible employment actions." Tangible adverse actions must "affect" the "terms and conditions" of an employee's employment, and include "ultimate employment decisions" (such as a termination or demotion) and "less obvious actions" that alter the "quality of an employee's duties," provided that these impacts have "tangible effects." In cases in which the alleged adverse action is "less obvious" than an ultimate employment action, a court must conduct an "evaluation" of the "entire effect" the action had on an employee's employment.[4]

The second category of adverse actions cognizable under the environmental whistleblower laws was adjudicated under the Department of Labor's "badmouthing" line of cases. In those cases, the DOL adopted a "prophylactic rule" prohibiting negative references or statements about an employee even if it did not result in the loss of the employee's job.[5]

The final category concerns on-the-job harassment, in which case a "tangible job detriment" is not required. This category includes "hostile work environment" cases. The DOL, in its cases under the hostile work environment theory, has interpreted that doctrine in an expansive manner:

> [O]ur determination regarding whether harassing incidents here rise to an actionable level ultimately turns on the question of how best to serve the whistleblower protection purpose of the ERA. As the Complainants argue and the Board has observed, the purpose of the ERA differs from that of federal anti-discrimination legislation such as Title VII, in that the ERA whistleblower provision is intended to "promote the public health and safety." . . . As the Supreme Court stated . . . [the whistleblower law] "encourages employees to report safety violations and provides a mechanism for protecting them against retaliation for doing so." . . . Title VII and other federal anti-discrimination case law provide guidelines for measuring the impact of harassment on a complainant's work environment, but the focal point of our analysis must be whether such harassment undermines the raising of safety concerns projected by the ERA.[6]

Various employer practices short of an actual termination have been held to be illegal discrimination, including the following:

- elimination of a position/reduction in force[7]
- transfers, and demotions[8]
- "constructive discharge" (or making working conditions so difficult as to force a resignation)[9]
- blacklisting[10]
- reassignment to a less desirable position[11]

- negative comments in evaluation that impact employment opportunities[12]
- a retaliatory order to undergo a psychological "fitness for duty" examination[13]
- denial of unescorted access to a work site[14]
- suspension of test certifications[15]
- denial of promotion[16]
- threats[17]
- retaliatory harassment[18] or acts constituting "intimidation and coercion"[19]
- transfer to position where employee could not perform supervisory duties[20]
- circulation of negative references and other forms of "bad mouthing"[21]
- moving an office and denying parking and access privileges[22]
- negative references provided to a reference-checking company[23]
- transfer to a position in which there was "less opportunity to earn overtime pay"[24]
- refusal to rehire or denial of employment[25]
- layoffs[26]
- failure to "recall" an employee back to work[27]
- denial of overtime or refusing to let an employee take time off[28]
- refusal to refer an employee for work with another employer[29]
- refusal to provide proper references and job referrals[30]
- denial of parking privileges[31]
- hostile work environment[32]
- offering an employee a "hush money settlement"[33]
- improperly coercive questioning concerning protected activities[34]
- harassment which reasonably could create a chilling effect on employee speech[35]
- enforcement of policies that directly impact or prohibit protected activity[36]

In a SOX case, a DOL judge noted that employer action that is "reasonably likely to deter employees from making protected disclosures" would constitute adverse action:

Whistle blower statutes are meant to encourage workers to disclose illegal and questionable activities, so their tests for unfavorable employment action encompass more than the adverse economic actions Title VII plaintiffs must prove; any action that would reasonably discourage a worker from making disclosures qualifies [as adverse action].[37]

It is also well settled that "not everything that makes an employee unhappy is actionable adverse action."[38] Actions that have no impact on "employment status" or are temporary in nature may not constitute adverse action.[39] In cases in which evidence of an actual concrete harm does not exist, courts often must "pore over each case to determine whether the challenged employment action reaches the level of 'adverse.'"[40]

Damages

The Sarbanes-Oxley corporate whistleblower law (SOX) contains two sections that are relevant to an award of damages. Both are substantially identical. First, in cases heard within the Department of Labor (DOL) the SOX statute incorporates by reference the "rules and procedures" contained in section (b) of the airline safety whistleblower law.[1] Under section (b), once the DOL determines that a "violation" of the statute "has occurred," the "Secretary of Labor shall order the person who committed such violation" to take specific steps to remedy the infraction, including "affirmative action to abate the violation," reinstatement of the employee, payment of back pay, restoration of the "terms, conditions, and privileges associated" with the employment, and payment of "compensatory damages to the complainant."[2]

In addition to the rules governing DOL proceedings incorporated by reference, the SOX also contains its own provision setting forth the damages required under the statute. This provision mirrors the damages set forth under the airline safety law. The statute states as follows:

(c) REMEDIES-(1) IN GENERAL- An employee prevailing in any action under subsection (b)(1) shall be entitled to all relief necessary to make the employee whole.

(2) COMPENSATORY DAMAGES- Relief for any action under paragraph (1) shall include-(A) reinstatement with the same seniority status that the employee would have had, but for the discrimination; (B) the amount of back pay, with interest; and (C) compensation for any special damages sustained as a result of the discrimination, including litigation costs, expert witness fees, and reasonable attorney fees.

The legislative history of the SOX demonstrates Congress's intent to ensure that employees who prevail in corporate whistleblower cases are properly compensated. The Senate Judiciary Committee's intention was to "require" "reinstatement of the whistleblower" and an award of "back pay and compensatory damages" to any claimant who prevailed in an action.[3]

The heart of a SOX damage award is a mandatory "make whole" remedy.[4] In *Albermarle Paper Company v Moody*,[5] the U.S. Supreme Court held that the "purpose" of the damage provisions in Title VII cases was to "make persons whole for injuries suffered on account of unlawful employment discriminations." The court then quoted from an 1867 case defining the "make whole" rule: "[The general rule is, that when a wrong has been done, and the law gives a remedy, the compensation shall be equal to the injury. The latter is the standard by which the former is to be measured. The injured party is to be placed, as near as may be, in the situation he would have occupied if the wrong had not been committed."[6]

Under the SOX, the "make whole" remedy authorizes a court or the DOL to award all relief necessary to make an employee "whole." This relief includes such things as reinstatement, back pay, interest, special damages, and attorney fees. Depending on the level of position held by an employee, and the type of adverse action at issue in a case, the amount of damages awarded can range from nonmonetary relief only (such as revoking a transfer or reassignment) to a multimillion-dollar award.

REINSTATEMENT

The single most important remedy available to a whistleblower is reinstatement.[7] A job represents a stream of income and benefits, which, over time, can be viewed as a very valuable asset. Given the difficulty many whistleblowers have obtaining comparable employment, reinstatement is often the only realistic method to protect a career. For example, Dr. Penina Glazer, the coauthor of a major study on whistleblowing, testified in one case that it was "extremely difficult, if not virtually impossible" for whistleblowers to find "comparable work in the same industry" after blowing the whistle.[8]

In the SOX, Congress expressly used the word "shall" in mandating reinstatement for wrongfully discharged employees.[9] Even where reinstatement is not expressly required under a statute, reinstatement is "normally an integral part of the remedy" and an employee is "presumed" to be entitled to such relief.[10] The rationale behind the presumption of reinstatement was articulated by Judge Robert Vance of the U.S. Court of Appeals for the 11th Circuit:

> This rule of presumptive reinstatement is justified by reason as well as precedent. When a person loses his job, it is at best disingenuous to say that money damages can suffice to make that person whole. The psychological benefits of work are intangible, yet they are real and cannot be ignored. Yet at the same time, there is a high probability that reinstatement will engender personal friction of one sort or another in almost every case in which a public employee is discharged for a constitutionally infirm reason. Unless we are willing to withhold full relief from all or most successful plaintiffs in discharge cases, and we are not, we cannot allow actual or expected ill-feeling alone to justify nonreinstatement. We also note that reinstatement is an effective deterrent in preventing employer retaliation against employees who exercise their constitutional rights. If an employer's best efforts to remove an employee for unconstitutional reasons are presumptively unlikely to succeed, there is, of course, less incentive to use employment decisions to chill the exercise of constitutional rights.[11]

This rule was adopted by the DOL.[12] In whistleblower cases, there is often significant animosity between the employee and the person or persons on whom the employee filed his or her whistleblower allegations. Yet even under these circumstances the DOL has ruled that reinstatement is the normal remedy.[13] Other federal courts have also rejected claims that "antagonisms" between an employee and employer should defeat the entitlement to reinstatement.[14] Indeed, employers' requests to deny reinstatement have been denied when evidence revealed that the employer was "determined to run" the employee "off the job."[15]

One of the goals of reinstatement is to "restore" the employee "as nearly as possible" to the position he or she would have been in if the discrimination had not occurred. Consequently "unlawfully discharged workers should ordinarily be returned to their original jobs."[16] Reinstatement to the original position sends a message that the "rights" of employees to engage in protected activity will "be protected."[17] Employees should be reinstated in a "substantially equivalent" position "only when the original position" is not available.[18] Moreover, an employee may be reinstated to a higher position if the record fully supports a finding that the employee would have received a promotion and has the qualifications for the higher position.[19]

Arguments that an employee's position no longer exists, therefore rendering reinstatement impossible, have been regularly rejected.[20] In such circumstances courts have ordered employees placed on full-pay status and instated into "the next available position" or to ensure that a comparable position is opened to the employee "within a reasonable period of time."[21] In cases under the NLRA, employers have been ordered to take extraordinary "affirmative action," such as geographically relocating an improperly transferred division of a company in order to properly reinstate employees.[22] However, ordering a company to "bump" an existing employee from his or her current position in order to immediately reinstate an employee is not a favored remedy.[23] Bumping should be used "sparingly and only when a careful balancing of the equities indicates" that absent bumping, an employee's "relief will be unjustly inadequate."[24]

FRONT PAY

Most whistleblower protection statutes, such as the SOX, reinstatement is the "automatic," "preferred," or "usual" remedy.[25] However, front pay is awardable by juries, courts, or administrative agencies "as a substitute for reinstatement" in circumstances when reinstatement is not possible in order to compensate an employee for loss of future earnings.[26]

The SOX, like most other employment laws, does not explicitly reference front pay as a remedy. However, as the Supreme Court has held, "front pay" is a "necessary part" of a "make whole" remedy in circumstances in which "reinstatement" is not a "viable option."[27] Front pay may be awarded where "irreparable animosity" exists between the employee and employer[28] or where "a productive and amicable working relationship would be impossible."[29] In the context of the DOL whistleblower statutes, the DOL permits front pay: "Where the record reflects a sufficient level of hostility between an employer and employee that would cause irreparable damage to the employment relationship, it may be appropriate, at the request of the complainant, to order front pay in lieu of reinstatement."[30]

One court set forth the following factors that can be weighed in deciding whether such a request can be granted:

> Certain factors may counsel against reinstatement in a particular case, including where the circumstances render it impracticable (the position no longer exists), where the employee's sincere and rational preference is against reinstatement, where friction exists between the employer and employee (unrelated to the discrimination), or where the burden of court supervision does not outweigh the gains achieved from reinstatement.[31]

In *Johnson v Old Dominion Security*, a Clean Air Act whistleblower case, the DOL held that "[f]ront pay may be awarded prospectively if reinstatement is impractical, impossible, or an inadequate remedy (e.g., reinstatement may not be feasible due to ongoing antagonism between the discriminated person and an employer)."[32]

BACK PAY

The "legitimacy of back pay as a remedy for unlawful discharge" is "beyond dispute."[33] The SOX statute requires a court or the DOL to award back pay when an employee prevails in his or her case.

The basic black letter law concerning the calculation of back pay was set forth in a whistleblower case as follows:

> The purpose of a back pay award is to make Complainant whole, which is to restore him to the same position he would have been in but for discrimination by Respondent. Back pay is measured as the difference "between actual earnings for the period and those she would have earned absent the discrimination by the defendant." Complainant has the burden of establishing the amount of back pay that Respondent owes. However, because back pay promotes the remedial statutory purpose of making whole the victims of discrimination, "unrealistic exactitude is not required" in calculating back pay, and "uncertainties in determining what an employee would have earned but for the discrimination should be resolved against the discriminating [party]." The courts permit the construction of a

hypothetical employment history for Complainant to determine the appropriate amount of back pay. Complainant is entitled to all promotions and salary increases which he would have obtained, but for the illegal discharge.[34]

Back pay awards are approximate and "uncertainties in determining what an employee would have earned but for the discrimination should be resolved against the discriminating employer."[35] It is fully appropriate when calculating the amount of damage to "recreate the employment history" of the victim and "hypothesize the time and place of each employee's advancement absent the unlawful practice."[36] Thus, sometimes courts must "engage" in this "imprecise process that will necessarily require a certain amount of estimation" in order to make an employee whole.[37]

Back pay awards should continue to "accrue" until an employer fully complies with a damage award, that is, until an employer makes an "unconditional offer of reinstatement."[38] The offer of reinstatement must be to a "comparable" job.[39] If reinstatement is not sought by the employee, back pay generally continues to "accrue until payment" of the damage "award."[40]

The DOL held that back pay awards could be adjusted upward in order to compensate an employee for adverse tax consequences based on the fact that back pay for a period of years is often obtained in one taxable calendar year.[41] However, it is incumbent upon an employee to introduce valid expert testimony in order to demonstrate the amount of additional tax liability.

Back pay awards are generally calculated on a quarterly basis. Specifically, an employee's interim earnings "in one particular quarter" have "no effect on back pay liability for another quarter."[42]

OTHER "MAKE WHOLE" REMEDIES AND INTEREST

Although reinstatement and back pay are usually the two most significant elements of a "make whole" remedy, courts and administrative agencies are usually authorized to award other damages and award equitable or "affirmative" relief in order to ensure that an employee is truly made whole. Often these other aspects of damages can be very significant in ensuring that the impact of an unlawful discharge is remedied.

Other forms of relief awarded employee whistleblowers have included the following: reimbursement for lost overtime;[43] an order to provide complainant with "only good recommendations";[44] interest on the back pay award;[45] restoration of all pension contributions;[46] restoration of health and welfare benefits;[47] restoration of seniority;[48] the provision of neutral employment references;[49] restoration of parking privileges;[50] the provision of necessary certifications for the employee;[51] prohibition against laying an employee off or terminating an employee in the future except when "good cause" exists;[52] cease and desist orders;[53] prohibition on future employer of "derogatory communications" that would impact future employment;[54] applicable promotions;[55] vacation pay;[56] salary increases;[57] training;[58] compensation for forced sale of assets;[59] job search expenses;[60] expungement of personnel file;[61] benefits;[62] and stock option and employee savings plan.[63] In the *Hobby v Georgia Power Company* case, the DOL and U.S. Court of Appeals affirmed a multimillion-dollar judgment on behalf of a corporate executive. In addition to back pay, the executive was awarded incentive pay, bonuses, medical and life insurance benefits, reinstatement of retirement programs, stock options, reimbursement for a tax penalty for early liquidation of retirement funds, job search expenses, compensation for loss of company car, lost vacation pay, compensatory damages for humiliation, prejudgment interest, and a requirement that the company issue a "welcome back" memo to be circulated to its employees.[64]

Damages are also fully available in a "refusal to hire" case. A court should conduct a similar analysis when evaluating damages due to a discharge versus damages due to failure to hire: "To differentiate between discrimination in denying employment and in terminating it, would be a differentiation . . . without substance."[65]

Prejudgment and postjudgment interest is fully available under the SOX.[66] The DOL uses the IRS rate for underpayment of taxes for calculating the applicable interest rate, and interest continues to accrue until the judgment is paid.

An employee must prove at trial each element of damage, including future pain and suffering and future medical expenses.[67] The record can be reopened for damages only if the employee was excusably unaware at the time of the hearing that such future damages would occur.[68]

SPECIAL AND COMPENSATORY DAMAGES

The SOX also permits employees to obtain compensation for "special damages."[69] Special damages include compensatory damages, such as "damages for emotional distress caused by an employer's retaliatory conduct."[70] Judge Frank H. Easterbrook of the U.S. Court of Appeals for the Seventh Circuit described "special damages" in a whistleblower case as follows:

> The phrase is an old one: "*special*, as contradistinguished from *general* damage, is that which is the natural, but not the necessary, consequence of the act complained of." Whether a particular kind of injury gives rise to "special" damages thus depends on the tort committed. The usual consequences of a wrong are "general" damages, and the unusual consequences of a wrong are "special."[71]

Judge Easterbrook then held that emotional distress could be classified as a special damage, and thus he sustained the $200,000 award issued in that case.

Compensatory damages are designed to make the injured party completely whole and include compensation for emotional distress, pain and suffering, mental anguish, and lost future earnings.[72] Compensatory damages are also available as compensation for harassment,[73] humiliation, loss of professional reputation,[74] ostracism,[75] depression,[76] "fear" caused by threats,[77] "panic,"[78] and for the "frustration experienced by victims of discrimination."[79] Marital or family problems caused by the retaliation may also be compensable.[80]

Compensatory damages cannot be used to punish the employer. In *Hedden v Conam Inspection Co.*, the administrative law judge held that "compensatory damages, however, are those necessary to make a wronged party whole and no more."[81]

An employee has the burden of proof in establishing compensatory damages with "competent evidence."[82] For example, in a nuclear whistleblower case, a DOL judge awarded $250,000 in compensatory damages based not only on the employee's subjective testimony of humiliation but also on other facts contained in the record, such as evidence of an employee's "unemployment and underemployment" during the course of his unemployment, "inability" to find comparable employment, expert testimony on loss of professional reputation and "negative" "attitude" employers had "toward whistleblowers," and the evidence that the employee would "face significant hostility and lack of professional respect upon his return" to work.[83]

MITIGATION OF DAMAGES

The SOX, like other employment discrimination laws, does not contain a statutory requirement that victims of discrimination mitigate their damages. However, employers can raise failure to mitigate as an affirmative defense to the amount of damages or scope of relief. The burden of proof to demonstrate that an employee failed to mitigate is on the employer, and the employee is given the "benefit of the doubt" on this issue:

> A claimant is only required to make reasonable efforts to mitigate damages, and is not held to the highest standards of diligence. The claimant's burden is not onerous, and does not require him to be successful in mitigation. The reasonableness of the effort to find substantially equivalent employment should be evaluated in light of the individual characteristics of the claimant and the job market.[84] In order to prevail in a mitigation defense, the DOL has held that an employer must meet an "extremely high" burden and demonstrate that an employee's efforts to obtain new employment were "so deficient as to constitute an unreasonable failure to seek employment."[85]

Attorney Fees and Costs

The Sarbanes-Oxley ("SOX") corporate whistleblower law is only one of four federal statutes that permit employees to obtain payment for reasonable attorney fees and costs as part of "special damages." In other words, fees and costs incurred by an employee are "part and parcel of the 'special damages sustained as a result of the discrimination.'"[1] An employee who prevails in a SOX case is entitled to fees and costs as part of the "make whole" remedy, and a court does not have the discretion to refuse to award reasonable fees and costs.

Under the statute, an employee "prevailing in any action" under the SOX "shall" be awarded "compensation for any special damages" "including litigation costs, expert witness fees, and reasonable attorney fees."[2] Unlike most other fee-shifting statutes, the SOX does not give the courts or the DOL the discretion to deny the payment of reasonable attorney fees to any employee if a violation of the SOX is upheld, does not permit the award of fees to an employer, and classifies fees as part of the "special" damages owed an employee.[3] Only the complainant may obtain reimbursement for expenses and attorney fees.[4] If the respondent (employer) wins, there is no provision for the payment of legal expenses.[5]

The SOX attorney fee provision provides for an award of fees at every step of the process, including the OSHA investigation,[6] the hearing, and the appeal.[7] Attorney fees and costs are also available in federal court actions under the SOX.[8] In *Thompson v U.S. Department of Labor*,[9] the court held that an employee was entitled to a fee under the Equal Access to Justice Act directly from the U.S. Department of Labor when the Secretary's decision against the employee was "not substantially justified." In some circumstances, even work performed outside of the formal adjudicatory process may be compensable.[10]

In administering statutory attorney fee provisions, the courts and the DOL generally follow, where appropriate, the case law developed under the Civil Rights Attorney's Fees Awards Act of 1976, codified as 42 U.S.C. § 1988 (commonly referred to as § 1988).[11] Section 1988 was the first major statutory attorney fee provision in which prevailing civil rights plaintiffs could obtain a fee from a defendant. In case law developed under § 1988 and similar laws, the U.S. Supreme Court explained the underlying reason why Congress, in a select number of public interest–related laws, permits requiring a losing defendant to pay the fees and costs of the plaintiff: "The purpose of § 1988 is to ensure effective access to the judicial process; for persons with civil rights grievances."[12] To achieve these goals, the fees awarded under that provision needed to be sufficiently "adequate" to ensure that employees could "attract competent counsel."[13] Similarly, in a whistleblower case under the DOL-administered laws upon which Sarbanes-Oxley was modeled, the DOL warned against setting a fee "standard that would chill attorneys from taking moderately complicated cases" where an employee "earned modest wages."[14]

Federal courts have recognized that, given the nonmonetary aspect of many civil rights or employment cases, attorney fees can be awarded without any direct relationship between the amount of fees and the amount of relief obtained for a client: "[u]nlike most private tort litigants, a civil rights plaintiff seeks to vindicate important civil and constitutional rights that cannot be valued solely in monetary terms. . . . Regardless of the form of relief he actually obtains, a successful civil rights plaintiff often secures important social benefits that are not reflected in nominal or relatively small damages awards."[15]

DETERMINING A REASONABLE ATTORNEY FEE

In determining a reasonable attorney fee, the basic starting point is the *lodestar* calculation. As defined by the U.S. Supreme Court,[16] the *lodestar* calculation is simply the product of multiplying a reasonable attorney fee rate by the number of hours reasonably expended on the litigation. In *Hensley v Eckerhart*[17] the U.S. Supreme Court held:

> The most useful starting point for determining the amount of a reasonable fee is the number of hours reasonably expended on the litigation multiplied by a reasonable hourly rate. This calculation provides an objective basis on which to make an initial estimate of the value of a lawyer's services. . . .
>
> The product of reasonable hours times a reasonable rate does not end the inquiry. There remain other considerations that may lead the district court to adjust the fee upward or downward, including the important factor of the "results obtained."[18]

Under the *lodestar* method, the first step in determining a reasonable attorney fee is to determine whether the number of hours that a complainant's counsel alleges he or she worked on the case and the requested hourly rate are "reasonable for the quantity and quality of the work performed."[19] Next, the reasonable fee would be established by multiplying the number of hours expended on the litigation by the established market hourly rate for attorney time.[20] The fact that an employee did not prevail on every issue does not automatically constitute a valid ground for reducing an attorney fee award,[21] but fees may be reduced when a plaintiff obtains "partial or limited" success.[22]

Once the amount of reasonable hours is determined, the next step is setting a reasonable market rate for each attorney who performed work on the case.[23] In the legislative history of the Civil Rights Attorney's Fee Award Act of 1976, Congress cited with approval 12 factors set forth in the case of *Johnson v Georgia Highway Express, Inc.*[24] for determining the fair market rate for which an attorney can collect fees.[25] Consequently, most courts use the 12 "Johnson factors" when evaluating fee petitions.[26] The Johnson factors are:

1. The time and labor required;[27]
2. The customary fee;
3. The novelty and difficulty of the questions;
4. The skill requisite to perform the legal service properly;

5. The preclusion of other employment by the attorney due to acceptance of the case;
6. The limitations imposed by the client or the circumstances; priority work that delays the lawyer's other legal work is entitled to some premium;
7. The amount involved and the results obtained;
8. The experience, reputation, and ability of the attorney; if a young attorney demonstrates the skill and ability, he or she should not be penalized merely for being admitted recently to the bar;
9. The "undesirability" of the case;
10. Awards in similar cases;
11. Whether the fee is fixed or contingent; and
12. The nature and length of the professional relationship with the client.[28]

It is recognized that "the most critical factor in determining a fee award's reasonableness is the degree of success obtained."[29] Additionally, civil rights or employment cases are often viewed as "complex civil litigation," and attorney fee rates must be set in order to "attract competent counsel" to work on such cases.[30]

The Department of Labor follows the "lodestar" method in determining a reasonable attorney fee: "In calculating attorney fees under these statutes, I employ the lodestar method which requires multiplying the number of hours reasonably expended in bringing the litigation by a reasonable hourly fee."[31]

The DOL requires an attorney for a prevailing whistleblower to meet the same standards for demonstrating a reasonable attorney fee as do the federal courts under § 1988: "Complainant's attorney's fee petition must include: adequate evidence concerning a reasonable hourly fee for the type of work the attorney performed and consistent for practice in the local geographic area; records indicating date, time and duration necessary to accomplish the specific activity, each activity being identifiable as pertaining to the case; and all claimed costs, specifically identified."[32]

Other factors that are not considered either in the lodestar approach or under the Johnson factors may impact an attorney fee. For example, attorneys for nonprofit organizations or public interest law firms should be awarded fees at the "prevailing market rates." In cases brought under 42 U.S.C. § 1988, the Supreme Court held that both private and nonprofit attorneys should be paid on the same market rate: "The statute and legislative history establish that 'reasonable fees' under § 1988 are to be calculated according to the prevailing market rates in the relevant community, regardless of whether plaintiff is represented by private or nonprofit counsel."[33] This analysis has been adopted by the DOL in whistleblower cases.[34]

The Supreme Court has also awarded attorney fees in cases where the plaintiff was only partially successful. Under traditional fee-shifting statutes, a "prevailing party" entitled to fees includes a party which was "awarded *some* relief."[35] The rule for calculating attorney fees in partially successful cases was spelled out in *Hensley v Eckerhart*:

> Where the plaintiff has failed to prevail on a claim that is distinct in all respects from his successful claims, the hours spent on the unsuccessful claim should be excluded in considering the amount of a reasonable fee. Where a lawsuit consists of related claims, a plaintiff who has won substantial relief should not have his attorney's fee reduced simply because the district court did not adopt each contention raised.[36]

Consistent with these holdings, the Department of Labor has awarded complainant's counsel their full fee, especially where the employee obtained "significant remedies" and remained a "prevailing party."[37]

If an attorney enters into a contingency fee agreement with a complainant, such an agreement will not automatically bar the attorney from being awarded a statutory fee greater than the contingency fee. Trial judges are not "limited" by any "contractual fee agreement between plaintiff and counsel."[38] But, if a case fully settles for a lump sum, that sum may include both damages for the client and attorney fees.[39] Under DOL case law, if a retainer agreement caps the maximum amount of money an employee may be billed for fees and costs, regardless of who wins or loses the case, that agreement may bar an employee's counsel from seeking fees in excess of the cap.

The "prevailing party" bears the burden for establishing the reasonable hourly rate applicable in any case.[40] This is usually accomplished through affidavits of nonparty attorneys who can attest to the local market rate[41] for attorneys of "comparable skill, expertise and reputation in complex federal litigation."[42] Attorneys are also required to properly document the amount of time spent on a case. If documentation is "inadequate," the fee may be reduced.[43] In *Washington v Philadelphia County*,[44] the Court of Appeals for the 3rd Circuit upheld the use of "computerized" time records, which set forth the date each activity took place with "sufficient specificity."

Attorneys who represent clients under a contingency fee arrangement are not permitted to obtain a fee enhancement because of the contingency nature of the retainer.[45] However, in complex cases, clients are "entitled to retain the most competent counsel available," and a court should be willing to pay counsel its "normal billing rate," even if that rate is higher than the local market fees.[46] Conversely, if a firm reduces its hourly rate in order to represent low-income or public interest clients, the firm should still be compensated at normal market rates.[47]

The amount of attorney fees may sometimes be larger than the damage award. In *City of Riverside v Rivera*,[48] the damage award amounted to $33,350.00, whereas the statutory attorney fee was $245,456.25.[49] Due to the significant size of the potential statutory attorney fee, complainants may reduce or waive it as part of a settlement.[50] In some jurisdictions, requiring such a waiver as a precondition to settle may constitute an ethical violation.[51]

In order to compensate for the delay of time between performing legal services and obtaining payment for these services, attorney fee awards are often paid at the rate in effect when awarded, not the rate in effect at the time the services are performed.[52] As the Supreme Court explained in *Missouri v Jenkins*:

> If no compensation were provided for the delay in payment, the prospect of such hardship could well deter otherwise willing attorneys from accepting complex civil rights cases that might offer great benefit to society at large; the result would work to defeat Congress' purpose in enacting § 1988 of "encourag[ing] the enforcement of federal law through lawsuits filed by private persons."[53]

In calculating "current rates," a court should not use an inflation index to merely increase a firm's "historic rate." Instead, the method most often utilized is to pay an attorney fee at the rate the attorney currently charges a client:

> Defendants correctly note that plaintiffs offer no evidence concerning the inflation rate during the last four years or how their 1999

rates compare to their rates in prior years as adjusted by inflation. However, plaintiffs have submitted evidence that their attorneys are representing them on a contingency basis. Therefore, payment to plaintiffs' attorneys has been delayed for four years. Such a lengthy delay in payment justifies the use of current rates.[54]

Attorney fees are awardable for "all phases of the litigation," including appeals and for work performed during administrative proceedings.[55] Attorney fees incurred in the preparation of an application for fees are also compensable.[56]

The calculation of a reasonable attorney fee should not result in a "second major litigation," and the fee petition need not "achieve technical perfection."[57] A fee application may be filed after the close of the administrative record.[58] Under the civil rights attorney fee law, applications for attorney fees have been filed after the 10-day period for motions to alter or amend a final judgment.[59]

Under SOX, attorney fees incurred by an employee are "special damages." Under 18 U.S.C. § 1514(A)(c)(2)(C), fees and costs incurred by an employee must be paid by an employer as part of the "compensation for any special damages sustained as a result of the discrimination." This language is very different from the language used by Congress in the Civil Rights Attorney Fee Act, 42 U.S.C. section 1988, which awards fees as part of "costs," not as part of damages. Based on this language, even if an employer voluntarily changed a discriminatory employment practice after a SOX claim was filed, an employee should still be permitted to pursue his or her discrimination case in order to recover "special damages," such as fees and costs incurred.[60]

COSTS AND EXPENSES

Consistent with most statutory fee provisions, the SOX requires that a prevailing employee be compensated for all costs reasonably incurred in pursuing the litigation. In this regard, costs "necessarily include all expenses incident to the litigation that are normally billed to fee-paying clients."[61] In a nuclear whistleblower case, the DOL held that the provision for an employer's payment of costs must be "interpreted broadly."[62] Like attorney fees, the costs must have been "reasonably incurred" and "sufficiently documented."[63] Recoverable costs have included items such as postage, reproduction, travel, meals,[64] lodging in a "deluxe hotel," paralegal expenses[65] and law clerk time,[66] supplemental secretarial costs, arbitration costs,[67] telephone costs, long-distance calls, messengers' fees,[68] certified mailings, gasoline, and parking.[69]

The U.S. Supreme Court held in *West Virginia University Hospitals, Inc. v Casey* that expert witness fees are only available to a prevailing party if they are explicitly authorized in the attorney fees and cost statute.[70] The SOX law explicitly permits an award of expert witness fees.[71]

Settlement of
SOX Complaints

In order to settle a Sarbanes-Oxley corporate whistleblower (SOX) case, the parties to the agreement must obtain the approval of the U.S. Department of Labor (DOL).[1] The controlling statutory language requires the DOL to "enter into" any agreement reached by the parties.[2] Under DOL case law, settlement agreements cannot be "entered into" unless they are fully reviewed by the DOL and the Labor Department finds that their "terms" are in the "public interest" and are "fair, adequate, and reasonable."[3]

The DOL's settlement-approval authority differentiates SOX cases from other administrative and civil legal actions. In most cases parties are free to settle cases without any government monitoring. Settlements are often confidential, and courts generally automatically dismiss proceedings upon the simple filing of a notice of dismissal after a settlement is reached. Because Congress authorized the DOL to "enter into" any private settlement agreement, the role of the government in SOX claims is different from the role played by a typical court in a civil case. The Secretary of Labor explained the DOL's unique public interest role in approving whistleblower settlements:

> This is not an ordinary lawsuit where a plaintiff's consent to settle a complaint ends the inquiry. The [DOL] does not simply provide a forum for private parties to litigate their private employment discrimination suits such that the parties are free to resolve the case as

they choose. Protected whistleblowing may expose not just private harms but health and safety hazards to the public, and the Secretary of Labor has been entrusted by Congress to represent the public interest in keeping channels of information open.[4]

Before the DOL aggressively enforced its settlement approval authority, employers in whistleblower settlements had abused their strong bargaining position and had insisted that "hush money" provisions be included in settlement agreements. These provisions would restrict the ability of employees to testify against their employers in regulatory enforcement proceedings, and in some cases actually prohibited employees from even informing federal authorities that an employer had violated the law.

In 1989, after a whistleblower publicly challenged the legality of a hush money settlement that restricted him from reporting nuclear safety violations, the U.S. Senate Subcommittee on Nuclear Regulation held public hearings on the DOL-whistleblower settlement practices.[5] In a bipartisan manner, both Democratic and Republican senators were highly critical of hush money agreements. Senator John Breaux (D-LA), who served as chairman of the Subcommittee, did not mix words when he reviewed the hush money practices of industry: "It is shocking to me that we should even have to hold a hearing on such questions. It seems self-evident that it is wrong to pay witnesses not to testify, regardless of the context. Any judicial procedure becomes a sham if witnesses can be paid to withhold evidence."[6]

Senator Alan K. Simpson (R-WY), the ranking minority member of the committee, also condemned the agreements: "This stinks. . . . I think there is a crude overreaching, and the next proceeding for those people ought to be a disbarment box somewhere. That's my view about their conduct when I look at it. And so they strapped together this document and put strictly confidential on it. No wonder they did. The Chairman has read some of it; not call [him] as a witness, or join him as a party. We've already heard that phrase, which is repugnant to any lawyer, to resist compulsory process."[7]

After these hearings, the DOL and the Courts of Appeal decided a number of settlement cases that resulted in strong administrative prohibitions against the practice. The case law, as it now stands, sets forth the following rules:

1. An agreement that contains restrictions on an employee's right to "blow the whistle" will be fully voided.[8] The entire

agreement will be voided even if only one small part of the agreement contains an improperly restrictive clause.[9]

2. A decision to void a settlement agreement and require the parties to proceed with the litigation is not subject to appeal under the collateral order doctrine.[10] Thus, once the DOL voids an agreement, the parties must go back to the hearing process. If the parties want to challenge the DOL's decision, they must wait until after the case is heard or dismissed on the merits, and then proceed to an appeal.

3. If a settlement agreement is voided due to restrictive or hush money terms, an employee is not required to return any monetary consideration he or she obtained as a result of the settlement, and the employee may still pursue his or her whistleblower case.[11] An employee's retention of the settlement proceeds obtained from a voided settlement agreement does not constitute a "ratification" of an illegal agreement.[12]

In addition to the settlement approval process, the DOL also ruled that employers who offer hush money agreements could be held liable in a separate discrimination claim. In *Delcore v. Barney Corp. et al.*,[13] the Secretary of Labor (SOL) ruled that offering an employee a hush money settlement constituted a separate violation of the law entitling the employee to relief (i.e., attorney fees incurred for opposing the hush money settlement). The U.S. Court of Appeals for the 2nd Circuit affirmed the Secretary's holding in *Delcore*: "[E]mployees have the right to be free from discriminatory action meant to deprive them of statutory rights. While in this case Delcore may have rejected the settlement, thereby maintaining his prerogative to communicate with the NRC, the behavior of employers to foist such restrictions on the employees through the guise of a choice does constitute adverse action with respect to employee's rights to communicate with regulatory agencies."[14] The court concluded that "proffering a settlement agreement containing provisions restricting an employee's access to judicial and administrative agencies violates" whistleblower law.[15]

The policies and case law prohibiting restrictive settlement agreements are fully applicable in SOX cases. For example, a federal court in the Northern District of California noted that Congress "indicated a public policy in favor of whistleblowers in securities cases" when it enacted the SOX. That policy prohibited employers from "muzzle(ing) their employees with overboard confidentiality agreements."[16]

SETTLEMENT APPROVAL PROCEDURES

The submission and approval of settlement agreements is a matter of routine procedure in the DOL. The DOL adheres to the principle that "settlements are to be encouraged."[17] Parties regularly execute settlements and submit them to an administrative law judge for approval. The Office of Administrative Law Judges has implemented regulations allowing both for a stay of proceedings (including discovery) in order to provide the parties time to execute agreement and for the appointment of "settlement judges" who can confidentially assist in the voluntary mediation of a dispute.[18] Likewise, under the DOL regulations, if a settlement agreement is approved by a presiding administrative law judge, the agreement may become final if no party files an appeal to the ARB within the 10-day period.[19] If an appeal of the merits decision has been filed with the ARB, then the ARB must approve the settlement.[20] If the case is settled during the OSHA investigation, OSHA must approve the agreement.[21]

The DOL will interpret the agreement— and the conduct of the parties when they negotiated the agreement—in accordance with contract law.[22] Parties must submit the entire agreement to the presiding DOL officer (usually the administrative law judge) for approval.[23] Any "side agreements" related to the whistleblower claims must also be submitted, or the parties to the agreement must certify that there are no other such agreements.[24] The agreement cannot be submitted "under seal,"[25] and the amount of money obtained by the employee, as well as the amount paid for attorney fees, must also be disclosed.[26] It is "error" for an act to dismiss the complaint without reviewing all the terms of the agreement.[27] Although the entire agreement must be submitted for approval and placed on the record in a case, a party may, pursuant to DOL Freedom of Information Act (FOIA) regulations codified in 29 C.F.R. § 70.26, designate some or all of the settlement as "confidential business information" and request that the agency not disclose the agreement.[28] However, designating the information as potentially nondisclosable under any FOIA does not automatically protect the confidentiality of the settlement:

The records in this case are agency records which must be made available for public inspection and copying under the FOIA. In the event a request for inspection and copying of the record of this case is made by a member of the public, that request must be responded to as provided in the FOIA. If an exemption is applicable to the record in this case or any specific document in it, the [DOL] would determine at the time the request is made whether to exercise its discretion to claim the exemption and withhold the document. If no exemption were applicable, the document would have to be disclosed.[29]

A settlement can only be approved by the DOL if the complainant consented to it.[30] The settlement should be signed by the complainant individually. If it is not, the complainant should certify in writing to the veracity of the agreement.[31] An "unequivocal agreement and all material terms" can be approved by the DOL even if a party has "second thoughts" about the settlement and attempts to back out of the agreement.[32] Oral agreements may be binding on the parties.[33] However, if the parties did not reach an agreement on all material terms, the SOL will not approve the agreement.[34] If the DOL determines that the parties cannot comply with a material term of the agreement, the DOL will not enter into the agreement.[35]

The DOL has jurisdiction to approve only those portions of a settlement that concern SOX whistleblower issues. If a settlement resolves other issues, the DOL's "approval" of the agreement does not constitute approval of the settlement as it relates to other potentially resolved claims.[36] A settlement agreement may contain the "final terms" of employment for a whistleblower.[37] Consequently, it is fully appropriate for an agreement to contain terms related to employment, such as an agreement that an employer provide "positive references" for an employee.[38] Attempts to require an employee to waive his or her right to file future discrimination claims that may arise after the settlement is executed have been voided.[39]

Settlements can be effective at their execution, and the parties are bound by the contract until the DOL renders a decision.[40] Allegations that one of the parties to the agreement breached the settlement agreement prior to the DOL's approval of the agreement may not, standing alone, provide adequate grounds for the DOL to refuse to approve an otherwise valid agreement.[41] The DOL can consider "bad faith" conduct by a party to a settlement when weighing whether the DOL will approve the agreement.[42]

A settlement agreement approved by the DOL constitutes an enforceable final order of the Secretary of Labor. The terms of a settlement may be enforced in federal court.[43] A suit for breach of contract based on a settlement agreement must be heard in federal court.[44]

13

Preemption and Arbitration

The Sarbanes-Oxley corporate whistleblower protection law (SOX) does not foreclose corporate employees from pursuing other federal legal remedies, even if they also file a claim under the SOX.[1] State laws that protect whistleblowers are not preempted, and employees can file other federal employment discrimination claims, even if they also file a SOX case.

In SOX subsection (d), Congress explicitly addressed the issue of federal preclusion and preemption.[2] That subsection states as follows:

> Nothing in this section shall be deemed to diminish the rights, privileges, or remedies of any employee under any Federal or State law, or under any collective bargaining agreement.[3]

Corporate whistleblowers are consequently free to pursue whatever legal remedies they deem most appropriate, and the fact that Congress passed the SOX does not negatively impact employee rights under other employee protection laws. Subsection (d) of Sarbanes-Oxley is fully consistent with U.S. Supreme Court precedent under the nuclear whistleblower law, which narrowly construed the preemptive effect of federal labor laws on state remedies.[4] In that case, even without the existence of a saving clause, such as subsection (d), no preemption was found, and the Supreme

Court held that whistleblowers were free to bypass federal statutory remedies and use state law as a source for their protection.

Subsection (d) is an extremely significant provision within the SOX. The SOX permits employees to file claims *de novo* in federal court if the U.S. Department of Labor (DOL) does not issue a final decision on the merits of a case within 180 days of the initiation of DOL proceedings. If an employee opts to file in federal court, any other potential federal claims can be joined with the case, and state pendent claims can also be joined. Conversely, if an employee files a SOX claim within the DOL, the employee can still pursue alternative remedies in state or federal court under various legal theories, including the public policy exception to the termination-at-will doctrine.[5] Under the public policy doctrine, some states have permitted corporate whistleblowers who expose financial wrongdoing to file claims under state law. For example, the Virginia Supreme Court permitted bank employees to file a wrongful discharge case after complaining about violations of securities law, and the Supreme Court of Tennessee upheld a tort cause of action for an employee who alleged that he was fired for reporting fraud to the state Department of Commerce and Insurance.[6]

Likewise, a SOX claim filed within the DOL can be joined with other DOL-administered claims. For example, the DOL has jurisdiction over corporate whistleblower cases that allege violations of environmental or nuclear safety laws. Thus, for example, a nuclear whistleblower may allege that he or she was terminated for disclosing information concerning fraud on stockholders (a SOX claim) and safety violations (a claim protected under the federal nuclear whistleblower law). The DOL has jurisdiction over both causes of action, and both claims could be filed together. The SOX does not mandate any form of election of remedies.[7]

ARBITRATION

In enacting the Sarbanes-Oxley (SOX) corporate whistleblower protections, Congress intended to create a "national floor" establishing minimum federal "employee protections in the context of publicly traded companies."[8] Congress required all employees seeking coverage under the SOX to file a claim with the U.S. Department of Labor. An arbitration agreement would not preclude an employee's filing such a claim with DOL or preclude OSHA from pursuing a claim on behalf of an employee.[9]

Additionally, the case law regarding DOL-administered whistle-blower laws in existence at the time Congress enacted the SOX unanimously reflected the view that DOL proceedings were not preempted by private contractual agreements,[10] including agreements to arbitrate, although the DOL was required to admit arbitration decisions into evidence during DOL proceedings. For example, in cases under the whistleblower provisions of the Surface Transportation Assistance Act, the Aviation Investment and Reform Act (AIR 21), and the Energy Reorganization Act, the DOL was not required to defer to the outcome of an arbitration.[11] Under the STAA, courts have affirmed holdings of the DOL that have differed with the results of arbitrators.[12] In the context of environmental whistleblowing, the DOL case law held that ALJs had the "discretion to determine the weight to be accorded an arbitral decision with regard to the facts and circumstances of each case."[13]

Congress required that the SOX DOL administrative proceedings be identical to the airline safety whistleblower proceedings administered by the DOL. The Senate Judiciary Committee explained that SOX cases heard before the DOL must be "governed by the same procedures" applicable in airline cases.[14] This intent was codified in the SOX statute itself.[15] In an airline safety case decided by a DOL judge less than one month before Congress passed the SOX, the judge explained why the DOL could not defer to private grievance processes:

> The [airline] industry, I argued, is heavily unionized and company-union agreements typically protect against discipline or discharge of workers without just cause. Yet by enacting the provisions of AIR 21 (the airline safety whistleblower law), Congress manifested the clear intent not to delegate protection of whistleblowers in this industry to an informal, private union/management employment grievance process. The legislative enactment protects not just the employee whose personal interests are at stake; AIR 21 triggers a Congressional mandate to foster the public interest in whistleblower activities involving commercial aviation safety issues. As such, deference to private processes is unwarranted.[16]

Under the SOX, an employee also has the right to file a private cause of action in federal court if the DOL does not issue a final order on the complaint within 180 days. The impact of a mandatory arbitration agreement on an employee's right to pursue a SOX claim in federal court has not been decided. Any such case would have to weigh the Congressional intent behind the SOX (including the nonpreclusion clause contained in subsection "d") with the specific terms of an arbitration agreement.[17]

Given the unpopularity of whistleblowers—both with management and coworkers—it would seem inappropriate for privately selected arbitrators to adjudicate SOX cases. Thus, the holdings of a number of cases that limit the applicability of arbitration agreement should be carefully weighed in evaluating whether to agree to or to pursue arbitration of a whistleblower case.[18]

Banking Whistleblower Protections

In addition to the Sarbanes-Oxley corporate whistleblower law (SOX), three relatively obscure federal laws broadly protect all employees within the banking system. The laws cover employees of credit unions, federally insured banks, and "financial institutions." Enacted in 1989, the laws were intended to "enhance the regulatory enforcement powers of the depository institution's regulatory agencies to protect against fraud, waste and insider abuse."[1] Consistent with this intent, courts have recognized that "laws protecting [banking] whistleblowers are meant to encourage employees to report illegal practices without fear of reprisal" and thus such laws should be "construe[d]" "broadly, in favor of protecting the whistleblower."[2] Moreover, courts should "avoid" "nonsensical result[s]" when interpreting the whistleblower laws.[3]

The first law covering the banking sector is the whistleblower provision of the Financial Institutions Reform, Recovery, and Enforcement Act of 1989 (FIRREA), which covers all whistleblowers who work for an "insured depository institution" or a "federal banking agency."[4] An insured depository institution covers most banks, and the law defines a "federal banking agency" as the Federal Deposit Insurance Corporation (FDIC), the Board of Governors of the Federal Reserve System, the Federal Reserve System, the Federal Housing Finance Board, the Comptroller of the Currency, and the Office of Thrift Supervision.[5] In addition to the FIRREA, the Federal Credit Union Act contains a similar provision covering credit unions and the National Credit Union Administration,[6] and the third law covers "financial institutions" involved in "monetary instrument transactions."[7]

The three laws are substantially identical, except the statutory burden of proof in the FIRREA provision was amended in 1993 to include a burden of proof formulation identical to the burden contained in the SOX. As explained in cases decided under FIRREA, the new burden overruled the traditional Title VII formula[8] and required FIRREA to follow the more pro-employee formulation set forth in the Whistleblower Protection Act, 5 U.S.C. § 1221(e).[9] As in the SOX, under the 1993 amendment, employees do not have to prove that retaliatory motive was the "motivating" factor in an adverse action. Instead, an employee must show that such improper motive was a "contributing factor" in the discharge. Once an employee meets the burden, the burden of proof actually shifts to the employer to demonstrate by "clear and convincing evidence" that the same employment decision would have been reached even if the employee did not engage in protected activity.[10]

Every court that has reviewed the new statutorily mandated burdens of proof under the 1993 amendments has agreed that the new burdens "quite clearly make it easier for the plaintiff to make her case . . . and more difficult for the defendant to avoid liability."[11] As the U.S. Court of Appeals for the Seventh Circuit explained:

> [T]he plaintiff, on the one hand, can make out a prima facie case of retaliation, and shift the burden of persuasion to the defendant, with circumstantial evidence that her disclosure was a contributing (not necessarily a substantial or motivating) factor in the adverse personnel action taken against her; and the defendant, once the burden has shifted, must prove not merely by a preponderance but by clear and convincing evidence that it would have taken the same action against the plaintiff even in the absence of her protected disclosure.[12]

Under all three laws, claims are filed in U.S. District Court (not the Department of Labor), and there is a two-year statute of limitations.[13] The statutory definition of protected activity under the banking laws is not as expansive as under the SOX. The banking laws protect employees who "provide information about violations of the law to the appropriate authorities."[14] Under the monetary transaction provision, protected activity includes providing "information" to the Secretary of Treasury, the Attorney General, and a "Federal supervisory agency."[15] The credit union law protects private sector employees who provide information to the Attorney General or the federal credit union board, and it protects employees of the National Credit Union Administration if they provide information to the Attorney General or the Administration.[16] The law covering "depository institutions" protects disclosures to all federal banking agencies (including the FDIC, the Attorney General, and the Federal Reserve).[17] Despite the differences in the statutory definition of protected activity, many courts have interpreted similar statutes in a manner consistent with the language Congress used in the SOX. In this regard, the Department of Labor has noted that Congress's broader definition of protected activity in its most recent statutes effectively "ratified" the prior judicial interpretation given similar statutes.

Consistent with the language in the SOX, the banking laws prohibit not only wrongful discharge but discrimination in the "conditions" of employment.[18] In order to obtain protection, employees need not demonstrate that there was an actual violation of the banking laws.[19] However, if the employee "deliberately" caused the violation at issue in a case, or if the employee "knowingly or recklessly provides false information" to the regulatory authorities, the "protections" afforded the employee under the whistleblower law "shall not apply."[20] If an employee prevails in his or her claim, he or she is entitled to reinstatement, compensatory damages, and "other appropriate actions to remedy any past discrimination."[21] Courts have also held that the language of the acts permits, in the appropriate case, punitive damages.[22] These damages can be significant. For example in *Haley v Retsinas*, the Court of Appeals for the 8th Circuit affirmed an award of $723,533 in back pay, future loss of income, and compensatory damages to a bank examiner employed by the Office of Thrift Supervision.[23] The one most significant difference between the remedies in the banking whistleblower laws and the SOX is the absence of a statutory attorney fee provision in the banking laws.

Employee-whistleblowers in the banking industry have the option of filing a SOX claim in the Department of Labor or a claim under the banking laws directly in federal court. If an employee were to file both claims, if the DOL did not render a final decision on the SOX claim within the 180 days, the employee could elect to file his or her SOX claim in federal court, and joint the two causes of action.

15

Attorneys as Whistleblowers

One of the most unique provisions of the Sarbanes-Oxley Act governs the conduct of attorneys. Under the law, attorneys who represent publicly traded companies in proceedings before the Securities and Exchange Commission (SEC) are now required to "blow the whistle" on misconduct. No other whistleblower law requires attorneys to be "blowing the whistle" on their own "clients."

Two separate provisions of the Act establish the framework governing attorney whistleblowers. First, in Section 307 of the Sarbanes-Oxley Act, Congress enacted a special provision setting forth "Rules of Professional Responsibility for Attorneys."[1] This provision required that any attorney "appearing and practicing"[2] in "any way" on behalf of a publicly traded company, report "evidence of a material violation of securities law or breach of fiduciary duty." The attorney's statutory reporting duty required him or her to report the wrongdoing to either the company's chief legal counsel or the company's chief executive officer. If the general counsel or CEO fails to take appropriate remedial action, the attorney must then disclose his or her concern to the company's audit committee, or an equivalent body.

Second, the whistleblower provision of Sarbanes-Oxley can shield the attorney who makes disclosures pursuant to Section 307 of the Act from retaliation.[3] In this regard, the SOX protects not just direct employees of a publicly traded corporation, but also protects contractors and agents of the company.[4] Thus an attorney who works either as in-house counsel or as outside counsel for a publicly traded corporation should be classified as a protected employee under the whistleblower law.

The SOX also fully protects employees who disclose material violations of securities laws directly to their supervisor, or any other person who has the "authority to investigate, discover, or terminate misconduct." Thus, an employee's disclosure to general counsel, a CEO, or an audit committee should constitute fully protected activity under the SOX. Consequently, adverse employment action taken by a law firm (or in-house counsel) against one of its own attorneys because that attorney reported a violation of securities law would be actionable under SOX.

Section 307 of the Sarbanes-Oxley Act also directs the SEC to implement rules establishing the minimum standards of professional conduct for any attorney "appearing and practicing" before the SEC. In response to this mandate, the SEC enacted 17 C.F.R. Part 205. These codified rules establish the "minimum standards of professional conduct for attorneys appearing and practicing before the Commission in the representation of an issuer,"[5] and govern how and to whom an "attorney"[6] must or may "report"[7] "evidence of a material violation"[8] of securities laws (including a "breach of fiduciary duty")[9] when evidence of a violation is uncovered, regardless of whether the violation has already occurred or is about to be committed by or on behalf of an "issuer."[10]

The failure of an attorney to follow these mandatory disclosure rules could have dire consequences for an attorney's career and ability to practice law. Any violation of SEC rules may subject the attorney to an SEC enforcement action in which the attorney may be subject to any of the "civil penalties and remedies for a violation of the federal securities laws available to the Commission," including censure or temporary or permanent denial of the privilege of appearing or practicing before the SEC. 17 C.F.R. § 205.6(b). Attorneys would also be subject to discipline by state attorney ethics committees.

REPORTING WRONGDOING UP THE LADDER

The SEC regulations governing the standards of professional conduct of attorneys place a great deal of emphasis on when, how, and to whom a lawyer must reveal credible evidence of a material violation of federal securities laws, including a violation of a fiduciary duty and other similar violations. The regulations are complicated and convoluted, and it may well turn out that the attorney who initially disclosed the wrongdoing could be blamed for the failure to rectify the wrongdoing unless the attorney documents every disclosure he or she makes.

The process used to report a material violation of the federal securities laws will differ based on the status of the lawyer—that is, is the lawyer classified as a "subordinate attorney," a "supervising attorney," the "chief legal officer"(CLO), or a member of a "qualified legal compliance committee"(QLCC) of an issuer?

A "subordinate attorney" is any attorney under the direct supervision or direction of an attorney other than the chief legal officer (or equivalent thereof) of a publicly traded company.[11] Without exception, all subordinate attorneys "shall" report to their supervising attorney "evidence of a material violation of which the subordinate attorney has become aware in appearing and practicing before the Commission."[12] Under the SEC rules, the subordinate attorney has no further obligation to report concerns.[13] The report need not be documented and can be made telephonically, orally, or in writing.[14] If a subordinate attorney believes that his or her supervisory attorney failed to comply with the up-the-ladder reporting requirements, then that subordinate attorney "may" report evidence of a material violation up the ladder as the supervisory attorney should have done.[15] Significantly, under Section 307 of the Sarbanes-Oxley Act, if appropriate corrective action is not taken by the general counsel or CEO, the subordinate attorney must take his or her concern to the audit committee.[16]

A "supervisory attorney" is any "attorney supervising another attorney who is appearing and practicing before the Commission in the representation of an issuer" as well as the "issuer's chief legal officer (or the equivalent thereof)."[17] The definition of a supervisory attorney also would include any attorney who is under the "direct supervision or direction of the issuer's chief legal officer (or the equivalent thereof)."[18] A supervisory attorney is deemed to appear and practice before the Commission if the subordinate attorney(s) reporting to the supervising attorney appear and practice before the Commission.[19] A supervisory attorney must take reasonable efforts to ensure that a subordinate attorney reports credible evidence of material violations to the supervisory attorney and to ensure that the mandatory reporting requirements are met if the supervisory attorney receives a report or otherwise uncovers evidence of a material violation.[20] A supervising attorney "may report" evidence of a material violation directly to a "qualified legal compliance committee" (QLCC).[21] By reporting such evidence to a QLCC, an attorney satisfies all the reporting requirements required under the SEC regulatory scheme.[22]

If the attorney "becomes aware of evidence of a material violation by the issuer, or by any officer, director, employee, or agent of the issuer, the attorney shall report such evidence to the issuer's chief legal officer (or the equivalent thereof) or to both the issuer's chief legal officer and its chief executive officer (or the equivalents thereof) forthwith."[23] If the attorney reasonably believes a report to the chief executive officer (CEO) or the Chief Legal Officer (CLO) would be "futile,"[24] the attorney "must" instead report the evidence of a material violation up the ladder to either a QLCC (if one exists) or to the audit committee or another independent committee of the issuer's Board of Directors.[25]

If a QLCC exists and the attorney reports the evidence of a material violation to the QLCC, then that attorney need not report the evidence of a material violation to either the CEO, CLO, Board of Directors, or one of its committees. Once a report is made to the QLCC, the attorney is under no obligation to take any further action and need not assess the issuer's response to the report.[26] A report other than to the QLCC requires the reporting attorney to evaluate the response and to determine whether a timely response was received and whether the response was appropriate.[27] No further action is required if the attorney reasonably believes that he or she received an "appropriate response"[28] to the report.[29]

Upon receipt of a report, the CLO can either investigate the report or turn it over to the QLCC and inform the reporting attorney that the report has been referred to the QLCC.[30] In that situation, the CLO has no further duty to forward the report further up the line or to investigate the report. Once the report is turned over to the QLCC, it has responsibility for investigating and resolving the reported evidence of a material violation. If the CLO elects not to investigate the report, he or she can turn the report over to a QLCC, if one exists.[31] If the CLO decides to conduct the investigation, then the CLO must conduct a reasonably appropriate inquiry into the report to determine whether the alleged material violation occurred, is ongoing, or is about to occur.[32] The CLO must report back to the attorney whether the investigation found that a violation is ongoing, has occurred or is about to occur. If a violation exists or is about to occur, then the CLO "shall take all reasonable steps to cause the issuer to adopt an appropriate response, and shall advise the reporting attorney thereof."[33] On the other hand, if no violation is detected, then the CLO "shall notify the reporting attorney and advise the reporting attorney of the basis for such determination."[34] The reporting attorney must then evaluate whether the response from the CLO was "appropriate" and "received within a reasonable time."[35] If the response is deemed inappropriate or if it was not submitted in a reasonable period of time, the reporting attorney "shall" report the evidence of a material violation to the issuer's board of directors or an appropriate committee of the Board.[36]

Because the SOX specifically protects employees and "agents" of publicly traded corporations who disclose misconduct to persons or corporate committees such as the CLO, the QLCC, the CEO, and an audit committee, the antiretaliation provisions of the SOX should fully protect attorney-whistleblowers, even if these attorneys never report their allegations outside the internal oversight committees mandated by the SEC regulations.

BLOWING THE WHISTLE TO THE COMMISSION

The most controversial regulation enacted by the SEC is the rule permitting—but not requiring—lawyers to disclose confidential information to the SEC. Reports to the SEC are permitted in three different circumstances. First, an attorney "may" reveal any confidential information to the Commission if the attorney "reasonably believes necessary"[37] to "prevent the issuer from committing a material violation that is likely to cause substantial injury to the financial interests or property of the issuer or investors."[38] What constitutes a "substantial injury" is not defined.

Second, an attorney "may" reveal confidential information to the Commission if the attorney "reasonably believes necessary" to prevent the issuer in the course of a "Commission investigation or administrative proceeding" from committing "perjury" or the "subornation of perjury" or any "act proscribed in 18 U.S.C. 1001 (i.e., knowingly and willfully '(1) falsifies, conceals, or covers up by any trick, scheme, or device a material fact; (2) makes any materially false, fictitious, or fraudulent statement or representation; or (3) makes or uses any false writing or document knowing the same to contain any materially false, fictitious, or fraudulent statement or entry') likely to perpetuate a fraud upon the Commission."[39] This provision is substantially broader in scope, as the "substantial injury" element is not included. Under this provision, if an attorney believes that false information was or is about to be presented during the course of an SEC investigation or proceeding, the attorney may provide the Commission with information to foil the plan or act.

Third, an attorney "may" reveal confidential information to the Commission to the extent he or she "reasonably believes necessary" to "rectify the consequences of a material violation by the issuer that caused or may cause, substantial injury to the financial interest or property of the issuer or investors in the furtherance of which the attorney's services were used."[40] The phrases "furtherance of which the attorney's services were used" and "substantial injury" are not defined but imply that the scope of the disclosure must be related to the actual legal services that were used.

As discussed later, if the issuer refuses or fails in any material respect to take appropriate action recommended by the QLCC in response to a report of a material violation, then the QLCC has the "responsibility, acting by a majority vote" to take all appropriate action that specifically includes "the authority to notify the Commission" of the issuer's refusal or failure.[41]

The SOX whistleblower provision directly protects employees who raise allegations of misconduct directly to the SEC from retaliation. Consequently, attorneys who "blow the whistle" to the SEC in a manner consistent with the SEC regulations governing attorney conduct should be fully protected against retaliation.

DUTIES OF A QUALIFIED LEGAL COMPLIANCE COMMITTEE (QLCC)

If evidence of a material violation is reported to the QLCC, then the QLCC must inform the CEO and CLO of the report unless the QLCC reasonably believes the report would be futile.[42] In any event, the QLCC must make an independent determination whether an investigation is necessary.[43] If a determination is made that an investigation is not necessary, the QLCC has no further obligations under the SOX Rules. If the QLCC determines that an investigation is necessary, then the QLCC must notify the Audit Committee or the full Board of Directors that an investigation is necessary, and the QLCC must commence the investigation.[44] The QLCC must be authorized to retain experts and other personnel the committee deems necessary to respond to a report.[45] An attorney retained by the QLCC to investigate or to assert a "colorable defense on behalf of the issuer" during the course of "any investigation or judicial or administrative proceeding" "shall not have any obligation to report evidence of a material violation."[46] At the conclusion of an investigation, the QLCC (by a majority vote) must recommend an appropriate response to the issuer and inform the CLO, CEO, and the full Board of Directors of the results of the investigation and the recommended remedial measures that need to be adopted.[47] If the issuer fails in any material respect to adopt the proposed appropriate response then the QLCC has the "responsibility, acting by a majority vote" to take all appropriate action "including the authority to notify the Commission" of the issuer's failure to take appropriate action.[48]

Consistent with these rules and regulations, attorneys and other employees who work for a QLCC engage in protected activity when they disclose the allegations of misconduct to their supervisors or to corporate committees with the authority to investigate or correct the misconduct. Under the case law on which the SOX was modeled, auditors who performed their job in an aggressive manner obtained full whistleblower protection.[49]

DUTIES OF THE CHIEF LEGAL OFFICER (CLO)

Once evidence of a material violation is brought to the attention of the CLO, he or she has two options. The CLO must cause a reasonably appropriate inquiry to determine whether a material violation has occurred, is ongoing, or is about to occur and take all reasonable steps to cause the issuer to adopt an appropriate response. The CLO also must advise the reporting attorney of what actions were taken or determined to have occurred.[50] If a QLCC exists, the CLO has the option of referring the report to QLCC for resolution.[51] If the report is forwarded to the QLCC, the CLO must inform the reporting attorney of the referral.[52] The referral to the QLCC and advising the reporting attorney of the referral satisfy all the CLO's mandatory reporting requirements.[53]

NOISY WITHDRAWAL

The SEC is still considering whether to require attorneys who withdraw from representation of public companies in certain circumstances to effect a so-called "noisy withdrawal"—that is, to notify the SEC that they are withdrawing for professional reasons.[54] The originally proposed SEC regulations contained a "noisy withdrawal" provision that would have required lawyers to withdraw from representation and inform the SEC if the matter in issue is not resolved. Although the noisy withdrawal provisions are not contained in the currently issued rules, the SEC appears to have only delayed action on the implementation of the rule and is also considering an alternative rule that would require the public company to notify the SEC of the withdrawal, as opposed to requiring the lawyer to notify the SEC.

THE USE OF CONFIDENCES AND SECRETS IN A SOX PROCEEDING

The SEC's Part 205 regulations permit attorneys "[a]ppearing and practicing before the Commission"[55] to utilize confidential communications to the detriment of the client. Relying on an explicit grant of statutory authority[56] and pursuant to the Supremacy Clause of the United States Constitution,[57] the SEC issued regulations restricting any state or other federal jurisdiction from interfering with an attorney's right to disclose confidences and secrets that would otherwise be permitted under the Commission's Part 205 regulations.[58] The SEC's Part 205 regulations permit "[a]ny report under this section (or the contemporaneous record thereof) or any response thereto (or the contemporaneous record thereof) may be used by an attorney in connection with any investigation, proceeding, or litigation in which the attorney's compliance with this part is in issue."[59] While the ARB has not yet considered whether this provision applies to a SOX whistleblower protection proceeding, the phrase "any investigation, proceeding or litigation" is extremely broad and presumably would encompass such proceedings. Such a conclusion is supported by the SEC's commentary accompanying the Federal Register publication of its Part 205 regulations.

According to the SEC, under Part 205, the use of confidential information was aimed at providing lawyers with the "equivalent" use of confidential information as contemplated under "the ABA's present Model Rule 1.6(b)(3)," i.e., the August 2002 edition.[60] Under this ABA Model Rule provision, attorneys are authorized to use confidential information "to the extent the lawyer reasonably believes necessary . . . to establish a claim or defense on behalf of the lawyer in a controversy between the lawyer and the client."[61] Moreover, well before the SEC equated the permissible use of confidential communications to this ABA Model Rule provision, the ABA published a formal ethics opinion clarifying that specifically under this provision lawyers are allowed to use confidential communications as the lawyer deems necessary to bring a wrongful discharge claim against a client.[62] Presumably the SEC was aware of the ABA's interpretation of its rule at the time the Commission enacted its Part 205 regulations. As such, there is little doubt that the SEC authorized the use of confidential communications consistent with the permissible uses contemplated under the ABA Model Rule.

In a recent decision the Department of Labor's ARB did restrict a lawyer's ability to use confidential information in a proceeding brought under several environmental whistleblower protection statutes, all of which significantly differ from the SOX in that the environmental whistleblower statutes do not address attorney conduct and did not provide for the promulgation of regulations governing attorney conduct.[63] The ARB concluded that where "Congress has not provided any exception to the rule on attorney-client privilege in the environmental whistleblower Acts,"[64] the ARB will ignore state bar rules and will apply "the federal common law" principles "'as they may be interpreted by the courts of the United States in light of reason and experience.'"[65] The ARB then concluded that the 1972 draft of Supreme Court Standard 503,[66] which was never enacted by Congress, reflects the current state of federal common law with respect to the use of confidential communications by an attorney.[67] Relying on this standard, the ARB concluded that a lawyer is permitted to bring the claim under Supreme Court Standard 503, but that the attorney must "prove his environmental whistleblower retaliatory discharge complaint, if at all, without the use of material protected under the attorney-client privilege."[68] Because the lawyer's claim was dependent on the use of confidential communications, the ARB dismissed the case. This holding may nonetheless apply to lawyers who do not fit the "appearing and practicing before the Commission" definition.

The ARB's current interpretation of the federal common law, which essentially reflects the prohibitions articulated in the ABA's older Code of Professional Responsibility, may give way to the modern standards adopted in ABA's modern rules. "This difference between the Model Rules and the Code of Professional Responsibility's Disciplinary Rules was clearly recognized by the Supreme Court of Tennessee,"[69] when that court concluded that the state bar rules would have to be changed to permit an in-house attorney to reveal confidences of a client in a retaliatory discharge claim. The Tennessee Supreme Court then expressly adopted a new provision paralleling Model Rule 1.6, thereby permitting the attorney to use confidential information.[70] As local jurisdictions adopt the approach set forth under ABA Model Rule 1.6(b)(3) (Aug. 2002),[71] the federal courts interpreting the federal common "in light of reason and experience"[72] may turn from the prohibitions generally recognized under the Code of Professional Responsibility to an approach consistent with the current Model Rule standard. It should be noted that the few federal courts that previously addressed whether a lawyer could bring a federal antidiscrimination claim against a client uniformly concluded that the "important public policies underlying federal antidiscrimination legislation and the supremacy of federal laws in determining federal anti-discrimination statutes take precedence over the at-will discharge principle."[73] Thus, while a lawyer "does not forfeit his rights simply because to prove them he must utilize confidential information,"[74] the federal courts can nonetheless utilize their equitable powers to limit the release of confidential information to third parties by sealing the record, conducting *in camera* proceedings, issuing protective orders, or restricting the use of testimony in successive proceedings.[75]

Audit Committees and Corporate Employee Concerns Programs

The Sarbanes-Oxley Act did not limit its whistleblower protection provisions merely to providing a cause of action for wrongfully discharged employees. When Congress investigated the Enron/World Com and other corporate scandals of 2001–2002, they expressed concern not only about corrupt accounting practices that harmed innocent investors, but also about a "culture of silence" that permitted unethical corporate misconduct to go unreported and a breakdown in corporate oversight that permitted illegal conduct to remain undetected. To remedy this problem, Congress looked toward whistleblowers. Employees were in the unique position to learn about unethical or illegal practices. The issue was, What could Congress do to encourage employee reporting?

The first step was to prohibit employer retaliation against whistleblowers and provide employees who alleged discriminatory practices a legal cause of action similar to other employee protection statutes. But Congress wanted to go further. Consequently, they required that every publicly traded corporation create an internal "employee concerns" type program that would permit employees, in confidence, to report "questionable accounting or auditing matters."[1]

Section 301 of the Sarbanes-Oxley Act (SOX) requires that every publicly traded corporation have an independent "audit committee," and that each such committee must thereafter "establish procedures" for employees to provide "confidential" and even "anonymous" allegations "regarding questionable accounting or auditing matters."[2] In order to emphasize the seriousness of providing a mechanism to encourage whistleblowing on corporate wrongdoing, Congress also provided that any company that fails to establish the procedures required by SOX Section 301 would be "de-listed" as a publicly traded company from the stock exchanges.

The Securities and Exchange Commission (SEC) has not yet adopted final rules regarding minimally acceptable procedures that audit committees must establish in order to comply with Section 301. However, the SOX statute, on its face, requires that audit committees provide for the "receipt, retention and treatment" of both "confidential" and "anonymous" complaints concerning company accounting, internal accounting controls, or auditing matters. Accordingly, audit committee procedures must contain at least three features in order to comply with Section 301:

- Ensuring that employees can make "confidential" and "anonymous" reports
- Requiring that employee complaints be handled independently from the management of the publicly traded company
- Mandating that employee complaints about company accounting, internal accounting controls, or auditing matters be independently investigated in a professional and effective manner

Obviously, in light of the Wall Street and accounting scandals, Congress was extremely concerned that publicly traded companies lacked the will to internally investigate themselves. In order to provide for a measure of accountability and to change corporate culture, Congress is now requiring as a condition of obtaining and maintaining the right to publicly trade securities that companies themselves provide for independent oversight and investigation of complaints concerning accounting and auditing problems.

In response to the enactment of SOX, the SEC proposed Exchange Act Rule 10A-3 to strengthen regulatory requirements regarding public company audit committees. Under the new rule, the SEC now requires that each member of the audit committee be a member of the company's board of directors, but the audit committee member must be "independent" of the company.[3] In addition, it is now required that each audit committee be "directly responsible" for the compensation and oversight of the work of any registered public accounting firm that is engaged for the purpose of auditing the company, that each public accounting firm report directly to the audit committee, that each audit committee independently establish the confidential and anonymous whistleblower procedures required by SOX Section 301, that each audit committee has the authority to engage independent contractors and advisors to carry out its duties, and that each company must provide appropriate funding for the audit committee.

In implementing SOX Section 301, the SEC expressly recognized that it is essential for the audit committee to maintain independence from the board of directors, as a whole, and company management so that the audit committee can fulfill its role in effectively performing oversight functions. The SEC also recognized that audit committee independence is paramount to ensure that there be "frank, open channels of communication so that information can reach the audit committee."[4]

The importance of maintaining the free flow of information from company employees has long been recognized as essential to uncover corporate fraud. Some federal courts have held that a stockholder may allege securities fraud violations under the Private Securities Litigation Reform Act (PSLRA) of 1995[5] based on confidential sources, such as allegations received from unnamed former or current employees.[6] One court has noted that "[e]mployees or others in possession of important information about corporate malfeasance may be discouraged from stepping forward if they must be identified at the earliest stage of a lawsuit."[7]

Mechanisms to receive and investigate employee complaints are not an alien concept to either corporate America or the federal government. Several companies in highly regulated industries—such as the nuclear power, defense contracting, and oil, gas, and chemical industries—have attempted to provide for so-called independent employee concerns or complaint programs. Likewise, the federal government has established various procedures, such as Inspector General programs and the Office of Special Counsel, to receive and investigate whistleblower complaints from federal employees. However, all of the currently established programs have met with dubious results and fall far short of the expectations and mandates envisioned by Congress when it enacted SOX.

Nonetheless, audit committees and human resources professionals would be well advised to study the problems and inherent flaws in these existing employee-concerns programs before attempting to establish the procedures required by SOX Section 301. In too many cases, the established employee-concerns programs have participated in the retaliation carried out against the employee-whistleblower. This must be avoided at all costs under SOX Section 301, or companies will risk being "de-listed" as a publicly traded company for failing to establish the required procedures.

In order to adhere to the reforms mandated by SOX Section 301, it is incumbent upon the audit committee to actively promote and enforce a corporate culture that encourages whistleblowing and that prohibits any retaliation against employees who make complaints protected under SOX Section 301. Once there exists the perception of retaliation against or unfair treatment of employees who report complaints to the audit committee, there will exist a lack of confidence in the program among employees, and the entire purpose of SOX Section 301 will be fatally undermined.

Take, for example, the system that NASA established in the wake of the *Challenger* accident in the mid-1980s to enable NASA workers to anonymously report potential safety problems. According to published reports, that system "logged an all-time high of 55 reports in 1990."[8] However, "that number dropped to nine in 1994 and 13 in 1995."[9] After the second shuttle exploded in early 2003, it was widely documented that NASA employees failed out of fear of retaliation to report safety problems that might have prevented the disaster.

Thus, in order for an audit committee to properly comply with SOX Section 301 it must build trust and instill confidence in employees to utilize whatever program and mechanisms the audit committee establishes to receive and investigate complaints.

Unlike the existing employee-concerns programs, SOX Section 301 requires that audit committees play a central role in changing or reforming corporate culture with respect to business ethics, generally, and in regard to the corporate view of whistleblowing on Section 301 matters in particular. As a result of this statutory mandate, audit committees are expected to be a driving independent force for corporate reform. By contrast, existing employee-concerns programs usually augment the role of management, and they lack the resources, independence, and clout to enforce reforms or make meaningful changes in corporate culture.

In short, if audit committees fully comply with SOX Section 301, there is the potential for a sea change in corporate culture and attitudes toward whistleblowers. That is precisely what Congress had in mind when it required, for the first time, that private companies establish independent procedures to encourage and facilitate corporate whistleblowing.

EMPLOYEE-CONCERNS PROGRAMS: "DON'T SHOOT THE MESSENGER"

It is well known that the prevailing view toward whistleblowers both within corporate America and in government is based on a "shoot the messenger" mentality. The precise reasons why whistleblowers are so ostracized and mistreated by corporate and governmental organizations are complex. However, it is not oversimplifying to say, as a general matter, that management, whether in the private or public sectors, instinctively detests whistleblowers. Naturally, nobody enjoys having their ethics questioned. Consequently, individuals and supervisors who are implicated by whistleblower allegations often overreact in a highly charged personal manner against the employee who is perceived or known to have raised the complaint.

When these disputes get out of hand, the whistleblower can be viewed by the organization itself as a threat to its mission or existence. If such situations persist, it can result in creation of a truly hostile work environment for the whistleblower. In the past, whistleblowers have been widely viewed by companies and coworkers as needlessly slowing down production, costing the company excessive amounts of money, threatening the shutdown of the plant and loss of jobs, and as being disloyal, traitors, or disgruntled. In many cases, companies and their management have permitted or even encouraged negative perceptions of whistleblowers to take hold within the organization as a whole.

Too often, existing employee-concerns programs have become part of this corporate "shoot the messenger" mentality. In the most extreme cases, employee-concerns programs have breached employee confidentiality and shared information with the company management or its lawyers to attack the whistleblower.

One of the most notorious cases of whistleblower retaliation involving employee-concerns programs, *Hill v TVA*, occurred in the mid-1980s at the Tennessee Valley Authority.[10] Just as TVA was about to obtain an operating license for one of its nuclear plants, the U.S. Nuclear Regulatory Commission (NRC) notified TVA that plant employees "had raised a number of safety concerns anonymously with NRC and congressional staff."[11] According to the Department of Labor, which investigated the matter, the employees had also expressed fear of retaliation, should they disclose their concerns to TVA management. At the urging of the NRC, the TVA hired an outside contractor, Quality Technology Company (QTC), "to interview TVA employees, so that their safety concerns might be identified, investigated, and resolved."[12] QTC's mission was "to develop and implement a program for the identification, investigation, and reporting of employee-raised issues, with special emphasis on issues dealing with nuclear safety."[13]

The Department of Labor noted that the "purpose of an employee concern program at a nuclear utility is to provide a confidential channel for the expression of employees, views and concerns."[14] That is remarkably similar to the purpose of the audit committee procedures that have been mandated by SOX Section 301.

At the time TVA hired QTC, TVA had its own employee-concern program in operation before hiring QTC, but, according to the Department of Labor, it "had proved ineffective."[15] After QTC began documenting and investigating employee complaints about the problems besetting TVA, "[m]anagers and consultants in the nuclear power industry became concerned that TVA's troubles would have repercussions on the entire industry, that other nuclear plants would be subjected to closer scrutiny by NRC."[16]

Not long after QTC began investigating employee complaints about nuclear safety, TVA management determined "that QTC was finding too many problems, reported them in a way that made them look serious, and that QTC was a cancer."[17] Members of TVA management also "complained that there was a direct link from QTC to Washington, D.C. and NRC" and "that QTC employees were communicating directly with members of Congress and NRC without obtaining TVA's permission."[18]

Notably, the Department of Labor found that TVA placed restrictions on QTC's contract, and then failed to renew it, "in retaliation for QTC's collection, investigation, and disclosure of safety-related problems."[19] Accordingly, the Department of Labor found that TVA violated the whistleblower provisions of Section 210 of the Energy Reorganization Act of 1974 when TVA restricted and failed to renew the contracts of QTC personnel.[20]

In another nuclear industry whistleblower case, *Mitchell v Arizona Public Service Co.*, the Department of Labor found that the company's employee-concerns program and the head of Quality Assurance, who oversaw the employee-concerns program, participated in a "hostile work environment" and other retaliation directed against the complainant for raising nuclear safety concerns.[21] The employee had "used the QA Hotline" established by the company "to raise safety concerns on a relatively regular basis."[22] However, the Department of Labor found "that Hotline personnel were hostile toward her."[23] To make matters worse, the head of QA, "who was responsible for ensuring that employees were not harassed or retaliated against for raising safety concerns," personally participated in the harassment of the complainant.[24] The Department of Labor found that the QA manager complained about the whistleblower to other company managers shortly after the NRC leveled a $250,000 fine against the company based in part on the whistleblower's safety allegations by calling her a "bitch" and by stating that she "is causing me and my people trouble."[25] He also indicated that the whistleblower was "telling a lot of lies" and said that the whistleblower and other engineers in her area "should be fired."[26]

In 1996, the NRC concluded that harassment and intimidation of workers who raised safety concerns at the Millstone nuclear power plant in Connecticut were widespread, and that conditions were so dangerous to public safety that the NRC ordered the operation of the plant shut down. Additionally, the NRC also ordered Northeast Utilities, the owner of Millstone Point, to hire independent, third-party oversight of employee complaints at the nuclear plant, and the NRC did not lift this restriction for three years, until Millstone management had shown "an acceptable level of performance in its employee concerns program and in creating a safety-conscious work environment."[27]

Unfortunately, such breakdowns in employee concerns and programs and widespread hostility toward workers who report significant problems that potentially violate regulatory requirements are not limited to the nuclear industry. Two other industries provide additional documented examples of a poor work culture resulting in intimidation against workers who report safety problems: NASA and the Trans-Alaska Pipeline System.

At NASA, the lack of a safety-conscious work environment was cited as a contributing factor to the *Challenger* disaster in the mid-1980s. However, shortly after the second major shuttle disaster occurred, when the *Columbia* was lost in early 2003, numerous complaints surfaced that NASA had continued to foster an atmosphere of intimidation against NASA workers "by fending off dissent, dragging its feet on safety initiatives and exiling detractors."[28] These repeated NASA failures are, according to some, caused by management's "change-resistant culture."[29] Rather than learn from its earlier mistakes that produced the first shuttle disaster, NASA failed to create a work environment that encouraged employees to report safety problems.

In 1997, the Bureau of Land Management (BLM) conducted a management evaluation of the Alyeska Pipeline Service Company, which operated the pipeline that carries one tenth of the oil produced in the United States from Alaska's North Slope to the port of Valdez. BLM's review showed that there existed a disturbing "shoot the messenger" attitude at Alyeska Pipeline, the employee-concerns program "is not being effectively implemented," and there "is a perceived tolerance for retaliation . . . resulting in a 'chilling' effect on employee willingness to be frank about concerns."[30] BLM suggested that federal and state regulatory agencies improve oversight over the Alyeska Pipeline employee-concerns program, citing "lack of written policies and procedures and a lack of confidence by concerned employees."[31]

In each of these examples, the employee-concerns programs failed, in large part, because they lacked the independence, resources, and effective oversight to change corporate culture. By contrast, SOX Section 301 provides congressionally mandated independence and requires that companies provide the necessary resources to implement and comply with SOX.

Though time will tell how well companies and audit committees comply with SOX Section 301, there exists additional protections in the law for auditors, investigators, accountants, human resources professionals, lawyers, and audit committee members who work to implement and comply with that provision. The courts have long held under the nuclear whistleblower protection law that auditors, and others whose job it is to inspect the quality of work performed at regulated companies, deserve special protection from retaliation because the very nature of their work is protected activity under the statute.[32] Employer hostility toward auditors and quality assurance inspectors cannot be tolerated, or else the entire system of encouraging complaints by workers will be thwarted. In order to ensure the independence of audit committees and to enforce SOX Section 301, companies and audit committees should be on notice that any retaliation or intimidation of auditors, investigators, and others hired to implement and enforce SOX Section 301 is prohibited as a matter of law.

Based on experiences of existing programs and precedents in cases arising under other whistleblower protection statutes administered by the Department of Labor, there are certain do's and don'ts when it comes to establishing employee-concerns programs. What follow are 10 suggestions that should assist audit committees in establishing effective procedures to comply with SOX Section 301.

TEN SUGGESTIONS FOR EFFECTIVE COMPLIANCE

1. Establish a companywide code of ethics as well as policies and procedures that encourage whistleblowing and prohibit retaliation. The audit committee must obtain a commitment from the company itself to establish a companywide code of ethics and company policies to encourage employees to report misconduct. In order for any such code of ethics or company policy to be believable and trustworthy, it must include provisions that retaliation against employees who engage in whistleblowing is strictly prohibited. Any failure on the part of companies to adopt such fundamental policies and codes of ethics, and to openly accept that whistleblower retaliation is prohibited, will doom the chance of success of any audit committee procedures under SOX Section 301. Moreover, the company policy must clearly inform employees of their right to file a retaliation case with the U.S. Department of Labor under Section 806 of the SOX. It should explain to the employees precisely how they can file a claim and should commit the employer to fully ensuring that the corporation will adhere to its obligations under the antiretaliation provision.

In order to succeed under SOX Section 301, the audit committees, human resources professionals, and company management must persuade employees that utilization of the established reporting procedures will not result in retaliation. They must also persuade employees that these internal reporting structures will effectively, objectively, and independently evaluate the merits of employee allegations. If employees believe that their identities will be revealed by the audit committee to management, or that employees will be subject to retaliation, there will not be an open and frank channel of communication between company employees and the audit committees that is required by SOX Section 301.

In order to instill the required trust and confidence in the program, companies should adopt strict policies of severely disciplining or terminating anyone who either breaches an employee's confidentiality or retaliates against an employee who reports corporate fraud or other misconduct protected by SOX Section 301.

2. Provide for confidential and anonymous reporting. Failure to do this can result in a publicly traded company being "de-listed" from the stock exchanges. Even in cases where an employee does not request confidentiality or anonymity in making a complaint, it is good practice to limit the identification of whistleblowers to the audit committee and its investigators. There is no need under any circumstances for an audit committee or its investigators to inform the company's board of directors, management, or legal department of the identity of a whistleblower. The most effective way to prevent retaliation against the employee is to restrict the number of people who know the identity of the whistleblower to the absolute minimum and to keep that information within the audit committee. Moreover, if information provided by employees to the audit committee is later revealed to management, or used by the company either to publicly discredit the employee or in litigation against the employee, it will create a chilling effect on other employees, and the audit committee's sources of information will quickly dry up.

Any reports issued by the audit committee or its investigators should not mention the employee's name, and audit committees should identify allegations by tracking number, or other anonymous identifier. Additionally, each audit committee should adopt procedures, such as those provided under the federal Whistleblower Protection Act, that prevent disclosure to management of any findings on the merits of the employee's complaint unless the employee consents to that disclosure.[33]

3. Maintain independence of investigators and audit committees. Once again, failure to do this can result in a company being "de-listed." This is perhaps the most important feature of SOX Section 301. It is only by maintaining the independence of the audit committee and its investigators and consultants with respect to whistleblower complaints that the Congressional mandate of reforming corporate culture can be realized. If employees do not have confidence in the independence of the audit committee from the company's board and management, then employees will not likely utilize the procedures established by the audit committee. Additionally, it is only through maintaining independence from management that audit committees can fulfill their oversight function and enforce meaningful reform of corporate culture.

It is also important for audit committees and companies to realize that auditors, investigators, and consultants who perform work to implement and comply with SOX Section 301 are protected, as a matter of law, from retaliation. Any retaliatory action taken against auditors, investigators, human resources professionals, attorneys, or other consultants who act to enforce or comply with SOX Section 301 would be actionable under the SOX whistleblower provisions.[34]

4. Investigate and keep track of each complaint. This is also required by SOX Section 301, and the failure of audit committees to act on and keep track of complaints could result in a company being "de-listed." Audit committees must ensure that competent and independent investigations are conducted. It will not be sufficient for audit committees to simply refer complaints to company management or corporate counsel to investigate. Additionally, if a company already has an existing employee-concerns program, the audit committee should insist that the existing program report directly to the audit committee and otherwise comply with SOX Section 301 requirements before utilizing any existing program. Most importantly, there must be a procedure designed to establish who is assigned to investigate and monitor complaints, one that avoids any conflicts of interest or compromise of an employee's confidentiality. In many cases, there may be a need for the audit committee, or its investigators, to hire outside consultants or technical experts to evaluate the merits of the employee's complaint. Care must be taken to ensure that such experts or consultants are unbiased and independent of management and that conflicts of interest are avoided.

5. Follow-up with the employee-whistleblower. Each audit committee or investigative authority assigned to handle the whistleblower complaint should regularly communicate with the employee who reported the misconduct to provide feedback on the investigation and to request additional information. Not only does this practice provide a measure of confidence in the investigation on the part of the employee, but it could also serve to save the investigators time and resources. Audit committees should avoid investigators expending months investigating a problem only to learn after the conclusion of the investigation that the complaint was not fully investigated or, even worse, that the wrong issue was investigated. These problems can be avoided if investigators regularly communicate with the complainant and/or his or her representatives during the course of the investigation.

6. Publicize the procedures and policies and regularly remind all employees and management to follow the procedures. Not only must employees know of the existence of the audit committee procedures that are created to comply with SOX Section 301, the audit committee should regularly publicize to all employees their rights under SOX to report misconduct. In addition, all employees should be informed in advance what they can expect to occur if they file a complaint with the audit committee, how complaints will be handled, how confidentiality will be maintained, and how the audit committee works to resolve complaints. Most important, both employees and management should be regularly reminded, at least on an annual basis, of the policies and procedures as well as the prohibition against retaliation against employees who report corporate fraud or other misconduct.

7. Incorporate the procedures into formal required training programs. Employees and management should be formally trained in the SOX requirements, including the antiretaliation provisions and potential criminal penalties that were enacted by Congress. Employees and management, particularly those who have supervisory authority, should be trained on the legal requirements and company policies concerning prohibitions on retaliation. It is important that training programs not turn into indoctrination sessions where employees and management are trained how to isolate, marginalize, or discriminate against employees who complain or are perceived to complain about matters protected by SOX Section 301. Moreover, training programs are likely to become subject to review by compliance audits by the audit committee, or even outside monitoring by regulators if there is an investigation by the SEC or Labor Department. Therefore, it is essential that training programs not simply be used to communicate ways to protect or defend the company against a whistleblower complaint.

8. Monitor and enforce compliance with the procedures. Audit committees should include as part of their procedures monitoring and enforcement of company compliance with SOX Section 301. Compliance audits should be conducted on a regular basis to ensure that the procedures are being effectively communicated to management and employees, that the procedures are part of the company's formal training requirements, and that appropriate enforcement action is taken in response to any violations of the procedures.

9. Avoid retaliation against employees who make complaints or who work as auditors. Companies should implement procedures that provide employees who make complaints to the audit committee with protection from personnel action. A company should establish a "zero tolerance" policy for retaliation against whistleblowers. In addition to informing employees of their rights under the SOX whistleblower provisions, employers should institute a mandatory disciplinary program for managers who are found guilty of having retaliated against employees. For example, if the Department of Labor makes a finding that a manager engaged in discriminatory practices against an employee, the employer needs to have a mechanism in place to hold the manager accountable.

Even if an employee does not file a formal SOX complaint with the Department of Labor, an employer should institute internal procedures both to assist and protect employees who have been subjected to retaliation and to internally investigate allegations of retaliation. There are many ways this can be done without identifying the employee as a whistleblower. If personnel changes are necessary after the filing of a confidential or anonymous complaint with the audit committee, companies should be encouraged to reassign the supervisor, not the employee who made the complaint.

Finally, the law provides special protections for persons employed as auditors or who are otherwise involved in corporate oversight functions. The SOX whistleblower statute itself directly protects employees who provide information in-house to persons with "authority to investigate, discover, or terminate misconduct."[35] This provision not only protects employees who provide information to auditors, but also protects the auditors themselves. The need to protect in-house auditors was explained in a case filed under the Energy Reorganization Act, one of the statutes upon which the SOX was modeled. In that case the Court of Appeals reasoned as follows:

> [I]nspectors play a crucial role in the . . . regulatory scheme. . . . At times, the inspector may come into conflict with his employer by identifying problems that might cause added expense and delay. [If the regulatory scheme] is to function effectively, inspectors must be free from the threat of retaliatory discharge for identifying safety and quality problems.
>
> [The employer] argues that the [Secretary of Labor's] ruling would require companies to retain "abrasive, insolent, and arrogant'" quality control inspectors. . . . Not so. The finding simply forbids discrimination based on competent and aggressive inspection work. In other words, [employers regulated under the whistleblower provision] may not discharge quality control inspectors because they do their jobs too well.[36]

Any internal audit committee, employee-concerns program, or "hotline" program that does not recognize the importance of prohibiting retaliation against employees, especially employees directly involved in the in-house oversight functions, will not succeed.

10. Create an effective liaison between the audit committee and company management. In order to carry out its obligations under SOX Section 301 in larger companies, it may become necessary for an audit committee to establish liaison officials, compliance officers, or even an Ombudsman office who work directly for the audit committee and not company management. The creation of such independent offices will further instill confidence among employees with the audit committee procedures required by SOX Section 301 and provide potential compliance, enforcement, and alternative dispute resolution mechanisms. Again, it is imperative that such liaison officials have operational independence and that the company's policies prohibiting retaliation equally apply to such officials, as well as to the formal audit committee itself.

17

Criminal Sanctions for Retaliation

The Sarbanes-Oxley Act does not merely provide whistleblowers with a traditional employment discrimination remedy within the U.S. Department of Labor or a federal court. The Act contains two very strong enforcement-related provisions that actually criminalize retaliation against whistleblowers. The first provision, contained in Section 1107 of the Act, amended the federal obstruction of justice statute and specifically criminalized retaliation against certain whistleblowers. The second provision, contained in Section 3(b)(1) of the Act, makes the violation of any of the whistleblower protection provisions within Sarbanes-Oxley also a violation of the Securities Exchange Act of 1934. This provision also criminalizes discrimination against whistleblowers and permits the SEC to independently enforce the whistleblower provisions of the Act.

OBSTRUCTION OF JUSTICE

One of the most significant reforms contained in the Sarbanes-Oxley Act was an amendment to the criminal obstruction of justice statute. Discrimination against whistleblowers who provided "truthful" information to a federal "law enforcement officer" concerning the "possible" violation of "any federal offense" was criminalized. Any person who retaliated against whistleblowers covered under this provision could be subject to federal criminal prosecution and fines, and could be "imprisoned" for 10 years.[1]

The new criminal law, 18 U.S.C. section 1513(e) states as follows:

> Whoever knowingly, with the intent to retaliate, takes any action harmful to any person, including interference with the lawful employment or livelihood of any person, for providing to a law enforcement officer any truthful information relating to the commission or possible commission of any federal offense, shall be fined under this title or imprisoned not more than 10 years, or both.

Section 1513(e) was introduced in the House of Representatives as part of the Corporate Fraud Accountability Act of 2002 by Congressman F. James Sensenbrenner, Jr., the Chairman of the House Judiciary Committee. The House passed the law by a 391-28 vote, and amendments were successfully added to the final Conference Report on the Sarbanes-Oxley Act and approved by both Houses of Congress. Congressman Sensenbrenner clearly intended this law to protect whistleblowers and alter the corporate culture that promoted employee silence concerning wrongdoing:

> The [Conference] report also contains House language that makes it a crime for someone to knowingly retaliate against a whistle blower and provides a criminal penalty of up to 10 years for such an offense. I would also point out that the restitution laws for all criminal activity are in place for these crimes as well, so the court can order restitution for those shareholders and employees who have been defrauded.
>
> By passing this conference committee report, America will know that those who abuse the law and tarnish corporate America's reputation will go to jail for a very long time. These are tough penalties that will crack down on the corporate crooks and go a long way to protecting the life savings of many Americans by making the price of such theft too high.[2]

The criminal statute's definition of protected activity is narrower than the definition contained in the employment discrimination section of Sarbanes-Oxley. The criminal law only protects disclosures to federal law enforcement officials, whereas the civil/administrative wrongful discharge provision protects a broader range of conduct, such as filing allegations of misconduct with an in-house audit committee, a supervisor, or members of Congress.

However, the scope of coverage under Section 1513(e) is far broader than the Sarbanes-Oxley wrongful discharge provision. Unlike the wrongful discharge provision of Sarbanes-Oxley, the criminal law covers every employer in the United States, and is not limited to publicly traded corporations. Moreover, the criminal law protects persons who blow the whistle on *any* violation of *any* federal law. Section 1513(e) is not limited to prohibiting retaliation against employees who "blow the whistle" on corporate fraud. It would cover any employee who reported violations of any federal law, including environmental, health and safety, or any other federal offense. Thus, the protections offered by Section 1513(e) are not limited to corporate whistleblowers who disclose potential fraud against shareholders. Any employee who reports any potential federal offense to a law enforcement officer could be protected.

Finally, although the criminal statute requires the employee-whistleblower to contact a federal law enforcement officer to obtain protection under the law, the definition of such an officer is very broad.[3] The definition of a "law enforcement officer" set forth in the obstruction of justice statute covers almost every federal investigative body that could be contacted by the whistleblower.[4]

SEC PENALTIES

Section 3(b)(1) of the Sarbanes-Oxley Act, 15 U.S.C. 7202(b)(1) provides that a violation of any provision of the Sarbanes-Oxley Act "shall be treated for all purposes" as a "violation of the Securities Exchange Act of 1934." Moreover, "any person" who violates any provision of Sarbanes-Oxley "shall be subject to the same penalties . . . as for a violation of" the Securities Exchange Act. The statutory provision states as follows:

> A violation by any person of this Act, any rule or regulation of the Commission issued under this Act, or any rule of the Board shall be treated for all purposes in the same manner as a violation of the Securities Exchange Act of 1934 (15 U.S.C. 78a et seq.) or the rules and regulations issued thereunder, consistent with the provisions of this Act, and any such person shall be subject to the same penalties, and to the same extent, as for a violation of the Act or such rules or regulations.

The penalties provided for under the Securities Exchange Act of 1934 are steep. Section 32 of the Act provides significant criminal penalties for any "willful" violation of the law, including 20 years in prison and a $5,000,000 fine for each violation. In addition to criminal penalties, various sections of the Securities Exchange Act of 1934 provide authority for the SEC to investigate and punish persons who violate the Act.

Simply stated, any person who violates any provision of the Sarbanes-Oxley Act, including any of the whistleblower protection provisions, also violates the Securities Exchange Act of 1934. The SEC would have jurisdiction to investigate and sanction any such violations. If the violations were "willful," the wrongdoer may face a long prison sentence.

Whether Section 3(b) (1) of the Sarbanes-Oxley Act also authorizes whistleblowers to pursue private causes of action under Section 10(b) of the 1934 Act has not been adjudicated. However, a corporation that violates any of the various whistleblower protections provisions contained in Sarbanes-Oxley may be liable to its shareholders under this section.

Thus, the failure of a publicly traded company to properly maintain the confidentiality of a whistleblower who contacts the audit committee, the failure of an attorney licensed to practice law before the SEC to properly disclose wrongdoing, and the wrongful discharge of a whistleblower within a publicly traded corporation all constitute separate and independent violations of the Securities Exchange Act of 1934.

The implications of Section 3(b) are enormous. First, it grants the SEC jurisdiction to investigate and sanction corporate contact that violates the various whistleblower provisions of Sarbanes-Oxley. Second, it subjects wrongdoers to potentially significant civil and criminal penalties should they be found guilty of discrimination against whistleblowers. Third, it authorizes the SEC to implement regulations protecting whistleblowers.

Subjecting corporations that discriminate against whistleblowers to multiple penalties is not without precedent. Under the Atomic Energy Act, whistleblowers are entitled to file employment discrimination cases within the U.S. Department of Labor under procedures nearly identical to the SOX law. Additionally, the Nuclear Regulatory Commission has implemented regulations that also prohibit discrimination against whistleblowers as a safety hazard. Under the NRC regulations codified at 10 C.F.R. 50.7, utilities that-discriminate against whistleblowers can be criminally prosecuted for willful violations of the Atomic Energy Act and can be subject to various administrative sanctions—including civil penalties and license revocation. In fact, the NRC regularly investigates whistle-blower-discrimination cases and regularly fines utilities that are found to have violated the rights of employee-whistleblowers.

The Sarbanes-Oxley Act authorizes a similar duel track for whistleblower cases. Employment discrimination cases may be filed with the Department of Labor, but whistleblowers are also free to utilize Section 3(b) (1) to request enforcement action against employers that discriminate against whistleblowers directly from the SEC.

DOES RICO OFFER A CIVIL REMEDY TO WHISTLEBLOWERS?

In 1970 Congress passed the Racketeering Influenced and Corrupt Organizations Act (RICO)[5] in order to aid in the eradication of organized crime causing great harm to "the general welfare of the Nation and its citizens."[6] Congress enacted RICO, in part, because corruption was harming "innocent investors and competing organizations."[7] The law contained criminal and civil penalties and provided a private right of action for treble damages and attorneys fees to "[a]ny person injured in his business or property by reason of a violation of section 1962" of the statute.[8] The passage of the federal RICO statute also resulted in the passage of numerous state RICO statutes, which generally reflect the language set forth in the federal statute.[9]

In order to bring a RICO civil action, the plaintiff must demonstrate that injury "to business or property" flowed from a violation of Section 1962. Section 1962, in turn, consists of four subsections that make it unlawful to: (a) invest income derived from a pattern of racketeering activity in an enterprise; (b) acquire or maintain an interest in any enterprise through a pattern of racketeering activity; (c) conduct the affairs of an enterprise through a pattern of racketeering activity; and (d) conspire to commit any of the above acts.[10] What constitutes a criminal enterprise is defined by the Act,[11] as is "racketeering activity."[12] The individual acts of racketeering activity are referred to as the predicate acts. Any civil remedy issued under RICO must flow from a predicate act. Every predicate act covered under RICO is listed in Section 1961(1) of the Act.

During the 1980s and 1990s a conflict among the Courts of Appeal emerged as to whether a person discharged or otherwise injured as a result of blowing the whistle on illegal racketeering activity could bring a private civil RICO claim for the injuries to employment and livelihood they suffered. In *Beck v Prupis*, a decision issued in 2000, the Supreme Court resolved this issue. The Court drew a distinction between injuries caused by one of the overt acts of racketeering specified under Section 1961(1) with the direct injuries flowing from any of the specific predicate acts set forth in Section 1961, as compared to indirect injuries caused in furtherance of one of the predicate acts of racketeering set forth in Section 1961. The Supreme Court determined that the injury to business or property flowing from an indirect act that was not one of the specific predicate acts designated under Section 1961(1)[13] did not give rise to a civil remedy.[14] Thus, in order to establish standing, a whistleblower must demonstrate that the harm suffered flowed directly from a violation of one of the predicate acts listed under Section 1961(1). Because harm flowing from discrimination against whistleblowers was not one of the predicate acts set forth in Section 1961(1), it was generally assumed that the *Beck* decision prevented whistleblowers from obtaining protection under RICO. However, because the Sarbanes-Oxley Act criminalized retaliation against certain whistleblowers, the roadblock created in *Beck* was removed. Under *Beck* it now appears as if numerous whistleblowers could set forth valid civil claims under RICO.

The Sarbanes-Oxley Act amended the federal obstruction of justice statute to specifically include a prohibition against discrimination against certain whistleblowers. This obstruction of justice law, codified 18 U.S.C. section 1513, is one of the statutes included in the list of predicate acts comprising a RICO claim.[15] The Sarbanes-Oxley Act amended section 1513 to create a new subsection (e) designed specifically to address the need to prohibit retaliation against whistleblowers. As a result of this amendment, it becomes unlawful for anyone to "knowingly . . . retaliate [or take] any action harmful to any person, including interference with the lawful employment or livelihood of any person" because that person provided "truthful information relating to the commission or possible commission of any Federal offense" to a "law enforcement officer."[16] It also became unlawful for anyone to "conspire to commit any offense under this section."[17]

Thus, retaliation against certain whistleblowers who report violations of federal law to law enforcement officials may be protected under RICO.

WHISTLEBLOWER STANDING UNDER RICO

Establishing a RICO claim is not easy. First, an "economic injury to business or property" must be established. Whether loss of employment or other employment-related injuries constitute injury to "business or property" is an unsettled issue. For the most part, the cases that denied standing to claims alleging employment-related injuries do not address the "business or property" clause; instead the courts were unable to confer standing because the employment injuries did not result from a predicate act.[18] Because Congress has now included retaliation against whistleblowers as one of the listed RICO predicate acts, the standing analysis set forth in these pre-SOX cases should no longer be applicable.

Inclusion of whistleblower retaliation under civil RICO is also supported by case law under the Clayton Act, a law upon which RICO's Section 1964(c) was modeled.[19] A number of cases interpreting the Clayton Act's "business or property" clause provide strong support for concluding that employment-related injuries are covered.[20]

A successful plaintiff will also have to establish the existence of a pattern of racketeering activity.[21] As explained by the U.S. Court of Appeals for the First Circuit: "Although showing two predicate acts is the only statutory requirement, case law establishes that this is not sufficient to prove a 'pattern'—the plaintiff also must demonstrate that the 'predicates are related, *and* that they amount to or pose a threat of continued criminal activity.'"[22] The relatedness prong simply requires that the predicate acts "have the same or similar purposes, results, participants, victims, or methods of commission, or otherwise are interrelated by distinguishing characteristics and are not isolated events."[23] The continuity requirement may be met by either showing a series of related predicate acts extending over a substantial period of time or establishing threat of continued racketeering activity.[24] It has been said that a "[s]hort term scheme threatening no future criminal activities is not sufficient to show pattern of racketeering activity within the meaning of RICO."[25] Given these parameters, a strong case for protecting employee whistleblowers under civil RICO could be demonstrated if the underlying wrongdoing at issue in the case was ongoing for a significant period of time and the whistleblower was terminated to hide that enterprise.

COLLATERAL ESTOPPEL, WAIVER
OF FIFTH AMENDMENT RIGHTS, AND
INCREASED RISK OF CRIMINAL PROSECUTION

The decision to litigate a whistleblower claim may bring with it unintended consequences. An administrative or court ruling in favor of a whistleblower could result in collateral estoppel on the facts necessary to establish liability in a RICO or other civil claims where punitive damages may be available.[26] Because a SOX wrongful discharge claim must be filed within 90 days of a discriminatory action, and civil RICO claims have a four-year statute of limitations, employees can initially file a discrimination case under the SOX wrongful discharge provisions, and later determine whether a civil RICO action may be appropriate.

It also seems likely that the federal government would be more apt to seek a criminal conviction for a violation of 18 U.S.C. § 1513(e) after a record is established where witnesses will be required to present sworn testimony under oath. Specifically, if a SOX employment claim is litigated, and the Department of Labor or a federal court hold that the employee was subjected to retaliation due to protected contacts with federal law enforcement officials, a local U.S. Attorneys Office could use these findings as part of its decision-making process in determining whether the defendants should be criminally charged under 18 U.S.C. § 1513(e).

Because the testimony elicited during a SOX employment case could be subsequently used in criminally prosecuting a corporate wrongdoer under the amended obstruction of justice statute, the corporate defendant(s) may need to invoke a Fifth Amendment privilege against self-incrimination during the SOX proceeding. If a corporate defendant invokes a Fifth Amendment self-incrimination privilege, the assertion of that privilege can have significant adverse consequences on the employment discrimination case. For example, if the privilege is pleaded, the Court can draw sufficiently strong adverse inferences to decide a case against the party (or witness) raising the privilege.[27]

Appendix: Key Practice Documents

Corporate and Criminal Fraud Accountability Act
Sec. 806, Sarbanes-Oxley Act of 2002
Protection for Employees of Publicly Traded Companies Who
Provide Evidence of Fraud
18 U.S.C. 1514A

(a) WHISTLEBLOWER PROTECTION FOR EMPLOYEES OF PUBLICLY TRADED COMPANIES—No company with a class of securities registered under section 12 of the Securities Exchange Act of 1934 (15 U.S.C. 78l), or that is required to file reports under section 15(d) of the Securities Exchange Act of 1934 (15 U.S.C. 78o(d)), or any officer, employee, contractor, subcontractor, or agent of such company, may discharge, demote, suspend, threaten, harass, or in any other manner discriminate against an employee in the terms and conditions of employment because of any lawful act done by the employee—

(1) to provide information, cause information to be provided, or otherwise assist in an investigation regarding any conduct which the employee reasonably believes constitutes a violation of section 1341, 1343, 1344, or 1348, any rule or regulation of the Securities and Exchange Commission, or any provision of Federal law relat-

ing to fraud against shareholders, when the information or assistance is provided to or the investigation is conducted by—

(A) a Federal regulatory or law enforcement agency;

(B) any Member of Congress or any committee of Congress; or

(C) a person with supervisory authority over the employee (or such other person working for the employer who has the authority to investigate, discover, or terminate misconduct); or

(2) to file, cause to be filed, testify, participate in, or otherwise assist in a proceeding filed or about to be filed (with any knowledge of the employer) relating to an alleged violation of section 1341, 1343, 1344, or 1348, any rule or regulation of the Securities and Exchange Commission, or any provision of Federal law relating to fraud against shareholders.

(b) ENFORCEMENT ACTION—

(1) IN GENERAL— A person who alleges discharge or other discrimination by any person in violation of subsection (a) may seek relief under subsection (c), by—

(A) filing a complaint with the Secretary of Labor; or

(B) if the Secretary has not issued a final decision within 180 days of the filing of the complaint and there is no showing that such delay is due to the bad faith of the claimant, bringing an action at law or equity for de novo review in the appropriate district court of the United States, which shall have jurisdiction over such an action without regard to the amount in controversy.

(2) PROCEDURE—

(A) IN GENERAL— An action under paragraph (1)(A) shall be governed under the rules and procedures set forth in section 42121(b) of title 49, United States Code.

(B) EXCEPTION— Notification made under section 42121(b)(1) of title 49, United States Code, shall be made to the person named in the complaint and to the employer.

(C) BURDENS OF PROOF— An action brought under paragraph (1)(B) shall be governed by the legal burdens of proof set forth in section 42121(b) of title 49, United States Code.

(D) STATUTE OF LIMITATIONS— An action under paragraph (1) shall be commenced not later than 90 days after the date on which the violation occurs.

(c) REMEDIES—

(1) IN GENERAL— An employee prevailing in any action under subsection (b)(1) shall be entitled to all relief necessary to make the employee whole.

(2) COMPENSATORY DAMAGES— Relief for any action under paragraph (1) shall include—

(A) reinstatement with the same seniority status that the employee would have had, but for the discrimination;

(B) the amount of back pay, with interest; and

(C) compensation for any special damages sustained as a result of the discrimination, including litigation costs, expert witness fees, and reasonable attorney fees.

(d) RIGHTS RETAINED BY EMPLOYEE— Nothing in this section shall be deemed to diminish the rights, privileges, or remedies of any employee under any Federal or State law, or under any collective bargaining agreement.

Corporate Responsibility
Sec. 301, Sarbanes-Oxley Act of 2002
Audit Committee
15 U.S.C. 78f(m)(4)

(4) COMPLAINTS— Each audit committee shall establish procedures for—

(A) the receipt, retention, and treatment of complaints received by the issuer regarding accounting, internal accounting controls, or auditing matters; and

(B) the confidential, anonymous submission by employees of the issuer of concerns regarding questionable accounting or auditing matters.

Corporate Responsibility
Sec. 307, Sarbanes-Oxley Act of 2002
Rules of Professional Responsibility for Attorneys
15 U.S.C. 7245

Not later than 180 days after the date of enactment of this Act, the Commission shall issue rules, in the public interest and for the protection of investors, setting forth minimum standards of professional conduct for attorneys appearing and practicing before the Commission in any way in the representation of issuers, including a rule—(1) requiring an attorney to report evidence of a material violation of securities law or breach of fiduciary duty or similar violation by the company or any agent thereof, to the chief legal counsel or the chief executive officer of the company (or the equivalent thereof); and (2) if the counsel or officer does not appropriately respond to the evidence (adopting, as necessary, appropriate remedial measures or sanctions with respect to the violation), requiring the attorney to report the evidence to the audit committee of the board of directors of the issuer or to another committee of the board of directors comprised solely of directors not employed directly or indirectly by the issuer, or to the board of directors.

Obstruction of Justice
Sec. 1107 of Sarbanes-Oxley
Retaliation Against Informants
18 U.S.C. 1513(e)

(e) Whoever knowingly, with the intent to retaliate, takes any action harmful to any person, including interference with the lawful employment or livelihood of any person, for providing to a law enforcement officer any truthful information relating to the commission or possible commission of any Federal offense, shall be fined under this title or imprisoned not more than 10 years, or both.

Sec. 3(b)(1) of Sarbanes-Oxley
Enforcement
15 U.S.C. 7202(b)(1)

(b)(1) A violation by any person of this Act [the Sarbanes-Oxley Act], any rule or regulation of the Commission issued under this Act, or any rule of the Board shall be treated for all purposes in the same manner as a violation of the Securities Exchange Act of 1934 (15 U.S.C. 78a et seq.) or the rules and regulations issued there under, consistent with the provisions of this Act, and any such person shall be subject to the same penalties, and to the same extent, as for a violation of that Act or such rules or regulations.

Aviation Investment and Reform Act
for the 21st Century
Administrative Provisions
49 U.S.C. 42121(b)
[Incorporated by reference into 18 U.S.C. § 1514A(b)(2)(A) and (C)]

42121(b) *Department of Labor Complaint Procedure.* (1) *Filing And Notification.* A person who believes that he or she has been dis-

charged or otherwise discriminated against by any person in violation of subsection (a) may, not later than 90 days after the date on
which such violation occurs, file (or have any person file on his or
her behalf) a complaint with the Secretary of Labor alleging such
discharge or discrimination. Upon receipt of such a complaint, the
Secretary of Labor shall notify, in writing, the person named in the
complaint and the Administrator of the Federal Aviation Administration of the filing of the complaint, of the allegations contained in
the complaint, of the substance of evidence supporting the complaint, and of the opportunities that will be afforded to such person
under paragraph (2).

(2) *Investigation; Preliminary Order.*

(A) *In General.* Not later than 60 days after the date of receipt of
a complaint filed under paragraph (1) and after affording the person named in the complaint an opportunity to submit to the Secretary of Labor a written response to the complaint and an opportunity to meet with a representative of the Secretary to present
statements from witnesses, the Secretary of Labor shall conduct an
investigation and determine whether there is reasonable cause to
believe that the complaint has merit and notify, in writing, the
complainant and the person alleged to have committed a violation
of subsection (a) of the Secretary's findings. If the Secretary of
Labor concludes that there is a reasonable cause to believe that a
violation of subsection (a) has occurred, the Secretary shall accompany the Secretary's findings with a preliminary order providing
the relief prescribed by paragraph (3)(B). Not later than 30 days
after the date of notification of findings under this paragraph,
either the person alleged to have committed the violation or the
complainant may file objections to the findings or preliminary
order, or both, and request a hearing on the record. The filing of
such objections shall not operate to stay any reinstatement remedy
contained in the preliminary order. Such hearings shall be conducted expeditiously. If a hearing is not requested in such 30-day
period, the preliminary order shall be deemed a final order that is
not subject to judicial review.

(B) *Requirements.*

(i) *Required Showing by Complainant.* The Secretary of Labor shall
dismiss a complaint filed under this subsection and shall not conduct an investigation otherwise required under subparagraph (A)
unless the complainant makes a prima facie showing that any
behavior described in paragraphs (1) through (4) of subsection (a)

was a contributing factor in the unfavorable personnel action alleged in the complaint.

(ii) *Showing by Employer*. Notwithstanding a finding by the Secretary that the complainant has made the showing required under clause (i), no investigation otherwise required under subparagraph (A) shall be conducted if the employer demonstrates, by clear and convincing evidence, that the employer would have taken the same unfavorable personnel action in the absence of that behavior.

(iii) *Criteria For Determination by Secretary*. The Secretary may determine that a violation of subsection (a) has occurred only if the complainant demonstrates that any behavior described in paragraphs (1) through (4) of subsection (a) was a contributing factor in the unfavorable personnel action alleged in the complaint.

(iv) *Prohibition*. Relief may not be ordered under subparagraph (A) if the employer demonstrates by clear and convincing evidence that the employer would have taken the same unfavorable personnel action in the absence of that behavior.

(3) *Final Order*.

(A) *Deadline For Issuance; Settlement Agreements*. Not later than 120 days after the date of conclusion of a hearing under paragraph (2), the Secretary of Labor shall issue a final order providing the relief prescribed by this paragraph or denying the complaint. At any time before issuance of a final order, a proceeding under this subsection may be terminated on the basis of a settlement agreement entered into by the Secretary of Labor, the complainant, and the person alleged to have committed the violation.

(B) *Remedy*. If, in response to a complaint filed under paragraph (1), the Secretary of Labor determines that a violation of subsection (a) has occurred, the Secretary of Labor shall order the person who committed such violation to

(i) take affirmative action to abate the violation;

(ii) reinstate the complainant to his or her former position together with the compensation (including back pay) and restore the terms, conditions, and privileges associated with his or her employment; and

(iii) provide compensatory damages to the complainant.

If such an order is issued under this paragraph, the Secretary of Labor, at the request of the complainant, shall assess against the person against whom the order is issued a sum equal to the aggregate amount of all costs and expenses (including attorneys and expert witness fees) reasonably incurred, as determined by the Secretary of Labor, by the complainant for, or in connection with, the bringing the complaint upon which the order was issued.

(C) *Frivolous Complaints.* If the Secretary of Labor finds that a complaint under paragraph (1) is frivolous or has been brought in bad faith, the Secretary of Labor may award to the prevailing employer a reasonable attorneys fee not exceeding $1,000.

(4) *Review.*

(A) *Appeal to Court of Appeals.* Any person adversely affected or aggrieved by an order issued under paragraph (3) may obtain review of the order in the United States Court of Appeals for the circuit in which the violation, with respect to which the order was issued, allegedly occurred or the circuit in which the complainant resided on the date of such violation. The petition for review must be filed not later than 60 days after the date of the issuance of the final order of the Secretary of Labor. Review shall conform to chapter 7 of title 5, United States Code. The commencement of proceedings under this subparagraph shall not, unless ordered by the court, operate as a stay of the order.

(B) *Limitation on Collateral Attack.* An order of the Secretary of Labor with respect to which review could have been obtained under subparagraph (A) shall not be subject to judicial review in any criminal or other civil proceeding.

(5) *Enforcement of Order by Secretary of Labor.* Whenever any person has failed to comply with an order issued under paragraph (3), the Secretary of Labor may file a civil action in the United States district court for the district in which the violation was found to occur to enforce such order. In actions brought under this paragraph, the district courts shall have jurisdiction to grant all appropriate relief including, but not limited to, injunctive relief and compensatory damages.

(6) *Enforcement of Order by Parties.*

(A) *Commencement of Action.* A person on whose behalf an order was issued under paragraph (3) may commence a civil action against the person to whom such order was issued to require compliance with such order. The appropriate United States district court shall have jurisdiction, without regard to the amount in controversy or the citizenship of the parties, to enforce such order.

(B) *Attorney Fees.* The court, in issuing any final order under this paragraph, may award costs of litigation (including reasonable attorney and expert witness fees) to any party whenever the court determines such award is appropriate.

LEGISLATIVE HISTORY
SOX WHISTLEBLOWER LAW

**Whistleblower Provision of Sarbanes-Oxley
(July 26, 2002)
Section-by-Section Analysis and Discussion of the Corporate
and Criminal Fraud Accountability Act
[Incorporated as Section 806 of Sarbanes-Oxley]**
Congressional Record, **pp. S7418 and 7420 (July 26, 2002)**

S.7414. Mr. LEAHY. Mr. President, yesterday during my floor remarks on the final passage of H.R. 2673, the Sarbanes-Oxley Act, I requested unanimous consent that a section by section analysis and discussion of Title VIII, the Corporate and Criminal Fraud Accountability Act, which I authored, be included in the *Congressional Record* as part of the official legislative history of those provisions of H.R. 2673. That unanimous consent request was granted, but due to a clerical error, this essential legislative history was not printed in yesterday's *Congressional Record.*

It is my understanding that this document will appear in yesterday's *Congressional Record* when the historical volume is compiled. However, in order to provide guidance in the legal interpretation of these provisions of Title VIII of H.R. 2673 before that volume is issued, I ask unanimous consent that the same document be printed in today's *Congressional Record* and be treated as legislative history for Title VIII, offered by the sponsor of these provisions, as if it had been printed yesterday.

There being no objection, the material was ordered to be printed in the *Record,* as follows: Section-by-Section Analysis and Discussion of the Corporate and Criminal Fraud Accountability Act (Title VIII of H.R. 2673)

Title VIII has three major components that will enhance corporate accountability. Its terms track almost exactly the provisions of S. 2010, introduced by Senator Leahy and reported unanimously from the Committee on the Judiciary. Following is a brief section by section and a legal analysis regarding its provisions.

SECTION-BY-SECTION ANALYSIS

Section 806.—Whistleblower protection for employees of publicly traded companies

This section would provide whistleblower protection to employees of publicly traded companies. It specifically protects them when they take lawful acts to disclose information or otherwise assist criminal investigators, federal regulators, Congress, supervisors (or other proper people within a corporation), or parties in a judicial proceeding in detecting and stopping fraud. If the employer does take illegal action in retaliation for lawful and protected conduct, subsection (b) allows the employee to file a complaint with the Department of Labor, to be governed by the same procedures and burdens of proof now applicable in the whistleblower law in the aviation industry. The employee can bring the matter to federal court only if the Department of Labor does not resolve the matter in 180 days (and there is no showing that such delay is due to the bad faith of the claimant) as a normal case in law or equity, with no amount in controversy requirement. Subsection (c) governs remedies and provides for the reinstatement of the whistleblower, back pay, and compensatory damages to make a victim whole, including reasonable attorney fees and costs, as remedies if the claimant prevails. A 90 day statute of limitations for the bringing of the initial administrative action before the Department of Labor is also included.

Congressional Record p. S7418.

* * *

S.7420. Section 806 of the Act would provide whistleblower protection to employees of publicly traded companies who report acts of fraud to federal officials with the authority to remedy the wrongdoing or to supervisors or appropriate individuals within their company. Although current law protects many government employees who act in the public interest by reporting wrongdoing, there is no similar protection for employees of publicly traded companies who blow the whistle on fraud and protect investors. With an unprecedented portion of the American public investing in these companies and depending upon their honesty, this distinction does not serve the public good.

In addition, corporate employees who report fraud are subject to the patchwork and vagaries of current state laws, even though most publicly traded companies do business nationwide. Thus, a whistleblowing employee in one state (e.g., Texas, see supra) may be far more vulnerable to retaliation than a fellow employee in another state who takes the same actions. Unfortunately, companies with a corporate culture that punishes whistleblowers for being "disloyal" and "litigation risks" often transcend state lines, and most corporate employers, with help from their lawyers, know exactly what they can do to a whistleblowing employee under the law. U.S. laws need to encourage and protect those who report fraudulent activity that can damage innocent investors in publicly traded companies. The Act is supported by groups such as the National Whistleblower Center, the Government Accountability Project, and Taxpayers Against Fraud, all of whom have written a letter placed in the Committee record calling this bill "the single most effective measure possible to prevent recurrences of the Enron debacle and similar threats to the nation's financial markets."

This provision would create a new provision protecting employees when they take lawful acts to disclose information or otherwise assist criminal investigators, federal regulators, Congress, their supervisors (or other proper people within a corporation), or parties in a judicial proceeding in detecting and stopping actions which they reasonably believe to be fraudulent. Since the only acts protected are ``lawful" ones, the provision would not protect illegal actions, such as the improper public disclosure of trade secret information. In addition, a reasonableness test is also provided under the subsection (a)(1), which is intended to impose the normal reasonable person standard used and interpreted in a wide variety of legal contexts (See generally Passaic Valley Sewerage Commissioners v. Department of Labor, 992 F. 2d 474, 478). Certainly, although not exclusively, any type of corporate or agency action taken based on the information, or the information constituting admissible evidence at any later proceeding would be strong indicia that it could support such a reasonable belief. The threshold is intended to include all good faith and reasonable reporting of fraud, and there should be no presumption that reporting is otherwise, absent specific evidence.

Under new protections provided by the Act, if the employer does take illegal action in retaliation for such lawful and protected conduct, subsection (b) allows the employee to elect to file an administrative complaint at the Department of Labor, as is the case for employees who provide assistance in aviation safety. Only if there is not final agency decision within 180 days of the complaint (and such delay is not shown to be due to the bad faith of the claimant) may he or she may bring a de novo case in federal court with a jury trial available (See United States Constitution, Amendment VII; Title 42 United States Code, Section 1983). Should such a case be brought in federal court, it is intended that the same burdens of proof which would have governed in the Department of Labor will continue to govern the action. Subsection (c) of this section requires both reinstatement of the whistleblower, back pay, and all compensatory damages needed to make a victim whole should the claimant prevail. The Act does not supplant or replace state law, but sets a national floor for employee protections in the context of publicly traded companies.

LEGISLATIVE HISTORY
"CONTRIBUTING FACTOR TEST"

Congressional Record — **Senate**
Thursday, March 16, 1989
101st Cong. 1st Sess.
135 Cong Rec S 2779

TITLE: WHISTLEBLOWER PROTECTION ACT OF 1989

[*S2779] The Senate continued with the consideration of the bill.

Mr. LEVIN. Mr. President, Government employees who "blow the whistle" on waste, fraud and abuse are front line soldiers in the battle to save the taxpayers' money. Giving real protection to these whistleblowers is a simple and effective way to cut cost overruns, wasteful spending, and the bottom line save taxpayers' dollars.

* * *

There has been a lot of give and take on both sides, and I am pleased that we have been able to agree upon an amendment that meets a number of the Attorney General's concerns without sacrificing important protections for whistleblowers. This amendment is a fair and balanced one.

* * *

First, our amendment would clarify that in order to prove retaliation a whistleblower must show that the protected disclosure was a contributing factor in the personnel action against [*S2780] him or her. This is not meant to change or heighten in any way the standard in S. 20, which is that the disclosure must be a factor in the action. The word "contributing" is only intended to clarify that the factor must contribute in some way to the action against the whistleblower.

I believe this was clear in the original statutory language. To me, there was no doubt that a factor in an action is something that contributes to that action. Indeed, my dictionary defines a "factor" as "one of the elements contributing to a particular result or situation."

The bottom line is that the words "a contributing factor," like the words "a factor," means any factor which, alone or in connection with other factors, tends to affect in any way the outcome of the decision. This test is specifically intended to overrule existing case law, which requires a whistleblower to prove that his protected conduct was a "significant," "motivating," "substantial," or "predominant" factor in a personnel action in order to overturn that action.

The Attorney General, in his letter to me agrees to that interpretation when he said:

We have agreed to clarify the word "factor" by adding the word "contributing" in the two places in which the Mt. Healthy test appears in the bill. A "contributing factor" need not be "substantial." The individual's burden is to prove that the whistleblowing contributed in some way to the agency's decision to take the personnel action.

Mr. President, I believe that the contributing factor test is the right one. By reducing the excessively heavy burden imposed on the employee under current case law, we will send a strong, clear signal to whistleblowers that we intend to protect them from any retaliation related to their whistleblowing and an equally clear message to those who would discourage whistleblowers from coming forward that reprisals of any kind will not be tolerated. Whistleblowing should never be a factor that contributes in any way to an adverse personnel action; the new test will make this the rule of law.

. . . at the same time, however, this new test will not shield employees who engage in wrongful conduct merely because they have at some point blown the whistle on some kind of purported misconduct. In such cases, the agency will, of course, be provided with an opportunity to demonstrate that the employee's whistleblowing was not a contributing factor in the personnel action.

If an employee shows by a preponderance of the evidence that whistleblowing was a contributing factor in a personnel action, the agency action may be upheld only if the agency can demonstrate, by clear and convincing evidence, that it would have taken the same action even in the absence of the whistleblowing. This is the standard in our bill, S. 20, and it is unchanged by our amendment.

"Clear and convincing evidence" is a high standard of proof for the Government to carry. It is intended as such for two reasons. First, this standard of proof comes into play only if the employee has proven by a preponderance of the evidence that whistleblowing was a contributing factor in the action against him or her — in other words, that the agency action was tainted. Second, this heightened burden of proof on the agency also recognizes that when it comes to proving the basis for an agency's decision, the agency controls most of the cards—the drafting of the documents supporting the decision, the testimony of witnesses who participated in the decision, and the records that could document whether similar personnel actions have been taken in other cases. In these circumstances, it is entirely appropriate that the agency bears a heavy burden to justify its actions.

* * *

EXHIBIT 1

Office of the Attorney General
Washington, DC, Mar. 3, 1989

Hon. Carl Levin,
U.S. Senate, Washington, DC

Dear Senator Levin: This letter will confirm our agreement regarding revisions in S. 20, the Whistleblower Protection Act of 1989. We are persuaded that the bill as revised by your proposed amendment will enhance the protections for individuals who report waste, fraud, and abuse while maintaining important safeguards in the federal personnel system. Moreover, I want to thank you for your efforts in working with us to forge a mutually acceptable resolution of our serious constitutional concerns as well as our objections to the Mt. Healthy test, as originally drafted.

We have agreed to clarify the word "factor" by adding the word "contributing" in the two places in which the Mt. Healthy test appears in the bill. A "contributing factor" need not be "substantial." The individual's burden is to prove that the whistleblowing contributed in some way to the agency's decision to take the personnel action.

Again, we appreciate your willingness to work with us to craft a product representing the good faith efforts of both sides. On behalf of the Administration, I pledge our cooperation to discourage any amendments, in either body of Congress, which might in any way interfere with this agreement. None of the changes to which we have agreed detracts in any way from Congress' intent to strengthen whistleblower protections.

The Office of Management and Budget has advised that there is no objection to the presentation of this report from the standpoint of the Administration's program.

Sincerely,
Dick Thornburg
Attorney General

* * *

JOINT EXPLANATORY STATEMENT

INTRODUCTION

The Senate, on August 8, 1988, passed S. 508, the Whistleblower Protection Act (See S. Rpt. 100-413). One year earlier, on August 5, 1987, the House Committee on Post Office and Civil Service favorably reported H.R. 25 (See H. Rpt. 100274).

From the time that the House Committee reported the legislation in August 1987 to the present, there have been extensive negotiations to develop a version of H.R. 25 which would be acceptable to the Administration and address the serious problems with the current federal employee whistleblower protection scheme. The negotiations culminated in a draft dated September 22, 1988. Due to the imminent end of the 100th Congress, Rep. Pat Schroeder and Rep. Frank Horton, the House sponsors of the legislation, decided that it would expedite consideration if differences between S. 508, as passed, and the September 22 draft of H.R. 25 could be resolved prior to House consideration.

The amendment brought to the House today, October 3, is the result of those negotiations with the Senate. If the House passes the Senate bill with the amendment, the same language will be presented to the Senate. Senate passage will clear the legislation for the President.

This joint explanatory statement explains new provisions of the version being considered. Some provisions in the amendment were contained in both H.R. 25, as reported, and S. 508, as passed. Those provisions are not discussed in this document but are fully discussed in the Senate report, the House report, or both.

* * *

[*S2784]

7. BURDEN OF PROOF

The bill makes it easier for an individual (or the Special Counsel on the individual's behalf) to prove that a whistleblower reprisal has taken place. To establish a prima facie case, an individual must prove that the whistleblowing was a factor in the personnel action. This supersedes the existing requirement that the whistleblowing was a substantial, motivating or predominant factor in the personnel action.

One of many possible ways to show that the whistleblowing was a factor in the personnel action is to show that the official taking the action knew (or had constructive knowledge) of the disclosure and acted within such a period of time that a reasonable person could conclude that the disclosure was a factor in the personnel action.

The bill establishes an affirmative defense for an agency. Once the prima facie case has been established, corrective action would not be ordered if the agency demonstrates by clear and convincing evidence that it would have taken the same personnel action in the absence of the disclosure. Clear and convincing evidence is a higher standard of proof than the preponderance of the evidence standard now used.

With respect to the agency's affirmative defense, it is our intention to codify the test set out by the Supreme Court in the case of MT. HEALTHY CITY SCHOOL DISTRICT v. DOYLE, 429 U.S. 274, 287 (1977). The only change made by this bill as to that defense is to increase the level of proof which an agency must offer from "preponderance of the evidence" to "clear and convincing evidence."

Notes

CHAPTER 1

1. 148 *Congressional Record*, pp. S7357–58 (July 25, 2002).

2. 148 *Congressional Record*, pp. S7357–58. Congress overwhelmingly approved the Sarbanes-Oxley Act on July 25, 2002. The final Senate vote on the law was 99-0 and the final House vote on the law was 423-3. 148 *Congressional Record* S7365 and H5480 (July 25, 2002).

3. Senate Judiciary Committee Report, "The Corporate and Criminal Fraud Accountability Act of 2002," Senate Report No. 107-146 (May 6, 2002). The portion of this report that directly concerned whistleblower protection was reprinted in the *Congressional Record*, pp. S7412–21 (July 26, 2002) and is reproduced in the appendix section of this book.

4. 148 *Congressional Record*, pp. S7357–58 (July 25, 2002).

5. 148 *Congressional Record*, pp. S7358 (July 25, 2002).

6. *Welch v Cardinal Bankshares Corp.*, 2003-SOX-15, Recommended D&O of ALJ, p. 35 (January 28, 2004).

7. 29 C.F.R. Part 24.

8. Explanatory Statement, reproduced in *Congressional Record* (March 21, 1989).

9. 15 U.S.C. 1514A(b)(2)(A) and (C).

10. *DeFord v Secretary of Labor*, 700 F.2d 281, 286 (6th Cir. 1983); accord., *NLRB v Schrivener*, 405 U.S. 117 (1972).

11. *Kansas Gas & Elec. Co. v Brock*, 780 F.2d 1505, 1512 (10th Cir. 1985); *Poulos v Ambassador Fuel Oil Co.*, 86-CAA-1, D&O of remand by SOL, at 6 (April 27, 1987).

12. *Polizzi v Gibbs & Hill, Inc.*, 87-ERA-38, Order Rejecting in Part, etc., by SOL, at 2-3 (July 18, 1989).

13. *Beliveau v Dept. of Labor*, 170 F.3d 83, 87-88 (1st Cir. 1999), quoting from Decision of the SOL in *Hoffman v Fuel Econ. Contracting*, 87-ERA-33 (August 4, 1989).

14. *DeFord v Secretary of Labor*, 700 F.2d 281, 286 (6th Cir. 1983) (citations omitted).

15. 992 F.2d 474, 479 (3rd Cir. 1993).

16. *Morefield v Exelon Services, Inc.*, 2004-SOX-2 , D&O of ALJ, p. 2 (January 28, 2004)

CHAPTER 2

1. 29 C.F.R. § 1980.103(a) defines "who may file" a complaint in the following manner: "An employee who believes that he or she has been discriminated against by a company or company representative in violation of the Act may file, or have filed by any person on the employee's behalf, a complaint alleging such discrimination."

2. 18 U.S.C. § 1514A(b)(2)(D).

3. Order of the Secretary of Labor No. 5-2002, 67 *Federal Register* 65008 (October 22, 2002). The OSHA Interim Rule is published at 29 C.F.R. Part 1980.

4. The OSHA Web site is located at http://www.osha.gov. The ALJ Web site is located at http://www.oalj.gov. In addition to DOL regulations, the ALJ Web site also posts various administrative rulings related to the SOX and other DOL-administered whistleblower laws.

5. 29 C.F.R. § 1980.104(a) ("Upon receipt of a complaint in the investigating office, the Assistant Secretary will notify the named person [or named persons] of the filing of the complaint, of the allegations contained in the complaint, and of the substance of the evidence supporting the complaint [redacted to protect the identity of any confidential informants]. . . . A copy of the notice to the named person will also be provided to the Securities and Exchange Commission.").

6. 29 CFR § 1980.103(d) ("The date of the postmark, facsimile transmittal, or e-mail communication will be considered to be the date of filing; if the complaint is filed in person, by hand-delivery, or other means, the complaint is filed upon receipt."). See *Sawyers v Baldwin Union Free School Dist.*, 85-TSC-1, D&O of remand by SOL, at 5 (October 10, 1988).

7. 29 CFR § 1980.103(c) ("The complaint should be filed with the OSHA Area Director responsible for enforcement activities in the geographical area where the employee resides or was employed, but may be filed with any OSHA officer or employee.").

8. 29 CFR § 1980.103(b) ("No particular form of complaint is required, except that a complaint must be in writing and should include a full statement of the acts and omissions, with pertinent dates, which are believed to constitute the violations.").

9. *Bassett v Niagara Mohawk Power Co.*, 86-ERA-2, Remand Order of SOL, slip op., at 5 (July 9, 1986); see also *Rudd v Westinghouse Hanford*, 88-ERA-33, D&O of ARB, at 24, n. 27 (November 10, 1997) (collecting cases). Accord., *Swierkiewicz v Sorema*, 534 U.S. 506 (2002).

10. 84-ERA-9-12, D&O of remand by SOL, slip op., at 9-10 (March 12, 1986).

11. *Rudd v Westinghouse Hanford*, 88-ERA-33, D&O of ARB, at 22-24 ("Supplementation should be freely permitted absent a showing, by the opposing party, of undue delay, bad faith, dilatory motive, or prejudice.").

12. *Hasan v U.S. DOL*, 296 F.3d 914 (10th Cir. 2002).

13. 29 C.F.R. § 1980.104(b)(1).

14. 29 C.F.R. § 1980.105(a).

15. *Walker v Aramark Corp.*, 2003-SOX 22, D&O of ALJ (August 26, 2003) (SOX claim dismissed because it was filed 105 days after the alleged discriminatory action).

16. *Hill v DOL*, 65 F.3d 1331, 1335 (6th Cir. 1995); *Larry v Detroit Edison*, 86-ERA-32, D&O of SOL, at 12-19 (June 28, 1991); aff'd sub nom. *Detroit Edison v SOL* (6th Cir. 1992) (unpublished decision); *Hall v DOL*, 960F.2d 149 (10th Cir. 1999).

17. 29 C.F.R. § 1980.103(d).

18. *Overall v TVA*, 97-ERA-53, D&O of ARB, p. 37 (April 30, 2001).

19. See *Delaware State College v Ricks*, 449 U.S. 250, 259 (1980); *English v Whitfield*, 858 F.2d 957, 961 (4th Cir. 1988). Notice of the decision must be "unequivocal." *Flor v U.S. Department of Energy*, 93-TSC-1, D&O of Remand by SOL, at 8 (December 9, 1994). *Ross v FP&L*, 96-ERA-36, D&O of ARB, at 3-5 (March 31, 1999); *McGough v U.S. Navy*, 86-ERA-18/19/20, at 9-10 (June 30, 1988) (collecting cases); *Rose v Dole*, 945 F.2d 1331 (6th Cir. 1991); *Pantanizopoulos v TVA*, 96-ERA-15, D&O of ARB, at 3-4 (October 20, 1997).

20. *Wagerle v The Hospital of the University of Pennsylvania*, 93-ERA-1, D&O of SOL, at 3 (March 17, 1995).

21. 01-ERA-19, D&O of ARB, p. 5 (February 26, 2004).

22. *National Railroad v Morgan*, 536 U.S. 101, 112-13 (2002); *English v Whitfield*, 858 F.2d 957, 961 (4th Cir. 1988).

23. *International Union v Robbins & Meyers, Inc.*, 429 U.S. 229, 236-240 (1976); *Prybys v Seminole Tribe of Florida*, 95-CAA-15, D&O of ARB, at 5 (November 26, 1996).

24. *Hill v DOL*, 65 F.3d 1331, 1335 (6th Cir. 1995) (citations and internal quotations omitted).

25. In *Hill v DOL*, 65 F.3d 1331, 1335 (6th Cir. 1995), the court delineated five factors to be weighed in determining whether to apply equitable tolling: (1) whether the plaintiff lacked actual notice of the filing requirements; (2) whether the plaintiff lacked constructive notice; (3) the diligence with which the plaintiff pursued his rights; (4) whether there would be prejudice to the defendant if the statute were tolled; and (5) the reasonableness of the plaintiff remaining ignorant of his rights.

26. *Prybys v Seminole Tribe of Florida*, 95-CAA-15, D&O of ARB, at 5 ("the doctrine of equitable tolling focuses on the question of whether a duly diligent complainant was excusably ignorant of his rights, whereas the principle of equitable estoppel focuses on the issue of whether the employer misled the complainant and thus caused the delay in filing the complaint.").

27. In *Hill v DOL*, 65 F.3d 1331, 1335 (citations omitted), the court identified three factors that would be necessary to toll the limitations period based on *fraudulent concealment*: (1) wrongful concealment by the defendants; (2) failure of the plaintiff to discover the operative facts; and (3) plaintiff's due diligence until discovery of the facts.

28. See, for example, *Varnadore v SOL*, 141 F.3d 625, 630 (6th Cir. 1998); *OFCCP v CSX Transportation, Inc.*, 88-OFC-24, D&O of Remand by SOL, at 22-26 (October 13, 1994), citing *Elliott v Sperry Rand Corp.*, 79 F.R.D. 580, 584-585 (D. Minn. 1978) (setting forth four basic fact patterns used in establishing a continuing violation);

Simmons v APS, 93-ERA-5, D&O of Remand by SOL, at 8-9 (May 9, 1995) (finding continuing violation due to a "pattern of discrimination"); *Egenrieder v Met. Ed.*, 85-ERA-23, Order of SOL, at 4 (April 20, 1987) (blacklisting); *Holden v Gulf States*, 92-ERA-44, D&O of SOL, at 12-13 (April 14, 1995) (discussing cases finding blacklisting to be a continuing violation); *Thomas v APS*, 89-ERA-19, D&O of SOL, at 10-16 (September 17, 1993) (denial of promotion held continuing in nature).

29. 657 F.2d 16, 19 (3rd Cir. 1981).

30. *Bausemer v TU Electric*, 91-ERA-20, D&O of SOL, at 9 (October 31, 1995). See also *Ross v FP&L*, 88-ERA-33, D&O of ARB, at 4 ("statute of limitations begins to run on the date when facts which would support the discrimination complaint were apparent or should have been apparent to a person similarly situated to Complaint with a reasonably prudent regard for his rights") (citations in internal quotations omitted); *Lawrence v City of Andalusia*, 95-WPC-6, D&O of ARB, at 2 (September 23, 1996) ("The doctrine of equitable tolling is generally inapplicable where a plaintiff is represented by counsel."); *Roberts v TVA*, 94-ERA-15, D&O of SOL, at 5 (August 18, 1995) (constructive knowledge).

31. *National Railroad v Morgan*, 536 U.S. 101, 114 (2002).

32. 536 U.S. 101, 113 (2002). Accord., *Belt v U.S. Enrichment Corp.*, 01-ERA-19 D&O of ARB, at 14 (February 26, 2004).

33. *National Railroad v Morgan*, 536 U.S. 101, 115-16 (2002).

34. *National Railroad v Morgan*, 536 U.S. 101, 115-16 (2002).

35. *National Railroad v Morgan*, 536 U.S. 101, 115, n. (2002).

36. *Connecticut Light & Power v Department of Labor*, 85 F.3d 89, 96 (2nd Cir. 1996).

37. 29 C.F.R. § 1980.105(a).

38. 29 C.F.R. § 1980.106(b)(1).

39. 29 C.F.R. § 1980.113.

40. *Taylor v Express One International, Inc.*, 2001-AIR-2, Order Denying Motion to Quash (December 6, 2001).

41. 5 U.S.C. §§ 552, 552a. A model Freedom of Information Act request is printed in the appendix.

42. *Getman v Southwest Securities, Inc.*, 2003-SOX-8, D&O of ALJ, at 11-12, 14 (February 2, 2004).

43. *English v General Electric Co.*, 85-ERA-2, D&O of SOL, at 7 (February 13, 1992).

44. *Rex v EBASCO Servs., Inc.*, No. 87-ERA-6, D&O of remand to the Wage and Hour Administrator by the SOL (April 13, 1987); *Kamin v Hunter Corp.*, 89-ERA-11, Order of SOL (March 12, 1990). See *Pickett v TVA*, 99-CAA-25, Order Remanding by ALJ (September 10, 1999) (granting uncontested remand, but recognizing remand not allowed under ERA).

45. *Friday v Northwest Airlines, Inc.*, 2003-AIR-19, Order of ALJ (June 27, 2003).

46. *Newton v State of Alaska*, 96-TSC-10, Order Denying Request for Hearing of the Chief ALJ (October 25, 1996). In *Newton*, the Chief ALJ held that a four-month delay in OSHA issuing its findings permitted a constructive appeal, whereas a three-month delay did not.

47. *Billings v TVA*, 91-ERA-12, D&O of ARB, at 8-9 (June 26, 1996).

48. 29 C.F.R. § 1980.104(b) ("A complaint of alleged violation will be dismissed unless the complainant has made a prima facie showing that protected behavior or

conduct was a contributing factor in the unfavorable personnel action alleged in the complaint.").

49. 29 C.F.R. § 1980.104(b)(1)(i)–(iv).

50. 29 C.F.R. § 1980.104(b)(2).

51. 29 C.F.R. § 1980.104(c).

52. 29 C.F.R. § 1980.104(c).

53. 29 C.F.R. § 1980.104(d) ("If the named person fails to demonstrate by clear and convincing evidence that it would have taken the same unfavorable personnel action in the absence of the behavior protected by the Act, the Assistant Secretary will conduct an investigation.").

54. "Investigations will be conducted in a manner that protects the confidentiality of any person who provides information on a confidential basis, other than the complainant, in accordance with part 70 of this title" (29 C.F.R. § 1980.104[d]).

55. 29 C.F.R. § 1980.104(e).

56. 29 C.F.R. § 1980.105(a).

57. 29 C.F.R. § 1980.105(b) ("The findings and the preliminary order will be sent by certified mail, return receipt requested, to all parties of record. The letter accompanying the findings and order will inform the parties of their right to file objections and to request a hearing, and of the right of the named person to request attorney's fees from the ALJ, regardless of whether the named person has filed objections, if the named person alleges that the complaint was frivolous or brought in bad faith. The letter also will give the address of the Chief Administrative Law Judge. At the same time, the Assistant Secretary will file with the Chief Administrative Law Judge, U.S. Department of Labor, a copy of the original complaint and a copy of the findings and order.").

58. 29 C.F.R. § 1980.105(a)(2).

59. 29 C.F.R. § 1980.105(a)(1) ("If the Assistant Secretary concludes that there is reasonable cause to believe that a violation has occurred, he or she will accompany the findings with a preliminary order providing relief to the complainant. The preliminary order will include all relief necessary to make the employee whole, including: Where appropriate, reinstatement with the same seniority status that the employee would have had but for the discrimination; back pay with interest; and compensation for any special damages sustained as a result of the discrimination, including litigation costs, expert witness fees, and reasonable attorney's fees. Where the named person establishes that the complainant is a security risk [whether or not the information is obtained after the complainant's discharge], a preliminary order of reinstatement would not be appropriate.").

60. 29 C.F.R. § 1980.105(c) ("The findings and the preliminary order will be effective 30 days after receipt by the named person pursuant to paragraph [b] of this section, unless an objection and a request for a hearing has been filed as provided at § 1980.106. However, the portion of any preliminary order requiring reinstatement will be effective immediately upon receipt of the findings and preliminary order.").

61. *McCafferty v Centerion*, 96-ERA-6, Order Denying Stay by ARB (October 16, 1996).

62. *Batts v TVA*, 82-ERA-5, slip op. of ALJ, at 1 (May 3, 1982).

63. *Majors v Asea Brown Boveri, Inc.*, 96-ERA-33, D&O of ARB, at 1 n. 1 (August 1, 1997).

64. 29 C.F.R. § 1980.106(a). See *Staskelunas v Northeast Utilities*, 98-ERA-8, D&O of ARB, at 2 n. 4, 3 n. 3 (May 4, 1998). The ARB recognizes that all of its administrative deadlines are subject to tolling or modification. See *Garcia v Wantz Equipment*, 99-CAA: 11 Order of ARB, at 2 (February 8, 2000), citing *American Farm Lines v Black Ball Freight*, 397 U.S. 532, 539 (1970).

65. Care should be given to ensure strict compliance with this procedural rule. If a technical error does occur in the filing procedure, there is authority supporting "substantial compliance" or "substantial equivalent" test for overcoming such errors. *Daugherty v General Physics Corp.*, 92-SDW-2, D&O of remand of ALJ, at 3 (December 14, 1992), adopted by SOL (April 19, 1995). But see *Degostin v Bartlett Nuclear*, 98-ERA-7, D&O of ARB, at 3 (May 4, 1998) ("time limit for filing a request for a hearing has been strictly construed"); *Backen v Energy Op. Inc.*, 95-ERA-46, D&O of ARB, at 3-4 (June 7, 1996) (time limits for filing a hearing request are "strictly construed").

66. 29 C.F.R. 1980.106(a).

67. *Hemingway v Northeast Utilities*, 99-ERA-14 (August 31, 2000).

68. 29 C.F.R. § 1980.105(c).

69. 29 C.F.R. 1980.106(a); 29 C.F.R. § 1980.106(b)(2) ("If no timely objection is filed with respect to either the findings or the preliminary order, the findings or preliminary order, as the case may be, will become the final decision of the Secretary, not subject to judicial review.").

70. *Shelton v Oak Ridge National Laboratories,*. 95-CAA-19, D&O of ARB, at. 5-6 (March 30, 2001); *Howlett v Northeast Utilities*, 99-ERA-1, D&O of ARB (March 31, 2001) (concurring opinion by Member Brown).

71. 29 C.F.R. 1980.106(a). These other parties should be served at the same time the notice of appeal is filed. However, failing to promptly serve these notices will not be fatal to an appeal. *See Pawlowski v Hewlett-Packard Co.*, 97-TSC-3, Order of ARB (September 15, 1999).

72. *English v General Electric Co.*, 85-ERA-2, D&O of SOL, at 11 n. 5 (February 13, 1992); *contra Allen v EG&G Defense*, 97-SDW-8 & 10, Order of ALJ (January 26, 1998).

CHAPTER 3

1. The implementing regulations require the DOL to follow the rules of practice set forth in 29 C.F.R. Part 18 in SOX adjudications. These are the same practice rules that DOL has used for other whistleblower adjudications, including cases under the Energy Reorganization Act and for airline and environmental whistleblowers. 29 C.F.R.§ 1980.1067(a). ("Except as provided in this part, proceedings will be conducted in accordance with the rules of practice and procedure for administrative hearings before the Office of Administrative Law Judges, codified at subpart A, part 18 of title 29 of the Code of Federal Regulations.").

2. 29 C.F.R.§ 1980.107(b) ("Hearings will be conducted as hearings *de novo*, on the record.")

3. See note 1.

4. In April 1996, the Secretary of Labor established the Administrative Review Board (ARB) with authority to issue final decisions on behalf of the Secre-

tary in whistleblower cases. *Varnadore v SOL*, 141 F.3d 625, 631-632 (6th Cir. 1998). ALJ rulings issued in SOX cases are subject to review, as a matter of right, before the ARB. The review is *de novo*, except that the review of the ALJ "factual determinations" are conducted under the "substantial evidence standard." 29 C.F.R. § 1980.110(b).

5. 29 C.F.R. § 1980.110(b).

6. 29 C.F.R. § 1980.109(a) ("Neither the Assistant Secretary's determination to dismiss a complaint without completing an investigation pursuant to § 1980.104(b) nor the Assistant Secretary's determination to proceed with an investigation is subject to review by the administrative law judge, and a complaint may not be remanded for the completion of an investigation or for additional findings on the basis that a determination to dismiss was made in error. Rather, if there otherwise is jurisdiction, the administrative law judge will hear the case on the merits.").

7. 29 C.F.R. § 1980.109(c) ("Any administrative law judge's decision requiring reinstatement or lifting an order of reinstatement by the Assistant Secretary will be effective immediately upon receipt of the decision by the named person, and may not be stayed. All other portions of the judge's order will be effective ten business days after the date of the decision unless a timely petition for review has been filed with the Administrative Review Board.").

8. 29 C.F.R. § 1980.113.

9. 29 C.F.R. § 1980.109(c).

10. 29 C.F.R. § 1980.108(a)(1).

11. 29 C.F.R.§ 1980.107(c) ("If the complainant and the named person object to the findings and/or order, the objections will be consolidated and a single hearing will be conducted.").

12. 29 C.F.R.§ 18.11.

13. 29 C.F.R. § 1980.108(a)(1).

14. 29 C.F.R. § 1980.108(a)(2) ("Copies of pleadings in all cases, whether or not the Assistant Secretary is participating in the proceeding, must be sent to the Assistant Secretary, Occupational Safety and Health Administration, and to the Associate Solicitor, Division of Fair Labor Standards, U.S. Department of Labor, Washington, DC 20210.") .

15. 29 C.F.R. § 1980.108(b).

16. 29 C.F.R. § 18.10.

17. 29 C.F.R. §§ 18.10 and 18.12.

18. *Young v Schlumberger Oil Field Services*, 2000-STA-28, D&O of ARB at 10 (February 28, 2003).

19. 29 C.F.R. § 1980.107(b).

20. 29 C.F.R. § 1980.107(b).

21. 29 C.F.R. §§ 18.4, 18.6(b), 18.24.

22. *Johnson v Transco Prods., Inc.*, 85-ERA-7, slip op. of ALJ, at 2 (March 5, 1985); *Bullock v Rochester Gas & Elec. Corp.*, 84-ERA-22, interim order on motion, slip op. of ALJ, at 2 (1984).

23. See, for example, *Donovan v Freeway Construction Co.*, 511 F. Supp. 869, 878 (D. R.I. 1982) ("The defendant may not pervert a statutory provision protecting employees.").

24. *Long et al. v Roadway Express, Inc.*, 88-STA-31, D&O of SOL, at 3-4 (March 9, 1990); *Poulos v Ambassador Fuel Co.*, 86-CAA-1, D&O of remand by SOL, at 12. For

authority on this issue, see also *Brock v Pierce County*, 106 S.Ct. 1834 (1986); *Logan v Zimmerman Brush Co.*, 455 U.S. 422, 432-437 (1982).

25. *Timmons v Mattingly Testing Services*, 95-ERA-40, D&O of ARB, at 5 (June 21, 1996).

26. 29 C.F.R. § 18.1(b); *Young v E. H. Hinds*, 86-ERA-11, D&O of remand by SOL, at 3 n. 2 (July 8, 1987). See *Forest v Williams Power Corp.*, 2000-ERA-16/17, D&O of ALJ (April 7, 2000) ("complainant who waives the statutory and regulatory deadline should be allowed time to conduct discovery").

27. *Timmons v Mattingly Testing Services*, 95-ERA-40, D&O of ARB, at 6-8.

28. *Khandelwal v Southern California Edison*, 97-ERA-6, Order of ARB (November 30, 2000).

29. 29 C.F.R. § 24.6(a). See also *Malpass v General Electric Co.*, 85-ERA-38/39, D&O of SOL (March 1, 1994) (discussing cases on granting continuances).

30. 29 C.F.R. § 1980.107(b).

31. 29 C.F.R. § 18.28(b) "Except for good cause arising thereafter, request for continuances must be filed within fourteen days prior to the date set for hearing.").

32. See *Abson v Kaiser Co.*, 84-ERA-8, slip op. of ALJ, at 2 (January 7, 1985); *Bullock v Rochester Gas & Elec. Corp.*, 84-ERA-22, decision and interim order on motion of ALJ (continuance ordered to allow *pro se* complainant time to find an attorney); *Guity v TVA*, 90-ERA-10, Remand Order of SOL (May 3, 1995) (delay due to psychological problems); *Rios-Berrios v INS*, 776 F.2d 859, 862-863 (9th Cir. 1985); *Lowe v City of E. Chicago*, 897 F.2d 272 (7th Cir. 1990).

33. *Unger v Saraflite*, 376 U.S. 575, 589-590 (1964); see also *Administrative Procedure Act*, 5 U.S.C. § 554. In *Khandelwal v Southern California Edison*, 97-ERA-6, Order of ARB (November 30, 2000), the ARB reversed the hearing results of an ALJ and remanded the case for an entirely new hearing on the ground that the ALJ failed to provide a complainant/employee adequate time to locate an attorney and conduct discovery.

34. The Department of Labor rules for time computation are located at 29 C.F.R. § 18.4.

35. See, for example, *O'Sullivan et al. v Northeast Nuclear Energy Co.*, 88-ERA-37/38, recommended D&O of ALJ, at 15-16 (August 18, 1989).

36. 29 C.F.R. §§ 18.40, 18.41.

37. See, for example, *Studer v Flowers Baking Co.*, 93-CAA-11, D&O of SOL, at 2 (June 19, 1995); *Varnadore v Oak Ridge National Laboratory*, 92-CAA-215 & 94-CAA-213, D&O of ARB, at 58 (June 14, 1996).

38. *Seetharaman v Stone & Webster*, 2003-CAA-4, Order Denying Motion for Summary Decision by ALJ (February 26, 2003); *Gillilan v TVA*, 91-ERA 31/34, D&O SOL, at 4-5 (August 28, 1995); *Kesterson v Y-12 Nuclear Weapons Plant*, 95-CAA-12, D&O of ARB, at 5-6 (April 8, 1997); *Johnson v Houston Nana, Inc.*, 99-TSC-4, D&O of ARB, p. 4 (January 27, 2003) (standard of appellate review for summary decision).

39. *Richter v Baldwin Assocs.*, 84-ERA-9/10/11/12, Order of SOL, at 13-14 (March 12, 1986); *Stauffer v Wal-Mart Stores*, 99-STA-21, D&O of ARB, at 6 (November 30, 1999).

40. *Flor v U.S. Department of Energy*, 93-TSC-1, at 9-12; *Moore v DOE*, 98-CAA-16, D&O of ARB, p. 4 (June 25, 2001).

41. *Reid v Methodist Medical Center*, 93-CAA-4, D&O of SOL, at 32 (April 3, 1995).

42. 29 C.F.R. § 24.6(e)(3).

43. *Ass't Secretary v Double Trucking, Inc.*, 98-STA-34, D&O of SOL, at 4 (July 16, 1999).

44. *Migliore v Rhode Island Dept. of Environmental Management*, 98-SWD-3, Order Regarding Discovery Dispute by ALJ, at 3 (October 14, 1998) ("It is clear from the aforementioned regulation and precedent that in determining whether to admit evidence at hearing over an objection of relevance, an ALJ should apply a broad scope of relevance. It logically follows that the scope of discovery is even broader").

45. See *Khandelwal v Southern California Edison*, 97-ERA-6, D&O of ARB, at 4 (March 31, 1998). See also *Timmons v Mattingly Testing Services*, 95-ERA-40, D&O of ARB, at 5-6 (June 21, 1996).

46. *Robinson v Martin Marietta Services*, 94-TSC-7, D&O of ARB, at 4 (September 23, 1996).

47. *Tracanna v Arctic Slope Inspection Svc.*, 97-WPC-1, D&O of ARB, at 5 n. 6 (November 6, 1997).

48. *Tracanna v Arctic Slope Inspection Svc.*, 97-WPC-1, D&O of ARB, at 5 n. 6

49. 29 C.F.R. §§ 18.18, 18.19, 18.20.

50. *Parshley v America West Airlines*, 2002-AIR-10 (April 17, 2002).

51. *Johnson v Oak Ridge Operations*, 95-CAA-201 21/22, D&O of ARB, at 12 (September 30, 1999).

52. *Tracanna v Arctic Slope Inspection Svc.*, 97-WPC-1, D&O of ARB, at 5.

53. *Timmons v Mattingly Testing Services*, 95-ERA-40, D&O or Remand by ARB, at 5-6. The time requirements for responding to discovery are set forth in administrative regulations. 29 C.F.R. Part 18. An initial request to extend these time limits are "routinely granted." *Tracanna v Arctic Slope Inspection Service*, 97-WPC-1, ARB No. 97-123, D&O of Remand by ARB, at 5 (November 6, 1997). The DOL adjudicatory rules applicable to whistleblower cases permit broad discovery in a manner consistent with the mechanisms available under the Federal Rules of Civil Procedure. *Malpass v General Electric Co.*, 85-ERA-38/39, D&O of SOL, at 12 (March 1, 1994).

54. In *Malpass v General Electric Co.*, the SOL stated that "it seems clear" that the SOL and ALJ have "no power under the ERA to issue subpoenas or to punish for contempt" the "failure to comply with a subpoena." 85-ERA-38/39, D&O of SOL, at 21 (March 1, 1994). The inability of the SOL to issue or enforce subpoenas does not render the DOL powerless to compel discovery. As pointed out in *Malpass*, the DOL "has the authority to impose sanctions for failure of a party to comply with discovery or other orders under 29 C.F.R. §18.6(d)(2)." *Malpass*, at 19, n.8. These sanctions include applying the adverse inference rule and issuing a default judgment. See 29 C.F.R. §§ 18.14-18.24. In *Childers v Carolina Power & Light*, 97-ERA-32, D&O of ARB (December 29, 2000) the ARB narrowed the holding in *Malpass* and held that the DOL could issue subpoenas. The decision did not address the enforceability of the subpoenas in federal court. Federal courts have not enforced DOL subpoenas in whistleblower cases. *Bobreski v EPA*, 2003 WL 22246796 (D.D.C. 2003).

55. *Assistant SOL, et al. v Gammons Wire Feeder Corp.*, 87-STA-5, D&O or SOL (September 17, 1987).

56. *Beliveau v Naval Undersea Warfare Center*, 97-SDW-1, Recommended D&O of ALJ (June 29, 2000) (entering judgment for whistleblower after employer

refused to comply with discovery). Accord., *Dickson v Butler Motor*, 01-STA-39, D&O of ARB, p. 4 (July 25, 2003); *In the Matter of Supervan, Inc.*, 94-SCA-14, D&O of ARB, p. 5 (September 30, 2002); *Webb v Government for the District of Columbia*, 146 F3d 964 (D.C. Cir. 1998) (default judgment in retaliatory discharge case for discovery abuses and destruction of documents); *International Union (UAW) v NLRB*, 429 F.2d 1329, 1338 (D.C. Cir. 1972) (setting forth "adverse inference rule").

57. See 5 U.S.C. §§ 552, 552(a). An excellent guide to using the Freedom of Information Act and Privacy Act is Allan Adler, ed., *Litigation under the Federal Freedom of Information Act and Privacy Act* (American Civil Liberties Union Foundation, 122 Maryland Avenue, N.E., Washington, D.C. 20002, published annually).

58. *Timmons v Mattingly Testing Services*, 95-ERA-40, D&O or Remand by ARB, at 5-6 (June 21, 1996); *Migliore v R.I Department of Environmental Management*, 98-SWD-3 "Order Regarding Discovery" (ALJ, October 14, 1998) (because rules of admissibility in DOL proceedings are relaxed, the "scope of discovery" is broad); *Holub v H. Nash Babcock, Babcock & King, Inc.*,93-ERA-25 Discovery Order of ALJ, at 9 (March 2, 1994).

59. *Khandelwal v Southern California* Edison, 97-ERA-6, ARB No. 97-50, D&O of ARB at 4 (March 31, 1998) ("opportunity for extensive discovery is crucial to serving ERA purposes of protecting employees and public interest"). The DOL ALJs also recognize that "extensive discovery" must be permitted in environmental whistleblower cases. *Mitchell v APS/ANPP*, 92-ERA-29, Order of ALJ, at 4 (May 3, 1992). Also see *Mulligan v Vermont Yankee*, 92-ERA-20, Order of ALJ, at 2 (April 17, 1992) ("Plaintiffs in equal employment cases should be permitted a very broad scope of discovery."). For example, in *Holub v H. Nash Babcock, Babcock & King, Inc.*, 93-ERA-25, Discovery Order of ALJ (March 2, 1994), the ALJ ruled that "the law is well settled regarding the appropriateness of extensive discovery in employment discrimination cases. Further, the courts have held that liberal discovery in these cases is warranted." *Timmons v Mattingly Testing Services*, 95-ERA-40, D&O or Remand by ARB at 6.

60. See Kohn, *Concepts and Procedures in Whistleblower Law*, pp. 276–80, 319–325 (Greenwood Press, Westport CT: 2000), for a full discussion of the subject matters held discoverable in whistleblower cases.

61. *Rockefeller v Carlsbad Area Office, DOE*, 98-CAA-10/11 and 99-CAA-1/4/6, D&O of ARB, p. 14 (October 31, 2000).

62. *Beliveau v Naval Undersea Warfare Center*, 97-SDW-6, Order Denying Motion for Reconsideration by ALJ (May 31, 2000); *Welch v Cardinal Bankshares Corp.*, 2003-SOX-15, Order of ALJ requiring *In Camera* Inspection (August 1, 2003) and Order Compelling Discovery (August 15, 2003).

63. *Shirani v Com/Exelon Corp.*, 02-ERA-28, Final Order Denying Emergency Appeal by ARB (December 10, 2002).

64. See *Kinser v Mesaba Aviation, Inc.*, 2003-AIR-7, Order Granting Motion to Compel by ALJ, p. 2 (March 4, 2003); *Khandelwal v Southern California Edison*, 97-ERA-6, Order of ARB, pp. 6-8 (November 30, 2000) (concurring opinion of Board Member Brown).

65. *Diego v United Parcel Service Co.*, 2003-AIR-27, Order Granting Motion to Compel by ALJ, p. 2 (September 24, 2003).

66. *Khandelwal v Southern California* Edison, 97-ERA-6, ARB No. 97-50, D&O of ARB at 4.

67. *Holden v Gulf States Utilities*, 92-ERA-44, D&O of Remand by SOL, at 8 (April 14, 1995). Accord., *Avirgan v Hull*, 118 F.R.D. 252 (D. D.C. 1987); *Alexander v FBI*, 186 F.R.D. 60, 65-66 (D. D.C. 1987) (citing cases). Protective orders should not prohibit a party's right to disseminate information obtained outside of the discovery process itself. *Holden*, at 9. ALJs have the authority to issue protective orders and are often asked to impose gag orders on a party's ability to publicly disclose information produced in discovery. Although such orders are often jointly presented to an ALJ for approval, ALJs have refused to enter such protective orders when they are viewed as too "all-encompassing and draconian." *Scott v Alyeska Pipeline Service Co.*, 92-TSC-2, ALJ Order Denying Protective Order (January 4, 1992). Once a protective order is issued by an ALJ, the ALJ maintains jurisdiction to modify the protective order, even after a case is dismissed. *Holden*, at 6.

68. 29 C.F.R. § 18.26. See also SWDA, 42 U.S.C. § 6971 (b); WPCA, 33 U.S.C. § 1367(b); CERCLA, 42 U.S.C. § 9610(b).

69. The APA, at 5 U.S.C. § 556(d) states:

> Any oral or documentary evidence may be received, but the agency as a matter of policy shall provide for the exclusion of irrelevant, immaterial, or unduly repetitious evidence. A sanction may not be imposed or rule or order issued except on consideration of the whole record or those parts thereof cited by a party and supported by and in accordance with the reliable, probative and substantial evidence. . . . A party is entitled to present his case or defense by oral or documentary evidence, to submit rebuttal evidence, and to conduct such cross examination as may be required for a full and true disclosure of the facts.

See also 29 C.F.R. § 24.5(e).

70. 29 C.F.R. § 18.26; *Melendez v Exxon*, 93-ERA-6, D&O of ARB, at 24-25.

71. *Masek v The Cadle Company*, 95-WPC-1, D&O of ARB, pp. 9-10 (April 28, 2000).

72. 29 C.F.R. § 18.34; See also *Seater v Southern California Edison*, 95-ERA-13, D&O of ARB, at 14-15 (September 27, 1996).

73. 29 C.F.R. § 1980.107(d). Application of the Federal Rules of Evidence is contrary to the regulatory mandate applicable to the DOL adjudicatory proceedings. *Melendez v Exxon*, 93-ERA-6, D&O of ARB, at 24-25 (July 14, 2000).

74. 29 C.F.R. § 1980.107(d).

75. *Timmons v Mattingly Testing Services*, 95-ERA-40, D&O of ARB, at 11. Accord., *Seater v Southern California Edison*, 95-ERA-13, D&O of ARB, at 5.

76. 29 C.F.R. §§ 18.52, 27.5(e)(2).

77. 29 C.F.R. § 18.29.

78. 29 C.F.R. § 18.1(a); *Steffenhagen v Securitas Sverige*, 2003-SOX-24, Order of ALJ, p. 2 (August 5, 2003).

79. 29 C.F.R. § 18.1(b).

80. 29 C.F.R. § 1980.115 ("In special circumstances not contemplated by the provisions of this part, or for good cause shown, the administrative law judge or the Board on review may, upon application, after three days notice to all parties and interveners, waive any rule or issue any orders that justice or the administration of the Act requires.").

81. *Yellow Freight v Martin*, 954 F.2d 353, 357 (6th Cir. 1992).

82. See *Matthews v Eldridge*, 424 U.S. 319 (1976) ("the fundamental requirement of due process is the opportunity to be heard at a meaningful time and in a mean-

ingful manner"); *English v General Electric Co.*, 85-ERA-2, D&O of SOL, at 7 (February 13, 1992), quoting *Matthews* at 335. See *Melendez v Exxon*, 93-ERA-6, D&O of ARB, at 24-25 (parties must be provided a "full and fair opportunity for the presentation of arguments and facts").

83. *In the Matter of Charles A. Kent*, 84-WPC-2, Remand D&O, at 9-10 (April 6, 1987), quoting from *Hornsby v Allen*, 326 F.2d 605, 608 (5th Cir. 1964). See also *Armstrong v Manzo*, 380 U.S. 545, 550-552 (1965); *Carson Products Co. v Califano*, 594 F.2d 453, 459 (5th Cir. 1979); *North Alabama Express, Inc. v United States*, 585 F.2d 783, 786-787 (5th Cir. 1978); 5 U.S.C. § 554(b) and (c) (1982). See *English v General Electric Co.*, 85-ERA-2, D&O of SOL, at 7-8 (February 13, 1992) (discussing due process requirements).

84. 29 C.F.R. § 1980.107(d).

85. *Frady v TVA*, 92-ERA-19/34, D&O of SOL, at 7-8 (October 23, 1995); see also *Seater v Southern California Edison*, 95-ERA-13, D&O of ARB, at 5-8.

86. *Ass't. Secretary of Labor for Occupational Safety and Health and Anthony Ciotti v Sysco Foods of Philadelphia*, 97-STA-30, D&O of ARB, at 6 (July 8, 1998).

87. 29 C.F.R. §§ 18.44(b), 24.5(e)(3). Major witnesses should, wherever possible, testify live at the hearing, not through prerecorded depositions. See *Carter v Electrical District No. 2*, 92-TSC-11, D&O of SOL, at 13 n.1 (July 26, 1995).

88. 29 C.F.R. § 18.47.

89. *Oliver v Hydro-Vac Services, Inc.*, 91-SWD-1, D&O of ARB, at 2 (January 6, 1998). *See* Stephen Smith, "Due process and the subpoena power in federal environmental health and safety whistleblower proceedings," 32 *University of San Francisco Law Review* 533 (1998).

90. *Immanuel v DOL*, 139 F.3d 889 (table), unpublished opinion, 1998 WL 129932 (4th Cir. 1998).

91. 29 C.F.R. § 18.45.

92. 29 C.F.R. § 18.47.

93. 29 C.F.R. § 18.50.

94. 29 C.F.R. § 18.46.

95. *Richardson v Perales*, 402 U.S. 389, 410 (1972); *Calhoun v Bailar*, 626 F.2d 145, 148 (9th Cir. 1980). See also *Ass't. Secretary of Labor for Occupational Safety and Health and Anthony Ciotti v Sysco Foods of Philadelphia*, 97-STA-30, D&O of ARB, at 6.

96. 29 C.F.R. § 18.45; *Davis v United Air Lines*, 2001-AIR-5, Order of ALJ (April 25, 2002).

97. 29 C.F.R. § 18.47.

98. *Seater v Southern California Edison*, 95-ERA-13, D&O of ARB, at 16.

99. 29 C.F.R. § 18.6(d)(2)(i)-(iv). See also *Seater v Southern California Edison*, 95-ERA-13, D&O of ARB, at 26; *Rockingham Machine-Lunex v NLRB*, 665 F.2d 303, 305 (8th Cir. 1981); *International Union (UAW) v NLRB*, 459 F.2d 1329, 1335-1342 (D.C. Cir. 1972); *Cram v Pullman-Higgins Co.*, 84-ERA-17, slip op. of ALJ, at 14 (July 24, 1984); *Pulliam v Worthington Service Corp.*, 81-WPCA-1, slip op. of ALJ, at 3 (May 15, 1981); J. Wigmore, *Evidence*, vol. 2 § 285 (3rd ed. 1940). But see *Fugate v TVA*, 93-ERA-9, D&O of SOL, at 4 (September 6, 1995) (admitting evidence due to parties' failure to file a timely motion to compel).

100. 29 C.F.R. § 18.54(c); see also *Madonia v Dominicki Finer Food*, 98-STA-2, Order of ARB, at 4 (January 29, 1999); *Foley v Boston Edison Co.*, 97-ERA-56, Order of ARB, at 4 (February 2, 1999) (admitted before ARB); *Nolan v AC Express*, 92-STA-

37, D&O of SOL, at 3 (January 17, 1995); *Ake v Ulrich Chemical, Inc.*, 93-STA-41, D&O of SOL, at 3 (March 21, 1994) (denying admission of evidence); *Timmons v Mattingly Testing Services*, 95-ERA-40, D&O of ARB, at 3-7 (admitting new evidence and remanding for discovery and new hearing); *Masek v Cadle Company*, 95-WPC-1, D & O of ARB (April 28, 2000) (denying admission of new evidence); *Varnadore v Oak Ridge Lab.*, 92-CAA-2/93-CAA-1/3, D&O of ARB (July 14, 2000) (rejecting admission of new evidence under FRCP 60).

101. *Timmons*, at 12; see, for example, *Seater v Southern California Edison*, 95-ERA-13, D&O of ARB, at 5-8.

102. *Delaney v DOL*, 69 F.3d 531 (1st Cir. 1995) (unpublished "Table" decision), 1995 WL 648107 (November 6, 1995). See also *Calhoun v Bailar*, 626 F.2d 145, 148 (9th Cir. 1980); *Hoonsilapa v Immigration & Naturalization Serv*, 575 F.2d 735, 738, modified, 586 F.2d 755 (9th Cir. 1978); *Marin-Mendoza v Immigration & Naturalization Serv*, 499 F.2d 918, 921 (9th Cir. 1974), cert. denied, 419 U.S. 1113, reh'g. denied, 420 U.S. 984. See also *Richardson v Perales*, 402 U.S. 389, 407-408 (1971).

103. See, for example, *Mackowiak v University Nuclear Systems, Inc.*, 82-ERA-8, D&O of remand by ALJ, at 4 (July 25, 1986).

104. *Calhoun v Bailar*, 626 F.2d 149, cert. denied, 452 U.S. 906 (1986).

105. *Richardson v Perales*, 402 U.S. 410.

106. *Consolidated Edison Co. of N.Y. v NLRB*, 305 U.S. 197, 230 (1938). But see *Richardson v Perales*, 402 U.S. 389, 410.

107. *Second Taxing District of City of Norwalk v Federal Energy Regulatory Comm'n.*, 683 F.2d 477, 485 (D.C. Cir. 1982); *National Airlines, Inc. v Civil Aeronautics Bd.*, 321 F.2d 380, 383 (D.C. Cir. 1963).

108. *Morgan v United States*, 298 U.S. 468 (1936).

109. 29 C.F.R. § 18.57(a).

110. 29 C.F.R. § 18.57(a).

111. 29 C.F.R. § 18.57(b) ("The decision of the administrative law judge shall include findings of fact and conclusions of law, with reasons therefore, upon each material issue of fact or law presented on the record. The decision . . . shall be based upon the whole record. It shall be supported by reliable and probative evidence.").

112. 29 C.F.R. §§ 1980.109(c).

113. *Garcia v Wantz Equipment*, 99-CAA-11, Order of ARB (February 8, 2000); *Duncan v Sacramento Met. Air*, 97-CAA-12, Order of ARB (September 1, 1999).

114. 29 C.F.R. § 1980.110(a) ("The decision of the administrative law judge will become the final order of the Secretary unless, pursuant to this section, a petition for review is timely filed with the Board. The petition for review must specifically identify the findings, conclusions or orders to which exception is taken. Any exception not specifically urged ordinarily will be deemed to have been waived by the parties. To be effective, a petition must be filed within ten business days of the date of the decision of the administrative law judge.").

115. 29 C.F.R. § 1980.109(c) ("Any administrative law judge's decision requiring reinstatement or lifting an order of reinstatement by the Assistant Secretary will be effective immediately upon receipt of the decision by the named person, and may not be stayed. All other portions of the judge's order will be effective ten business days after the date of the decision unless a timely petition for review has been filed with the Administrative Review Board.").

116. 29 C.F.R. §§ 1980.106(a), 1980.109(b) and 1980.109(a).

117. 29 C.F.R. § 18.36(a).

118. 29 C.F.R. § 18.36(b). See *Johnson v Oak Ridge Operations Office*, 95-CAA-20/21/22, Order to Show Cause by ALJ (January 6, 1997). Appeals from an ALJ disqualification order are filed with the Chief ALJ. 29 C.F.R. § 18.36(b); Rockefeller v. DOE, 98-CAA-10/11 (Chief ALJ, October 6, 1998).

119. 29 C.F.R. § 18.36(b). See *Hufstetler v Roadway Express*, 85-STA-8, SOL Order, at 2 (April 8, 1986) (rejecting motion to reassign ALJ); *Robinson v Martin Marietta Services*, 94-TSC-7, D&O of ARB, at 5; *Flor v U.S. Department of Energy*, 93-TSC-1, Order of SOL, at 13 (December 9, 1994). ALJs are "presumed to be impartial," and any party seeking their disqualification must meet a "substantial burden." See *Billings v TVA*, 91-ERA-12, D&O of ALJ, at 5-7 (June 26, 1996).

120. *Johnson v DOE*, 95-CAA-20/21/22, ALJ (February 4, 1997). *See also Rockefeller v DOE*, 98-CAA-10/11, Order Barring Counsel from Future Appearances, ALJ (September 28, 1998); *Hasan v NPS*, 86-ERA-24, ALJ Order of Disqualification (appealed October 21, 1986; settlement reached without concession as to legality of ALJ's decision; joint motion to vacate pursuant to terms of settlement granted) (February 4, 1987).

121. 29 C.F.R. § 18.36(b).

122. *Webb v CP&L*, 93-ERA-42, D&O of ARB, at 9 (August 26, 1997) ("Where the integrity of the department's adjudicative process is at stake, the presiding ALJ should take all appropriate steps to resolve uncertainty surrounding questionable conduct.").

123. *Young v CBI Servs., Inc.*, 88-ERA-8, D&O of remand by SOL (August 10, 1988).

124. 29 C.F.R. § 24.6(e)(4)(b)(ii).

125. *Young v CBI Servs., Inc.*, 88-ERA-8, D&O of remand by SOL, at 2. See also *National Hockey League v Metropolitan Hockey Club*, 427 U.S. 639 (1976); *Iowa Beef Packers, Inc. v NLRB*, 331 F.2d 176, 185 (8th Cir. 1964). In *Tracanna v Arctic Slope Inspection Svc.*, 97-WPC-1, D&O of ARB, at 4, the DOL quoted from its basic rule on default judgment: "Dismissal with prejudice is warranted only where there is a clear record of delay or contumacious conduct and a lesser sanction would not better serve the interests of justice."

126. *Young v CBI Servs., Inc.*, 88-ERA-8, D&O of remand by SOL, at 2-3; *Coupar v DOL*, 105 F.3d 1263, 1267 (9th Cir. 1997) (default denied because respondent had good cause for not appearing at the hearing).

127. *Ass't. Sec'y. v Gammon Wire Feeder Corp.*, 87-STA-5, D&O of SOL (September 17, 1987).

128. *Ridings v Commonwealth Edison*, 88-ERA-27, recommended order by ALJ, at 14-15 (March 10, 1989).

129. *Ass't. Sec'y. v Brenner Ice, Inc.*, 94-STA-10, Order of SOL (July 26, 1994).

130. *Billings v TVA*, 91-ERA-12, D&O of ALJ, at 9-10.

131. *White v "Q" Trucking Co., Alliance Trucking and Employment Services of Michigan*, 93-STA-28, Order of SOL (December 2, 1994); *Wellman v Dipple*, 85-ERA-019, order of dismissal by ALJ, at 3 (November 27, 1985).

132. *Ass't. Sec'y. v Gammon Wire Feeder Corp.*, 87-STA-5, D&O of SOL at 3.

133. See, for example, *Rex v EBASCO Services, Inc.*, No. 87-ERA-6; *Hasan v NPS et al.*, 86-ERA-24, decision of ALJ regarding motion to disqualify (appealed October 21, 1986), settlement reached without concession as to legality of ALJ's deci-

sion; joint motion to vacate pursuant to terms of settlement agreement (granted February 4, 1987).

134. *Cox v Lockheed Martin,* 97-ERA-17, D&O of ARB, pp. 5-6 (March 30, 2001); *Graf v Wackenhut Services,* 1998-ERA-37, Order of recusal by ALJ (April 28, 2000).

135. *Cable v Arizona Public Service Co.,* 90-ERA-15, D&O of SOL (November 13, 1992).

136. *Cable v Arizona Public Service Co.,* 90-ERA-15, D&O of SOL at 5.

137. *Rogers v MultiAmp Corp.,* 85-ERA-16, D&O of SOL, at 2 (December 18, 1992). See also *TVA v Reich,* 25 F.3d 1050 (Table), 1994 WL 236487 (6th Cir. 1994) (upholding DOL denial of costs to a respondent-employer).

138. Rex v EBASCO Services 87-ERA-6/40, D&O of SOL (March 4, 1994).

139. 87-ERA-6/40, D&O of SOL, at 5.

140. 87-ERA-6/40, D&O of SOL, at 6.

141. *Rex v EBASCO Services, Inc.,* No. 87-ERA-6 D&O of SOL, at 6 (March 4, 1994). Attorneys who prevail in a debarment are not entitled to counsel fees under the Equal Access to Justice Act. See 87-ERA-6/40, D&O of ARB (January 7, 1997). See *In the Matter of the Disqualification of Edward A. Slavin* 03-CAA-2, ARB Case No. 02-109 (June 30, 2003).

142. *Malpass v General Electric Co.,* 85-ERA-38/39 D&O of SOL, at 20-21 (March 1, 1994).

143. *Malpass v General Electric Co.,* 85-ERA-38/39 D&O of SOL, at 21-22.

144. *Ridings v Commonwealth Edison,* 88-ERA-27, D&O of SOL (September 20, 1991).

145. *Willy v Coastal Corp.,* 85-CAA-1, D&O of SOL, at 22 (June 1, 1994); see also *ABF Freight System v NLRB,* 114 S.Ct. 835 (1994).

146. 29 C.F.R. § 1980.106(a).

147. 29 C.F.R. § 1980.109(b).

148. 29 C.F.R. § 1980.109(a).

149. *Sylvester v ABB/Power Systems Energy,* D&O of SOL, 93-ERA-11 (March 21, 1994); *Blevins v TVA,* 90-ERA-4, D&O of SOL (June 28, 1993); *Mosbaugh v Georgia Power Co.,* 90-ERA-58, D&O of SOL (September 23, 1992).

150. *Mosbaugh,* D&O of SOL, at 2.

151. *Mosbaugh,* D&O of SOL, at 3-4. Accord., *Carter v LANL,* 93-CAA-10, D&O of SOL (March 21, 1994).

152. *Mosbaugh,* at 5-6.

153. See *Anderson v DeKalb Plating Co.,* 97-CER-1, Order of ARB (July 27, 1999) (applying "legal prejudice" standard in evaluating request for dismissal without prejudice).

154. *Brown v Holmes* 90-ERA-26, D&O of SOL, at 2 (August 31, 1992).

155. *Brown v Homes & Narver, Inc.,* 90-ERA-26, D&O of remand of ALJ, at 3 (December 19, 1990) (citations omitted), adopted by SOL (August 31, 1992). Accord., *Young v CBI Services, Inc.,* 88-ERA-19, D&O of remand of ALJ (April 6, 1993) (case dismissed without prejudice after telegram appeal had been filed by moving party).

156. *Wood v Lockheed Martin Energy Systems,* 97-ERA-58, ARB Order (May 14, 1998).

157. *Mosbaugh v Georgia Power Co.,* 91-ERA-1/11, D&O of SOL, at 5-6 n. 4.

158. *Billings v TVA*, 91-ERA-12, D&O of ARB, at 14 (June 26, 1996) (discussing *res judicata* effect of administrative ruling); *Thompson v DOL*, 885 F.2d 551, 556, 557 (9th Cir. 1989).

CHAPTER 4

1. 29 C.F.R. § 1980.110(a).
2. 29 C.F.R. § 1980.110.
3. 29 C.F.R. § 1980.112.
4. 29 C.F.R. § 1980.113.
5. *Macktal v Chao*, 286 F.3d 822, 825-26 (5th Cir. 2002).
6. *Saavedra v Donovan*, 700 F.2d 496, 498 (9th Cir. 1983) cert. denied, 464 U.S. 892; *Director, Office of Workers' Comp. v Robertson*, 625 F.2d 873, 876 (9th Cir. 1980); *NLRB v Interboro Contractors, Inc.*, 388 P.2d 495, 499 (2nd Cir. 1967).
7. 29 C.F.R. § 1980.110(b).
8. *Director et al. v Brandt Airflex Corp.*, 645 F.2d 1053, 1057 (D.C. Cir. 1981).
9. *Director, Office of Workers' Comp. v Congleton*, 743 F.2d 428, 429-430 (6th Cir. 1984).
10. *Congleton*, at 430.
11. See, for example, *Peabody Coal Co. v Helms*, 859 P.2d 486, 492 (7th Cir. 1988); *Burnett v Bowen*, 830 F.2d 731, 735 (7th Cir. 1987).
12. 29 C.F.R. § 1980.113.
13. *Herchak v American West Airlines*, 02-AIR-12, D&O of ARB (May 14, 2003). In *Reid v Niagara Mohawk Power Corp.*, 2000-ERA-23, Notice of Review by ARB, pp. 1-2 (September 26, 2000), the ARB accepted an untimely review on the basis that no party would be prejudiced and the appellate had attempted, in good faith, to comply with the time requirements.
14. *Johnson v Roadway Express*, 99-STA-5, D&O of ARB, p. 8 (December 30, 2003); *Exxon Chemicals v Chao*, 298 F.3d 464 (5th Cir. 2002).
15. It is anticipated that any change to the interim rule will also be published on the OSHA and DOL ALJ Web sites, located at http://www. osha.gov and http://www.oalj.gov respectively.
16. 29 C.F.R. § 1980.110(a). This filing deadline may be subject to equitable tolling. See *Gutierrez v Regents of the University of California*, 98-ERA-19, Order of ARB, at 3-4 (November 8, 1999) (finding tolling under other DOL whistleblower statutes).
17. 29 C.F.R. § 1980.110(a). See *Gutierrez v Regents of the University of California*, 98-ERA-19, Order of ARB, at 3-4 (November 8, 1999). See *Pawlowski v Hewlett-Packard Corp.*, 97-TSC-3, Order of ARB (September 15, 1999).
18. *Berkman v U.S. Coast Guard*, 97-CAA-2/9, D&O of ARB, p. 15 (February 29, 2000).
19. *Eash v Roadway Express*, 2000-STA-47, D&O of ARB, p. 3 (June 27, 2003).
20. *Bushway v Yellow Freight*, 00-STA-52 D&O of ARB, p. 2 (December 13, 2002).
21. *Hall v EG&G Defense*, 97-SDW-9, D&O of ARB, p. 4 (September 30, 1998).
22. *Ashcraft v University of Cincinnati*, 83-ERA-7, decision of SOL, at 11 n. 3 (November 1, 1984); 5 U.S.C. § 556(e). The ARB applies the rule set forth in 29 C.F.R. 18.54(c) in weighing the admissibility of new evidence on appeal. *Hasan v Commonwealth Edison*, 99-ERA-17, D&O of ARB, p. 3 (December 28, 2000).

23. See, for example, *Boyd v Belcher Oil Co.*, 87-STA-9, D&O of SOL, at 3 (December 2, 1987); *McDaniel v Boyd Bros. Transp.*, 86-STA-6, order of dismissal by SOL, at 4 (March 16, 1987). The admission of new evidence is generally governed by 29 C.F.R. § 18.54(c).

24. *Thomas v APS*, 89-ERA-19, D&O of SOL, at 22 n. 10 (September 17, 1993).

25. *Crosby v Hughes Aircraft Co.*, 85-TSC-2, D&O of SOL, at 14 (August 17, 1993).

26. *Boyd v Belcher Oil Co.*, 87-STA-9, D&O of Deputy SOL, at 3-4 (December 2, 1987).

27. *High v Lockheed Martin Energy Systems, Inc.*, 96-CAA-8, Order of ARB (October 2, 1998) (giving party "extraordinary" amount of time to file a brief and denying "sixth request" for enlargement).

28. ERA, 42 U.S.C. § 5851(c)(1); CAA, 42 U.S.C. § 7622(c)(1); SDWA, 42 U.S.C. § 300j-9(i)(3)(A); SWDA, 42 U.S.C. § 6971(b); WPCA, 33 U.S.C. §§ 1367(b) and 1369(b); CERCLA, 42 U.S.C. § 9610(b); TSCA, 15 U.S.C. § 2622(c)(1). Appeals are filed in the U.S. Court of Appeals, not the District Court. See *Rhode v City of West Lafayette*, 850 F. Supp. 753 (N.D. Ind. 1993).

29. *Waters v Transport, Inc.*, 84-STA-8, D&O of SOL, at 3 (October 24, 1984) (quoting, in part, from the Administrative Procedure Act, 5 U.S.C. § 557).

30. *Calmat Co. v U.S. Department of Labor*, 364 F.3d 1117, 1121-22 (9th Cir. 2004) (setting forth identical standard under the Surface Transportation Act).

31. *Stout v Yellow Freight System, Inc.*, 99-STA-42, D&O of ARB, at 2 (January 31, 2003) (citations and internal quotations omitted). *Accord Peck v Safe Air International*, 2001-AIR-3, D&O of ARB, pp. 3-4 (January 30, 2004).

32. *BSP Trans, Inc. v Department of* Labor, 160 F.3d 38, 46-47 (1st Cir. 1998). A recent unpublished decision by the U.S. Court of Appeals for the Tenth Circuit noted, in dicta, that some commentators had questioned whether the Secretary of Labor could be required to defer to ALJ rulings under a substantial evidence standard, noting that the Administrative Procedure Act vests an agency's final decision-making authority with *de novo* decision-making powers. *Dalton v DOL*, 2002 WL 356780 (10th Cir. 2003).

33. *BSP Trans, Inc. v Department of* Labor, 160 F.3d 38, 48, n. 2 (1st Cir. 1998) (discussing cases).

34. *Ellis Fischel State Cancer Hospital v Marshall*, 629 F.2d 563, 566 (8th Cir. 1980).

35. See, for example, *Brooks Cameras, Inc.*, 691 F.2d 912, 915 (9th Cir. 1982); *Penasquitos Village Inc. v NLRB*, 565 F.2d 1074, 1078 (9th Cir. 1977), quoting 369 U.S. 404, 408 (1982): "Weight is given to the [administrative law judge's] determinations of credibility for the obvious reason that he or she sees the witnesses and hears them testify, while the Board and the reviewing court look only at cold records." Accord., *Jackson v Ketchikan Pulp Co.*, 93-WPC-793-WPC-7, D&O of SOL, at 6 (March 4, 1996) ("substantial weight" given to ALJ: findings on witness credibility).

If a credibility determination is not based upon the demeanor of the witnesses but on an analysis of testimony, the opinion of the administrative law judge will deserve "less than the usual deference." *Consolidated Coal Co. v NLRB*, 669 F.2d 482, 488 (7th Cir. 1982).

36. 940 F.2d 1287 (9th Cir. 1991).

37. 940 F.2d 1287 (9th Cir. 1991). Accord., *Simon v Simmons Industries, Inc.*, 87-TSC-2, D&O of SOL, at 8 (April 4, 1994): "Although I am not bound by the credibility determinations of the ALJ, these findings must be considered in light of 'the con-

sentency [*sic*] and inherent probability of testimony . . .' and are entitled to weight because the ALJ 'sees the witnesses and hears them testify'" (citation omitted).

38. *Bartlik v TVA*, 88-ERA-15, Final D&O of SOL, at 4-5 (April 7, 1993).

39. *McCafferty v Centerion*, 96-ERA-6, Order of ARB, at 16 n. 23 (September 24, 1997).

40. *Spencer v Hatfield Elec. Co.*, 86-ERA-33, D&O of SOL, at 3-4 (October 24, 1988) (quoting from the rule laid out in *Beavers v Secretary of Health*, 577 F.2d 383, 387 [6th Cir. 1978]); *Smith v Norco Technical Servs., etc.*, 85-ERA-17, D&O of SOL, at 4 (October 2, 1987).

41. *Perez v Guthmiller Trucking Co., Inc.*, 87-STA-13, D&O of SOL, at 13-14, 27 (December 7, 1988).

42. *NLRB v Miller Redwood Corp.*, 407 F.2d 1366, 1369 (9th Cir. 1969).

43. See *Bartlik v DOL*, 1994 WL 487174 (6th Cir. 1994), vacated en banc on other grounds and withdrawn from bound volume, 34 F.3d 368.

44. *Macktal v Brown & Root, Inc.*, 86-ERA-23, Order Granting Reconsideration by ARB (November 20, 1998), affirmed U.S. Court of Appeals for the Fifth Circuit.

45. *Wells v KG&E*, 85-ERA-22, Order of SOL, at 2 (June 28, 1991).

46. See, for example, *Amato v Assured Transportation*, 98-TSC-6, ARB Order (January 31, 2000); *Hasan v Commonwealth Edison Co.*, 99-ERA-17, Order of ARB (September 16, 1999); *Shusterman v EBASCO Services, Inc.*, 87-ERA-27, Order Denying Remand by SOL, at 2 (July 2, 1987); *Plumley v Federal Bureau of Prisons*, 86-CAA-6, order denying interlocutory appeal by SOL (April 29, 1987).

47. See, for example, *In re Willy*, 831 F.2d 545, 549 (5th Cir. 1987).

48. Even in a case in which the ALJ recommended granting interlocutory reviews, the SOL declined the invitation. See *Porter v Brown & Root*, 91-ERA-4, Order of SOL (September 29, 1993).

49. *Beliveau v Naval Undersea Warfare Center*, 97-SDW-1/4, Order of ARB (August 14, 1997); *Plumley v Federal Bureau of Prisons*, 86-CAA-6, order denying interlocutory appeal by SOL, at 2-3 (April 29, 1987).

50. *Puckett v TVA*, 2002-CAA-15, Order of ARB (September 26, 2002); *Greene v EPA Chief Judge*, 02-SWD-1, Order Dismissing Interlocutory Appeal by ARB (September 18, 2002).

51. The Eleventh Circuit has held in DOL whistleblower cases that an order establishing liability is not "final" until all issues related to the amount of damages have been decided. *Bechtel v SOL*, No. 92-5176 (11th Cir. April 8, 1993), citing *Redden v Director, OWCP*, 825 F.2d 337, 338 (11th Cir. 1987). If the only issue remaining relates to attorney's fees, the order is final and must be appealed. *Fluor Constructors, Inc. v Reich*, 111 F.3d 94 (11th Cir. 1997).

52. See, for example, 29 C.F.R. § 1980.112(a). *Bartlick v DOL*, 62 F.3d 163 (6th Cir. 1995) (appeal timely if 60th day falls on a Saturday, Sunday, or federal holiday and the appeal is docketed on the next business day).

53. 49 U.S.C. § 42121(b)(4)(A), incorporated into SOX by 18 U.S.C. § 1514A(b)(2)(A).

54. 49 U.S.C. § 42121(b)(4)(A), incorporated into SOX by 18 U.S.C. § 1514A(b)(2)(A).

55. For a discussion on what constitutes the administrative record and some of the grounds for a court to go beyond that record, see *Thompson v DOL*, 885 F.2d 551, 555-556 (9th Cir. 1989).

56. 735 F.2d 1159, 1163 (9th Cir. 1984). See also *Thompson,* at 555.

57. *Universal Camera Corp. v NLRB,* 340 U.S. 474 (1981).

58. See *Passaic Valley Sewerage Comm'ns v DOL,* 992 F.2d 474, 480 (3rd Cir. 1993) (substantial evidence); *Pogue v DOL,* 940 F.2d 1287, 1289 (9th Cir. 1991) (substantial evidence); *Rose v Dole,* 945 F.2d 1331, 1334 (6th Cir. 1991) (*de novo* review of relevant questions of law).

59. *Passaic Valley Sewerage Comm'ns v DOL,* 992 F.2d 478, citing *Chevron, U.S.A., Inc. v NRDC,* 467 U.S. 837, 843 (1984).

60. *Rose v Dole,* 945 F.2d 1331, 1334 (6th Cir. 1991).

61. *Rose v Dole,* 945 F.2d 1335 (6th Cir. 1991).

62. *Lockert v DOL,* 867 F.2d 513, 518 (9th Cir. 1989) (review of Secretary's interpretation of whistleblower statute is "deferential").

63. 467 U.S. 837 (1984).

64. See, for example, *Stone & Webster Engineering v Herman,* 115 F.3d 1568, 1571 (11th Cir. 1997), citing *Chevron v NRDC,* 467 U.S. 837, 843 (1984); *A.N.R. v DOL,* 134 F.3d 1292, 1294 (6th Cir. 1998) ("defer somewhat to the agency"); *Connecticut Light & Power v SOL,* 85 F.3d 89, 94 (2nd Cir. 1996) (defer to "permissible construction of the statutory mandate").

65. 380 U.S. 1, 16 (1965). See also *Chevron v NRDC,* 467 U.S. 837, 843 (1984).

66. *A.N.R. v DOL,* 134 F.3d 1292, 1294 (6th Cir. 1998).

67. *Thompson v DOL,* 885 F.2d 551, at 557. See also *Secretary of Agriculture v United States,* 347 U.S. 645, 653 (1954).

68. *Talley v Mathews,* 550 P.2d 911, 919 (4th Cir. 1977).

69. 5 U.S.C. § 706(2)(e); *Couty v Dole,* 886 F.2d 147, 148-149 (8th Cir. 1989).

70. *Universal Camera Corp. v NLRB,* 340 U.S. 477.

71. *Universal Camera Corp. v NLRB,* 340 U.S. at 474-94.

72. *Arnold v Secretary of H.E.W.,* 567 F.2d 258, 259 (4th Cir. 1977). See also *Moon v U.S. Dep't of Labor,* 727 F.2d 1315, 1318 (D.C. Cir. 1984).

73. *Arnold,* 567 F.2d at 259. See also *Peabody Coal Co. v Helms,* 859 F.2d 486, 492 (7th Cir. 1988); *Zeigler Coal Co. v Sieberg,* 839 F.2d 1280, 1283 (7th Cir. 1988).

74. *Lockert v U.S. DOL, v DOL,* 867 F.2d 520 (9th Cir. 1989).

75. *Burnett v Bowen,* 830 F.2d 734-735 (7th Cir. 1987); *Janik, Paving & Const., Inc. v Brock,* 828 F.2d 84, 93 (2nd Cir. 1987).

76. See, for example, *Ethyl Corp. v EPA,* 541 F.2d 1, 34-36 (D.C. Cir. 1976).

77. *Home Owners Loan Corp. v Huffman,* 134 F.2d 314, 317 (8th Cir. 1943). See also *Conway v Chemical Leaman Tank Lines, Inc.,* 610 F.2d 360, 367 n. 9 (5th Cir. 1980); *NLRB v Guernsey-Muskingum Electric Co-op, Inc.,* 285 F.2d 8, 11 (6th Cir. 1960).

78. *Hobby v Georgia Power,* 90-ERA-30, Order Denying Stay (April 20, 2001).

79. 5 U.S.C. § 705; Federal Rules of Appellate Procedure, Rule 18; *Commonwealth-Lord Joint Venture v Donovan,* 724 F.2d 68.

80. See *Virginia Petroleum Jobbers Assn. v Federal Power Comm'n.,* 259 F.2d 921, 925 (D.C. Cir. 1958); see, for example, DOL decisions applying the four-factor test in whistleblower proceedings: *Hobby v Georgia Power,* 90-ERA-30, Order Denying Stay (April 20, 2001). *Hoffman v Bossert,* 94-CAA-4, SOL Order (November 20, 1995); *Guttman v Passaic Valley Sewerage Comm'ns,* 85-WPC-2, SOL Order Denying Stay (June 4, 1992) (compiling cases); *OFCCP v University of North Carolina,* 84-OFC-20, SOL Order Denying Stay (April 25, 1989).

81. *Rexroat v City of New Albany*, 85-WPC-3, order denying stay by SOL (October 8, 1986).

82. See also ERA, 42 U.S.C. § 5851(c)(1); CAA, 42 U.S.C. § 7622(c)(1); SDWA, 42 U.S.C. § 300j-9(i)(3)(A); TSCA, 15 U.S.C. § 2622(c)(1).

83. 5 U.S.C. § 705.

84. See, for example, *Arcamuzi v Continental Air Lines, Inc.*, 819 F.2d 935, 938-939 (9th Cir. 1987); *Garcia v Lawn*, 805 F.2d 1400, 1405 (9th Cir. 1986).

85. *Sampson v Murray*, 415 U.S. 61, 90 (1974); *Meyers v Bethlehem Shipbuilding Corp.*, 303 U.S. 41, 51-52 (1938); *Rexroat v City of New Albany*, 85-WPC-3 at 2-3.

86. *Commonwealth-Lord Joint Venture v Donovan*, 724 F.2d 68. See also *Rexront* at 2-3.

87. 724 F. 2d 67 (7th Cir. 1983).

88. *Goldstein v EBASCO Constructors, Inc.*, 86-ERA-36, Order Denying Stay by SOL (August 31, 1992); *Wells v KG&E Co.*, 85-ERA-22, Order of SOL (June 28, 1991).

89. *Dutkiewicz v Clean Harbors*, 95-STA-34 ARB Order Denying Stay (September 23, 1997) (denying stay of "monetary portion" of DOL's final order).

90. 29 C.F.R. § 1980.113. Enforcement actions are "ministerial" in nature. *Kansas Gas and Elec. v Brock*, 780 F.2d 1505, 1515 (10th Cir. 1985).

91. *Scott v Roadway Express, Inc.*, 98-STA-8, Order of ARB, p. 2 (May 29, 2003), citing Secretary of Labor Order No. 5-2002, 4.a.(1)(h) (October 10, 2002).

92. 29 C.F.R. § 1980.113. Enforcement actions are "ministerial" in nature. *Kansas Gas and Elec. v Brock*, 780 F.2d 1505, 1515 (10th Cir. 1985).

93. *Kansas Gas and Elec. v Brock*, 780 F.2d 1505, 1515 (10th Cir. 1985).

94. *Kansas Gas and Elec. v Brock*, 780 F.2d 1505, 1515; 49 U.S.C. 42121(b)(5) and (6).

95. *Martin v Yellow Freight Sys., Inc.*, 793 F.Supp. 461, 473-74 (S.D.N.Y. 1992), aff'd 983 F.2d 1201 (2nd Cir. 1993); *Martin v Castle Oil Corp.*, No. 92, Civ 2178, 1992 U.S. Dist. LEXIS 4568 (S.D.N.Y 1992).

CHAPTER 5

1. 18 U.S.C. 1514A(b)(1); *Murray v. TXU Corp.*, 279 F.Supp.2d 799 (N.D. Tex. 20037).

2. *Congressional Record*, S7414 (July 26, 2002) (reprinting Senate Judiciary Committee Report).

3. *Congressional Record*, S7420 (July 26, 2002) (reprinting Senate Judiciary Committee Report).

4. 18 U.S.C. 1514A(b)(1); *Livingston v Wyeth Pharmaceuticals*, 2003-SOX-25 (October 6, 2003).

5. 29 C.F.R. 1980.114(b)(Interim Rule).

6. *Murray v TXU Corp.*, 279 F.Supp.2d 794 (N.D. Tex. 20003).

7. See *Stone v Duke Energy Corp.*, 3:03-vc-256, unpublished Order (W.D.N.C., June 10, 2003).

8. Senate Report No. 107-146, pp. 19–29 ("Should such a case be brought in federal court, it is intended that the same burdens of proof which would have governed in the Department of Labor will continue to govern the action."); 18 U.S.C. 1514A(b)(2)(C), reprinted in *Congressional Record*, S7420 (July 26, 2002).

9. *Knox v U.S. Department of Interior*, 2001-CAA-3, Recommended D&O of ALJ, p. 3 (December 30, 2002).

10. *English v General Electric*, 496 U.S. 72 (1990).

11. See Kohn, *Concepts and Procedures in Whistleblower Law*, pp. 21–77 (Greenwood Press, 2000), setting forth a state-by-state review of nonfederal whistleblower remedies.

12. See Kohn, *Concepts and Procedures in Whistleblower Law*, pp. 81–95, 201–216 (Greenwood Press, 2000), setting forth federal causes of action which may be available to private sector employees.

13. See, for example, *Charvat v Eastern Ohio Regional Wastewater Authority*, 246 F.3d 607 (6th Cir. 2001) (permitting employee to file a Section 1983 claim in federal court even after employee obtained a ruling from an Administrative Law Judge in a DOL whistleblower case).

14. 29 C.F.R. Parts 24, 1979, and 1987.

CHAPTER 6

1. Congress fully explained its intent in creating the "contributing factor" test in its Joint Explanatory Statement contained in the legislative history of the Whistleblower Protection Act of 1989. This Statement is reproduced in the Key Practice Documents appendix of this book.

2. *Addington v Texas*, 441 U.S. 418, 423 (1979) (internal quotes and citations omitted).

3. *Addington v Texas*, 441 U.S. 418, 423 (1979).

4. *Rouse v Farmers State Bank of Jewell*, 866 F. Supp. 1191, 1208 (N.D. Iowa 1994) ("the legislative history reveals that the burden on the plaintiff was intended to be lessened").

5. 135 *Congressional Record* S2784 (1989).

6. *Rouse v Farmers State Bank of Jewell*, 866 F. Supp. 1208 (explaining difference between "contributing factor" test and traditional Title VII formulation). See also *Trimmer v DOL*, 174 F.3d 1098, 1101 (10th Cir. 1999) (Congress established a "burden-shifting framework distinct from Title VII").

7. *Stone & Webster Engineering v Herman*, 115 F.3d 1572-1573 (11th Cir. 1997); *Gutierrez v Regents of the University of California*, 98-ERA-19, D&O of ARB, pp. 5-6 (November 13, 2002); *TVA v Secretary of Labor*, 2003 WL 932433, p. 6 (6th Cir. 2003); *Stoneking v Avbase Aviation*, 2002-AIR-7, D&O of ALJ, p. 10 (March 17, 2003).

8. In *Kester v Carolina Power & Light Co.*, 2000-ERA-31, D&O of Remand by ARB, p. 3 (September 30, 2003) the DOL Administrative Review Board sets forth the complete standard of proof that must be established in a contributing factor test case. The ARB set forth this burden as follows:

> The burden [on the employee] is to prove by a preponderance of evidence that he engaged in protected activity under the [SOX], that [the employer] knew about this activity and took adverse action against him, and that his protected activity was a contributing factor in the adverse action. . . . Then, if [the employee] meets this burden, the [court or DOL] will proceed to determine whether [the employer] demonstrated by clear and convincing evidence that it would have taken the same unfavorable personnel action in the absence of the protected activity.

9. *Peck v Safe Air International*, 2001-AIR-3, D&O of ARB, p. 6 (January 30, 2004).

10. *Marano v Department of Justice*, 2 F.3d 1137, 1140 (Fed. Cir. 1993), citing 135 Cong. Rec. 5033 (1989) (Explanatory Statement on S. 20). Accord., *Rouse v Farmers State Bank of Jewell*, 866 F. Supp. 1208; *Taylor v Express One International*, 2001-AIR 2, R.D&O of ALJ, p. 27 (February 15, 2002).

11. *Kewley v Department of Health and Human Services*, 153 F.3d 1357, 1362 (Fed. Cir. 1998) (citations and internal quotations omitted).

12. *Kester v Carolina Power & Light Co.*, 2000-ERA-31, D&O of Remand by ARB, p. 3 (September 30, 2003). In evaluating whether an employee can meet the "contributing factor" test based solely on circumstantial evidence, the ARB, in an airline safety case, stated that the DOJ judges should also "examine the legitimacy of the employer's articulated reasons for the adverse personnel action in the course of concluding whether" an employee can prove that protected activity "contributed to the dismissal." *Peck v Safe Air International*, 2001-AIR-3, D&O of ARB, p. 7 (January 30, 2004).

13. *Welch v Cardinal Bankshares Corp.*, 2003-SOX-15, Recommended D&O of ALJ, p. 36 (January 28, 2004); *Getman v Southwest Securities*, 2003-SOX-8, D&O of ALJ, p. 10 (February 2, 2004).

14. *Rouse v Farmers State Bank of Jewell*, 866 F. Supp. 1209 (temporal proximity between the whistleblower disclosures and the adverse action, combined with employer knowledge of the disclosures, is sufficient, standing alone, to meet the "contributing factor" test). Accord., *Kewley* at 1361-1362; *Frobose v American Savings & Loan Association*, 152 F.3d 602, 609 (7th Cir. 1998).

15. The parameters of this test were discussed by the Supreme Court in *Cruzan v Director, Missouri Department of Health*, 497 U.S. 261, 282-83 (1990).

16. *Stone & Webster Engineering v Herman*, 115 F.3d 1572. See *Grogan v Garner*, 498 U.S. 297 (1991) (discussing "clear and convincing evidence standard"). The SOL applies the *Grogan* analysis in whistleblower cases. See *Timmons v Mattingly Testing Services*, 95-ERA-40, D&O of Remand by ARB, at 16.

17. *Colorado v New Mexico*, 467 U.S. 310, 316 (1984); *Duprey v Florida Power & Light*, 2000-ERA-5, D&O of ARB, p. 6, n. 22 (February 27, 2003).

18. *Am-Pro Protective Agency, Inc. v U.S.*, 281 F.3d 1234, 1240 (Fed. Cir. 2002).

19. *Williams-Moore v Dept. of Veterans Affairs*, 2000 WL 369678 (Table), (unpublished Fed. Cir. April 10, 2000) quoting *Carr v Social Security*, 185 F.3d 1318, 1323 (Fed. Cir. 1999).

20. *Kester v Carolina Power & Light Co.*, 2000-ERA-31, D&O of Remand by ARB, p. 3, n. 12 (September 30, 2003).

21. *U.S. Postal Service v Aikens*, 460 U.S. 711, 715 (1983) (the main question at a hearing is whether a plaintiff can prove that the defendant "intentionally discriminated against" him or her).

22. *Kester v Carolina Power & Light Co.*, 2000-ERA-31, D&O of Remand by ARB, p. 3, n. 19 (September 30, 2003).

23. *Kane v Krebser*, 44 F. Supp.2d 542, 547 (S.D. N.Y. 1999); *Melendez v Exxon*, 93-ERA-6, D&O of ARB, at 27.

24. *Calmat Co. v U.S. Department of Labor*, 364 F.3d 1117, 1122 (9th Cir. 2004).

25. *Tyler v Bethlehem Steel*, 958 F.2d 1175, 1183-1184 (2nd Cir. 1992) (collecting cases setting forth the various definitions of "direct evidence").

26. *Merritt v Dillard Paper Co.*, 120 F.3d 1181, 1189-1190, quoting *Caban-Wheeler v Elsea*, 904 F.2d 1549, 1555 (11th Cir. 1990) (collecting cases finding direct evidence of discrimination).

27. *Talbert v Washington Public Power Supply*, 93-ERA-35, D&O of ARB, at 4 (September 27, 1996). Accord., *Stacks v Southwestern Bell*, 996 F.2d 200, 202 (8th Cir. 1993).

28. *Simas v First Citizens Federal Credit Union*, 170 F.3d 37, 48 (1st Cir. 1999).

29. *Aka v Washington Hospital Center*, 156 F.3d 1284, 1292 (D.C. Cir. 1998) (*en banc*). Accord., *U.S. Postal Service v Aikens*, 460 U.S. 711, 714 n. 3, 717 (1983).

30. *Desert Palace v Costa*, 123 S.Ct. 2148, 2154 (2003).

31. *Simas v First Citizens Federal Credit Union*, 170 F.3d 37, 48 (1st Cir. 1999) ("Normally, employers do not leave behind direct evidence of their discriminatory animus. . . . Therefore, generally the plaintiff-employee must make do with circumstantial evidence, leaving it to the jury whether to infer from the nature of the materially adverse employment conditions that the defendant-employer harbored a retaliatory animus"). Accord., *Desert Palace v Costa*, 123 S.Ct. 2148 (2003); *Donovan v Zimmer America, Inc.*, 557 F. Supp. 642, 651 (D. S.C. 1982), quoting from *Polynesian Cultural Center, Inc. v NLRB*, 582 F.2d 467, 473 (9th Cir. 1978); *Kester v Carolina Power & Light Co.*, 2000-ERA-31, D&O of Remand by ARB, p. 3, n. 19 (September 30, 2003).

32. *Kester v Carolina Power & Light Co.*, 2000-ERA-31, D&O of Remand by ARB, p. 3, n. 19 (September 30, 2003)) ("The Act requires only that the complainant prove by a preponderance of sufficient evidence, direct or circumstantial, that the protected activity contributed to the employer's decision.").

33. *Housing Works, Inc. v City of New York*, 72 F. Supp.2d 402, 422 (S.D. N.Y. 1999), citing to *Ramseur v Chase Manhattan Bank*, 865 F.2d 460 (2nd Cir. 1989) ("employers are rarely so cooperative as to include a notation . . . that their actions are motivated by factors expressly forbidden by law").

34. 629 F.2d 563, 566 (8th Cir. 1980), cert. denied, 450 U.S. 1040 (1981). See also *Couty v Dole*, 886 F.2d 147, 148 (8th Cir. 1989) (holding that "temporal proximity is sufficient as a matter of law" to establish discriminatory motive).

35. See also *Mackowiak v University Nuclear Systems, Inc.*, 735 F.2d 1159, 1162 (9th Cir. 1984); *Zoll v Eastern Allamkee Community School Dist.*, 588 F.2d 236, 250 (8th Cir. 1978); *Rutherford v American Bank of Commerce*, 565 F.2d 1162, 1164 (10th Cir. 1977); *Ertel v Giroux Bros. Transp., Inc.*, 88 STA-24 D&O of SOL, at 24 (February 16, 1989).

36. *Timmons v Mattingly Testing Services*, 95-ERA-40, D&O of Remand by ARB, at 10 (June 21, 1996).

37. *Reeves v Sanderson Plumbing*, 120 S. Ct. 2097, 2108 (2000).

38. *Getman v Southwest Securities*, 2003-SOX-8, D&O of ALJ, pp. 15-18 (February 2, 2004).

39. *Overall v TVA*, 97-ERA-53, pp. 16-17, D&O of ARB (April 30, 2001), affirmed, *TVA v DOL*, 2003 WL 932433 (6th Cir. 2003); *Ellis Fischel State Cancer Hosp. v Marshall* 629 F. 2d 563, 566 (8th Cir. 1980); *Keene v EBASCO Constructors, Inc.*, 95-ERA-4, D&O of Remand by ARB, at 10; *Cram v Pullman-Higgins Co.*, 84-ERA-17, slip op. of ALJ, at 10 (July 24, 1984), adopted in part by SOL (January 14, 1985); *Hedden v Conam Inspection Co.*, 82-ERA-3, slip op. of ALJ, at 4 (January 22, 1983), adopted in part by SOL (June 30, 1983). See also *Brown & Root-Northrop*, 174 NLRB 1048, 1050-1051 (1969); *DeFord v TVA*, 81-ERA-1, slip op. of ALJ, at 6 (January 7, 1981), adopted in part by SOL (March 4, 1981), aff'd, *DeFord v Secretary of Labor*, 700 F.2d 281 (6th Cir. 1983); *Richter v Ellis Fischel State Cancer Hosp.*, 79-ERA-1, slip op. of ALJ, at 2-4 (July 6, 1979), adopted by SOL (August 10, 1979).

40. *Landers v Commonwealth-Lord Joint Venture*, 83-ERA-5, slip op. of ALJ, at 12. See also *Kendall Co.*, 188 NLRB 805, 809 (1971).

41. *Georgia Power Company v DOL*, No. 01-10916, p. 15 (11th Cir. 2002) (unpublished decision); *Poll v R.J. Trucking*, 96-STA-35, pp. 6, D&O of ARB (June 28, 2002); *Tracanna v Arctic Slope*, 97-WPC-1, D&O of ARB, p. 8 (July 31, 2001); *Moon v Transportation Drivers, Inc.*, 836 F.2d 226, 229 (6th Cir. 1987); *Couty v Dole*, 886 F.2d 147, 148 (8th Cir. 1989); *Creekmore v ABB Power Systems*, 93-ERA-24, D&O of Remand by SOL, at 11 (February 14, 1996); *Wells v Kansas Gas & Elec. Co.*, 83-ERA-12, slip op., at 6-7 (February 27, 1984), adopted by SOL (June 14, 1984); *Landers v Commonwealth-Lord Joint Venture*, 83-ERA-5, slip op. of ALJ, at 12; *Richter v Ellis Fischel State Cancer Hosp.*, 79-ERA-1, slip op. of ALJ, at 3-4. See also *Jim Causley Pontiac v NLRB*, 620 F.2d 122, 125 (6th Cir. 1980); *Womack v Munson*, 619 F.2d 1292, 1296 (8th Cir. 1980); *Melchi v Burns Int'l. Security Servs., Inc.*, 597 F. Supp. 575, 584 (E.D. Mich. 1984); *McCarthy v Cortland County Community Actions Program*, 487 F. Supp. 333, 340 (N.D. N.Y. 1980); *G & S Metal Prods. Co.*, 199 NLRB 705, 708 (1972), enforced, 489 F.2d 441 (6th Cir. 1973). An employee can establish a *prima facie* case of discriminatory motive by showing that the employee engaged in protected activity and suffered from an adverse action "shortly thereafter." *Priest v Baldwin Assocs.*, 84-ERA-30, decision of SOL, slip op., at 10 (June 11, 1986).

42. *Wells v Kansas Gas & Elec. Co.*, 83-ERA-12, slip op., at 11-12. *See also Viracon, Inc. v NLRB*, 736 F.2d 1188, 1192 (7th Cir. 1984); *M & S Steel Co.*, 148 NLRB 789, 795 (1964), enforced, 353 F.2d 80 (5th Cir. 1965); *Housing Works, Inc. v City of New York*, 72 F. Supp.2d 402, 422 (S.D. N.Y. 1999) (collecting cases); *Sumner v U.S. Postal Service*, 899 F.2d 203, 209 (2nd Cir. 1990) ("The causal connection . . . can be established indirectly with circumstantial evidence, for example . . . through evidence of disparate treatment of employees who engaged in similar conduct."); *O'Brien v Stone & Webster Eng. Corp.*, 84-ERA-31, slip op. of ALJ, at 19, n. 12 (February 28, 1985); *Clifton v UPS*, 94-STA-16, D&O of SOL, at 13 (May 9, 1995); *Donovan v Zimmer America, Inc.*, 557 F. Supp. 642, 652 (D. S.C. 1982), citing *Midwest Regional Joint Board v NLRB*, 564 F.2d 434, 442 (D.C. Cir. 1977) and *NLRB v Hecks's Inc.*, 386 F.2d 317, 320 (4th Cir. 1967) ("enforcement of an otherwise valid rule only against those engaged in [protected] activities is discriminatory").

43. *Wells v Kansas Gas & Elec. Co.*, 83-ERA-12, slip op. of ALJ, at 15; *Hedden v Conam Inspection Co.*, 82-ERA-3, slip op. of ALJ, at 3; *Haney v North American Car Corp.*, 81-SWD-1, slip op. of ALJ, at 17-18 (August 10, 1981), supplemental decision and order (December 15, 1981), adopted by SOL (June 30, 1982); *Johnson v Old Dominion Security*, 86-CAA-3/4/5, D&O of SOL, at 18 (May 29, 1991); *Francis v Bogan*, 86-ERA-8, slip op. of ALJ, at 15 (March 21, 1986); *Nix v NEHI-RC Bottling Co., Inc.*, 84-STA-1, D&O of SOL, at 12 (July 13, 1984) ("inconsistent application of company politics has also been held to be evidence of retaliatory motive").

44. *DeFord v TVA*, 81-ERA-1, slip op. of ALJ, at 6. See also *Landers v Commonwealth-Lord Joint Venture*, 83-ERA-5, slip op. of ALJ, at 12 (May 11, 1983), adopted by SOL (September 9, 1983), stay denied, *Commonwealth-Lord Joint Venture v Donovan*, 724 F.2d 67 (7th Cir. 1983); *Cotter v Consolidated Edison Co. of N.Y.*, 81-ERA-6, slip op. of ALJ, at 17 (July 7, 1981), adopted by SOL (November 5, 1981), aff'd, *Consolidated Edison Co. of N.Y. v Donovan*, 673 F.2d 61 (2nd Cir. 1982); *Diaz-Robainas v FP&L*, 92-ERA-10, D&O of Remand by SOL, at 18 (January 19, 1996).

45. *Haney*, slip op. of ALJ at 18; *DeFord v TVA*, 81-ERA-1, slip op. of ALJ, at 6.

46. *Murphy v Consolidation Coal Co.*, 83-ERA-4, slip op. of ALJ, at 28.

47. *Simons v Simmons Indus., Inc.*, 87-TSC-2, recommended D&O of ALJ, at 5 (July 14, 1988); *Hale v Baldwin Assocs.*, 85-ERA-37, recommended D&O of ALJ, at 18 (October 20, 1986).

48. *Blake v Hatfield Elec. Co.*, 87-ERA-4, recommended decision of ALJ, at 22 (August 13, 1987); *Fischer v Town of Steilacoom*, 83-WPC-2, slip op. of ALJ, at 8-9; *Haney v North Am. Car Corp.*, 81-SWD-1, slip op. of ALJ, at 17; *Hill v Lockheed Martin*, 314 F.3d 657, 665 (4th Cir. 2003).

49. *Hedden v Conam Inspection Co.*, 82-ERA-3, slip op. of ALJ at 4-5; *Cram v Pullman-Higgins Co.*, 84-ERA-17, slip op. of ALJ, at 16.

50. *Murphy v Consolidation Coal Co.*, 83-ERA-4, slip op. of ALJ, at 16 (August 2, 1983), settlement approved by SOL (January 17, 1985).

51. *Cram v Pullman-Higgins Co.*, 84-ERA-17, slip op. of ALJ, at 10; *Lewis Grocer Co. v Holloway*, 874 F.2d 1008 (5th Cir. 1989). See also *G & S Metal Prods. Co.*, 199 NLRB 705, 708 (1972), enforced, 489 F.2d 441 (6th Cir. 1973); *Wedderspoon v City of Cedar Rapids, Iowa*, 80-WPC-1, slip op. of ALJ, at 9-10 (July 11, 1980), adopted by SOL (July 28, 1980).

52. *Hobby v Georgia Power Co.*, 90-ERA-30, D&O of Remand by SOL, at 20, affirmed (11th Cir. Court of Appeals, 2002); *James v Ketchikan Pulp Co.*, 94-WPC-4, D&O of SOL, at 4 (March 15, 1996); *Bechtel Construction v SOL*, 50 F.3d 926, 935 (11th Cir. 1995); *Edwards v U.S. Postal Service*, 909 F.2d 320, 324 (8th Cir. 1990) ("In light of this record, filled with changing and inconsistent explanations, we can find no legitimate, nondiscriminatory basis for the challenged action that is not mere pretension.").

53. *St. Mary's Honor Center v Hicks*, 509 U.S. 502, 511 (1993); *Aka v Washington Hospital Center*, 156 F.3d 1284, 1292-1293 (D.C. Cir. 1998).

54. *Cram v Pullman-Higgins Co.*; *Fischer v Town of Steilacoom*, 83-WPC-2, slip op. of ALJ, at 9 (May 2, 1983), settlement approved by SOL (August 22, 1983). See also *NLRB v Wright Line, A Div. of Wright Line*, 662 F.2d 899, 907-908 (1st Cir. 1981), cert. denied, 455 U.S. 989 (1982); *Hedden v Conam Inspection Co.*, slip op. of ALJ at 4.

55. *Stone & Webster v Herman*, 115 F.3d 1568, 1574.

56. *Larry v Detroit Edison Co.*, 86-ERA-32, slip op. of ALJ at 7 (October 17, 1986).

57. *Timmons v Mattingly Testing Services*, 95-ERA-40, D&O of Remand by ARB, at 12, 14-15.

58. *Lewis Grocer Co. v Holloway*, 874 F.2d 1008 (5th Cir. 1989); *Keeneway v Matlock, Inc.*, 88-STA-20, D&O of SOL, at 5; *Dartey v Zack Co.*, 82-ERA-2, D&O of SOL, at 10 (April 25, 1983); *Thomas v APS*, 89-ERA-19, recommended D&O of ALJ, at 8 (April 13, 1989); *Zinn v University of Missouri*, 93-ERA-34/36, D&O of SOL, at 13 (January 18, 1996). In *Timmons v Mattingly Testing Services*, the Department of Labor noted that "antagonism toward activity that is protected . . . may manifest itself in many ways, *e.g.*, ridicule, openly hostile action or threatening statements, or in the case of a whistleblower who contacts the NRC, simply questioning why the whistleblower did not pursue corrective action through the usual internal channels." 95-ERA-40, D&O of Remand by ARB, at 11 (June 21, 1996).

59. *Housing Works, Inc. v City of New York*, 72 F. Supp.2d 402, 25.

60. *Seater v Southern California Edison Co.*, 95-ERA-13, D&O of Remand by ARB, at 4-6 (September 27, 1996).

61. *Reeves v Sanderson Plumbing*, 120 S. Ct. 2097, 2108 (2000) ("Proof that the defendant's explanation is unworthy of credence is simply one form of circumstantial evidence that is probative of intentional discrimination and it might be quite persuasive. . . . In appropriate circumstances, the trier of fact can reasonably infer from the falsity of the explanation that the employer is dissembling to cover up a discriminatory purpose."). Accord., *Getman v. Southwest Securities*, 2003-SOX-8, D&O of ALJ, p. 17 (February 2, 2004) (dishonesty regarding material fact). In *Getman* the DOL ALJ found that an employer's false statement on a U-5 form regarding the reason for an employee's discharge constituted evidence of retaliation. *Id.*

62. S. Kohn, *Concepts and Procedures in Whistleblower Law*, pp. 266-71 (Greenwood Publishing Group, Westport, CT, 2000) (setting forth extensive list of factors relied upon by courts in finding circumstantial evidence of discriminatory motive).

63. *Newkirk v Cypress Trucking Lines, Inc.*, 88-STA-17, D&O of SOL, at 8 (February 13, 1989); *Housing Works, Inc. v City of New York*, 72 F. Supp.2d 402, 422 (collecting cases).

64. *Newkirk v Cypress Trucking Lines, Inc.*, 88-STA-17, D&O of SOL, at 8 (February 13, 1989); *Housing Works, Inc. v City of New York*, 72 F. Supp.2d 402, 422 (collecting cases). See also *Bechtel Construction v SOL*, 50 F.3d 926, 934 (11th Cir. 1995); *Ertel v Giroux Bros. Transp., Inc.*, 88-STA-24, D&O of SOL, at 24-25 (February 16, 1989); *Priest v Baldwin Assocs.*, 84-ERA-30, D&O of SOL, at 10 (June 11, 1986). Accord., *Couty v Dole*, 886 F.2d 147 (8th Cir. 1989). However, the discriminatory inference created by "timing" may be broken by any number of factors. See *Bartlik v DOL*, 73 F.3d 100, 103 (6th Cir. 1996); *Schulman v Clean Harbors Environmental Service*, 98-STA-24, D&O of ARB, at 9 (October 18, 1999). For example, in *Carson v Tyler Pipe Co.*, 93-WPC-11, D&O of SOL, at 10 (March 24, 1995), because the misconduct that precipitated the employee's removal was "wholly unprotected" and "immediately preceded" the discharge, the SOL held that the discharge was not "pretextual."

65. *White v The Osage Tribal Council*, 95-SDW-1, D&O of Remand by ARB, at 4 (August 9, 1997), citing *Bechtel Construction v SOL*, 50 F.3d 926, 934.; *Welch v. Cardinal Bankshares Corp.*, 2003-SOX-15, Recommended D&O of ALJ, p. 42 (January 28, 2004); *Getman v. Southwest Securities*, 2003-SOX-8, D&O of ALJ, p. 16-17 (February 2, 2004) (distinguishing case which held that temporal proximity analysis did not apply due to intervening events).

66. 509 U.S 502, 511 (1993). Accord., *Reeves v Sanderson Plumbing*, 530 U.S. 133, 147-48 (2000).

67. *Aka v Washington Hospital Center*, 156 F.3d 1293 (en banc). Accord., *Reeves v Sanderson Plumbing*, 120 S.Ct. 2097.

68 *Poll v R.J. Vyhnalek Trucking*, 96-STA-35, D&O of ARB, at 5 (June 28, 2002) (citations and internal quotations omitted).

69. *Timmons v Mattingly Testing Services*, 95-ERA-40, D&O of ARB, at 13 (collecting cases).

70. *Donovan on Behalf of Chacon v Phelps Dodge Corp.*, 709 F.2d 86, 93 (D.C. Cir. 1983).

71. *Borel Restaurant Corp. v NLRB*, 676 F.2d 190, 192-193 (6th Cir. 1982). See *NLRB v Faulkner*, 691 F.2d 51, 56 (1st Cir. 1982); *NLRB v Clark Manor Nursing Home Corp.*, 671 F.2d 657, 661-663 (1st Cir. 1982); *Clifton v UPS*, 94-STA-16, D&O of SOL,

at 13 (May 9, 1995). For some cases where the court failed to find disparate treatment, see *Viracon, Inc. v NLRB*, 736 F.2d 1188, 1193 (7th Cir. 1984); *Airborne Freight Corp. v NLRB*, 728 F.2d 357, 358 (6th Cir. 1984).

72. *Timmons v Mattingly Testing Services*, 95-ERA-40, D&O of ARB, at 13 n. 8.

73. *Donovan v Zimmer America, Inc.*, 557 F. Supp. 642 (D. S.C. 1982), quoting *Midwest Regional Joint Board v NLRB*, 564 F.2d 434, 442 (D.C. Cir. 1977).

74. *Adams v Coastal Production Op., Inc.*, 89-ERA-3, D&O of SOL, at 11 (August 5, 1992). Accord., *Marcus v U.S. EPA*, 92-TSC-5, R. D&O of ALJ, at 26 (December 3, 1992). Also see *Pogue v U.S. DOL*, 940 F.2d 1287, 1291 (9th Cir. 1991) ("substantially disproportionate" discipline is evidence of retaliation).

75. *Welch v Cardinal Bankshares Corp.*, 2003-SOX-15, Recommended D&O of ALJ, p. 42 (January 28, 2004).

76. *McCoy v WGN Continental Broadcasting Co.*, 957 F.2d 368, 373 (7th Cir. 1992) (citations omitted).

77. *McCoy v WGN Continental Broadcasting Co.*, 957 F.2d 368, 373.

CHAPTER 7

1. 15 U.S.C. 1514A(a) and (b)(1) (emphasis added).

2. The statute applies to two classes of publicly traded corporations, "companies required to register their securities" under sections 12 and 15(d) of the Securities Exchange Act of 1934. Companies exempt from the registration requirements of these two provisions are not considered "publicly traded" for purposes of the SOX. *Flake v New World Pasta Company*, 2003-SOX-18, D&O of ARB (February 25, 2004).

3. *In re Five Star Products, Inc.*, CLI-93-23, M&O of NRC Commission, 38 NRC 169 (October 21, 1993).

4. See *Moland v Bil-Mar Foods*, 994 F. Supp. 1061, 1073 (N.D. Iowa 1998) (finding liability where employer "controls an individual's access to employment opportunities").

5. *Landers v Commonwealth-Lord Joint Venture*, 83-ERA-5, slip op. of ALJ at 5, adopted by SOL (September 9, 1983).

6. *Robinson v Shell Oil Co.*, 519 U.S. 843, 848 (1997). Accord., *Board of County Commissions v Umbehr*, 518 U.S. 668 (protecting contractors from retaliation under First Amendment); *O'Hare Truck Service, Inc. v City of Northlake*, 518 U.S. 712 (1996) (protecting independent contractors from retaliation on basis of First Amendment).

7. *Palmer v Western Truck Manpower*, 85-STA-6, D&O of Remand by SOL, at 4-5 (January 16, 1987); *Stephenson v NASA*, 94-TSC-5 (February 13, 1997). See also *Boire v Greyhound Corp.*, 376 U.S. 473 (1964); *Tanforan Park Ford v NLRB*, 656 F.2d 1358, 1360 (9th Cir. 1981); *Schweitzer v Advanced Telemarketing Corp.*, 104 F.3d 761, 763-64 (5th Cir. 1997).

8. *McIntyre v Merrill Lynch*, 2003-SOX-23, Order Denying Respondent's Motion for Summary Decision by ALJ (September 4, 2003).

9. See, for example, *Hill et al. v TVA*, 87-ERA-23/24, D&O of Remand by SOL, at 7-8; *St. Laurent v Britz, Inc. et al.*, 89-ERA-15, recommended D&O of ALJ, at 6-7 (April 12, 1989); *Faulkner v Olin Corp.*, 85-SWDA-3, recommended decision of ALJ,

at 6-7 (August 16, 1985), adopted by SOL (November 18, 1985). See *Board of County Commissions v Umbehr*, 518 U.S. 668; *O'Hare Truck Service, Inc. v City of Northlake*, 518 U.S. 712 (1996).

10. Under securities law, courts have upheld claims against publicly traded corporations based on the material misrepresentations made by a subsidiary. *Gebhardt v Conagra Foods, Inc.*, 335 F.3d 824 (8th Cir. 2003); *In re Reliance Securities Litigation*, 91 F.Supp.2d 706, 721 (D.Del.2000) (defendant "argues that, as an officer of the Company's subsidiary, he cannot be held liable for the misconduct by the parent company's officers. The court finds no support for this notion, however, and concludes that a reasonable shareholder of the Company might have detrimentally relied on his statements."). Additionally, Section 20 of the Securities Act provides for liability against "controlling persons"—that is,"every person who, directly or indirectly, controls any person liable under any provision [of the Securities Act] . . . shall also be liable jointly and severally with and to the same extent as such controlled person . . . unless the controlling person acted in good faith." 15 U.S.C. 78t. See *Neely v Bar Harbor Bankshares*, 270 F.Supp. 50, 54 (D. Maine 2003) (discussing liability under controlling persons test).

11. Compare *McIntyre v Merrill Lynch*, 2003-SOX-23, Order Denying Respondent's Motion for Summary Decision by ALJ (September 4, 2003) (granting motion to amend complaint to include publicly traded parent corporation filed before hearing on the merits) with *Hobby v Georgia Power Company*, 90-ERA-30, Final Decision and Order on Damages of ARB, p. 35 (noting that liability against a parent corporation could not be imposed if the parent corporation was not joined as a party in the lawsuit).

12. *McIntyre v Merrill Lynch*, 2003-SOX-23, Order Denying Respondent's Motion for Summary Decision by ALJ, p. 9 (September 4, 2003). However, the issue of whether non-publicly traded corporations that are subsidiaries of publicly traded corporations is currently an issue.

13. *Morefield v. Exelon Service*, 2004-SOX-2, D&O of ALJ (January 28, 2004).

14. *Hill et al. v TVA*, 87-ERA-23/24, D&O of Remand by SOL, at 8 (May 24, 1989).

15. *Hill et al. v TVA*, 87-ERA-23/24, D&O of Remand by SOL, at 8. See also *Hudgens v NLRB*, 424 U.S. 507, 510 n. 3 (1976); *Phelps Dodge Corp. v NLRB*, 313 U.S. 177, 192 (1941); *Seattle-First National Bank v NLRB*, 651 F.2d 1272, 1273 n. 2 (9th Cir. 1980), *Sibley Memorial Hosp. v Wilson*, 488 F.2d 1338, 1341-1342 (D.C. Cir. 1973); *Flanagan v Bechtel Power Corp., et al.*, 81-ERA-7, decision of SOL (June 27, 1986).

16. *Hill et al. v TVA*, 87-ERA-23/24, D&O of Remand by SOL, at 7-8, citing *Seattle-First Nat'l. Bank v NLRB* at 1273 n.2 (9th Cir. 1980).

17. Use of the term "person" in definition of employer permits findings of individual liability. *Assistant Secretary of Labor v Bolin Associates*, 91-STA-4, D&O of SOL, 5-6 (December 30, 1991), citing *Donovan v Diplomat Envelope, Inc.*, 587 F. Supp. 1417, 1425 (E.D. N.Y. 1984). But if statute uses the term "employer" instead of "person," individual liability does not attach. *Varnadore v Oak Ridge National Laboratory*, 92-CAA-2/5, 93-CAA-2, 94-CAA-2/3, D&O of ARB, at 57 (June 14, 1996).

18. *Hill et al. v TVA*, 87-ERA-23/24, D&O of Remand by SOL, at 7; *Young v Philadelphia Elec. Co.*, 87-ERA-11/35, 88-ERA-1, order of ALJ, at 4 (February 4, 1988) ("It has long been recognized that . . . [an] employer may violate the Act with respect to employees other than his own.").

Notes 209

19. See *Stephenson v NASA*, 94-TSC-5, D&O of Remand by ARB, at 3 (February 13, 1997) ("A parent company or contracting agency acts in the capacity of an employer establishing, modifying or otherwise interfering with an employee of a subordinate company regarding the employee's compensation, terms, conditions or privileges of employment. For example, the president of a parent company who hires, fires or disciplines an employee of one of its subsidiaries may be deemed an 'employer.' . . . A contracting agency which exercises similar control over the employees of its contractors or subcontractors may be a covered employer.").

20. *Chase v Buncombe County, N.C., etc.*, 85-SWD-4, D&O of Remand by SOL, at 4 (November 3, 1986).

21. *Proud v Cecos Int'l.*, 83-TSC-1, slip op. of ALJ, at 2 (September 30, 1983), adopted by SOL; *Royce v Bechtel Power Co.*, 83-ERA-3, slip op. of ALJ, at 3 (March 24, 1983); *Flanagan v Bechtel Power Corp. et al.*, 81-ERA-7, decision of SOL (June 27, 1986), slip op. of ALJ, at 7-10 (November 19, 1981), adopted by SOL (June 27, 1986).

22. *Samodurov v General Physics Corp.*, 89-ERA-20, D&O of SOL, at 5-7 (November 16, 1993); *Cowan v Bechtel Constr., Inc.*, 87-ERA-24, D&O of Remand by SOL, at 3 (August 8, 1989); *Hill et al. v TVA*, 87-ERA-23/24, D&O of Remand by SOL, at 7; *Faulkner v Olin Corp.*, 85-SWDA-3, recommended decision of ALJ, at 6-7 (August 16, 1985), adopted by SOL (November 18, 1985).

23. *Hill et al. v TVA*, 87-ERA-23/24, D&O of Remand by SOL, at 10; *Chase v Buncombe County, N.C., etc.*, 85-SWD-4, D&O of Remand by SOL, at 2-4 (November 3, 1986); *Flanagan v Bechtel Power Corp. et al.*, 81-ERA-7, decision of SOL (June 27, 1986), decision of SOL (June 27, 1986).

24. *O'Brien v Stone & Webster Eng. Corp.*, 84-ERA-31, recommended D&O of ALJ, at 12 (February 28, 1985).

25. *Figueroa v Aponte-Roque*, 864 F.2d 947 (1st Cir. 1989).

26. *Wells v Kansas Gas & Elec. Co.*, 83-ERA-12, slip op. of ALJ, at 3, adopted and modified by SOL (June 14, 1984).

CHAPTER 8

1. Senate Report No. 107-146, p. 19.
2. *Knox v U.S. Department of Interior*, 2001-CAA-3, D&O of ALJ, p. 3 (December 30, 2002).
3. Senate Report No. 107-146, p. 19.
4. 18 U.S.C. § 1514A(a).
5. 18 U.S.C. § 1514A(a).
6. *Adams v Kinder-Morgan*, 340 F.3d 1083 (10th Cir. 2003); *Gebhardt v Conagra Foods, Inc.*, 335 F.3d 824 (8th Cir. 2003); *Bovee v Coopers & Lybrand*, 216 F.R.D. 596 (E.D. Ohio 2002); *In re Tyson Foods*, 2003 WL 22316548 (D.Del. 2003); *In re PSS World Medical, Inc.*, 250 F.Supp.2d 1335 (M.D. Fla. 2002).
7. *Lambert v Ackerley*, 180 F.3d 997, 1002-1008 (9th Cir. 1999) (en banc) (collecting cases and discussing protected activity under various antiretaliation laws).
8. *NLRB v Scrivener*, 405 U.S. 117, 121-126 (1972).
9. 405 U.S. at 122-24.
10. Fair Labor Standards Act: *Lambert v Ackerley*, 180 F.3d 997, 1002-1008 (9th Cir. 1999) (en banc) (collecting cases and discussing protected activity under vari-

ous antiretaliation laws). Surface Transportation Act: *Clean Harbors Environmental Services v Herman*, 146 F.3d 12 (1st Cir. 1998). 1969 Federal Mine Safety Act: *Baker v Board of Mine Operations Appeals*, 595 F.2d 746 (D.C. Cir. 1978); *Munsey v Morton*, 507 F.2d 1202 (D.C. Cir. 1974); *Phillips v Board of Mine Operations Appeals*, 500 F.2d 772, 781-782 (D.C. Cir. 1974), cert. denied, 420 U.S. 938 (1974). OSHA: *Donovan v Peter Zimmer America, Inc.*, 557 F. Supp 642 (D. S.C. 1982); *Dunlop v Hanover Shoe Farms Inc.*, 441 F. Supp. 385 (M.D. Pa. 1976). NLRA: *NLRB v Retail Store Employees' Union*, 570 F.2d 586, 591 (6th Cir. 1978), cert. denied, 439 U.S. 819 (1978). 1977 Federal Mine Safety Act: *Donovan v Stafford Constr. Co.*, 732 F.2d 954, 960-961 (D.C. Cir. 1984). False Claims Act: *U.S. ex rel. Yesudian v Howard University*, 153 F.3d 731 (D.C. Cir. 1998). Energy Reorganization Act: *Bechtel Construction v SOL*, 50 F.3d 926, 931-933 (11th Cir. 1995). Clean Water Act: *Passaic Valley Sewerage Commissioners v DOL*, 992 F.2d 474, 478-479 (3rd Cir. 1993).

11. *Lopez v West Texas Utilities*, 86-ERA-25, D&O of SOL, at 5-6 (July 26, 1988); *Wilson v Bechtel Constr., Inc.*, 86-ERA-34, D&O of SOL, at 2-5 (February 9, 1988); *Smith v Norco Technical Services et al.*, 85-ERA-17, D&O of SOL, at 4 (October 2, 1987) (see cases cited therein); *Nunn v Duke Power Co.*, 84-ERA-27, D&O of Remand by Deputy SOL, at 11-13 (July 13, 1987).

12. *Nunn v Duke Power Co.*, 84-ERA-27, D&O of Remand by Deputy SOL, at 12 (July 30, 1987).

13. *Richter et al. v Baldwin Associates*, 84-ERA-9/10/11/12, D&O of Remand by SOL, at 11-12 (March 12, 1986).

14. *Wilson v Bechtel Constr., Inc.*, 86-ERA-34, D&O of SOL, at 2-5 (February 9, 1988).

15. *Wilson v Bechtel Constr., Inc.*, 86-ERA-34, D&O of SOL, at 2-5 (February 9, 1988); *Consolidated Edison Co. of N.Y. v Donovan*, 673 F.2d 61 (2nd Cir. 1982).

16. *Keeneway v Matlack, Inc.*, 88-STA-20, D&O of SOL, at 6-7, 10-13 (June 15, 1989).

17. 18 U.S.C. § 1514A(a)(1)(A), (B) and (a)(2).

18. See, for example, *Tyndall v EPA*, 93-CAA-6/95-CAA-5, D&O of Remand by ARB, at 6 (June 14, 1996),

19. 18 U.S.C. § 1514A(a)(1)(B).

20. *Sasse v Office of the U.S. Attorney*, 98-CAA-7, D&O of ARB, p. 11 (January 30, 2004).

21. 42 U.S.C. 5852(a).

22. 18 U.S.C. § 1514A(a)(C).

23. 500 F.2d 772 (D.C. Cir. 1974).

24. Federal Coal Mine Health and Safety Act of 1969, Section 110(b)(1).

25. *Phillips*, 500 F.2d at 778.

26. See *Lambert v Ackerley*, 180 F.3d 997, 1002-1008 (9th Cir. 1999) (en banc) (collecting cases and discussing protected activity under various antiretaliation laws). Banking whistleblower law: *Haley v Retsinas*, 138 F.3d 1245, 1250-1251 (8th Cir. 1998); Atomic Energy Act cases: *Bechtel Construction v DOL*, 50 F.3d 926, 931-933 11th Cir. 1995); *Mackowiak v University Nuclear Systems*, 735 F.2d 1159 (9th Cir. 1984); *Kansas Gas & Electric v Brock*, 780 F.2d 1505 (10th Cir. 1985); False Claim Act cases: *U.S. ex rel. Yesudian v Howard University*, 153 F.3d 731, 741-743 (D.C. Cir. 1998) (collecting cases). Fair Labor Act cases: *Love v Re/Max of America Inc.*, 738 F.2d 383, 387 (10th Cir. 1984); *Marshall v Parking Co. of America Denver, Inc.*, 670 F.2d 141

(10th Cir. 1982). 1969 Federal Mine Safety Act cases: *Baker v Board of Mine Operations Appeals*, 595 F.2d 746 (D.C. Cir. 1978). Federal Railroad Safety Act cases: *Rayner v Smirl*, 873 F.2d 60, 64 (4th Cir. 1989). Clean Water Act cases: *Passaic Valley Sewerage Commissioners v DOL*, 922 F.2d 474, 478 (3rd Cir, 1993). ERISA cases: *Hashimoto v Bank of Hawaii*, 999 F.2d 408, 411 (9th Cir. 1993). OSHA cases: *Donovan v Peter Zimmer America, Inc.*, 557 F. Supp. 642 (D. S.C. 1982). NLRA cases: *NLRB v Retail Store Employees' Union*, 570 F.2d 586 (6th Cir. 1978), cert. denied, 439 U.S. 819 (1978). Surface Transportation Act cases: *Clean Harbors Environmental Services v Herman*, 146 F.3d 12 (1st Cir. 1998). See also *Givhan v Western Line Consolidated School District*, 439 U.S. 410 (1979) (upholding internal whistleblowing under First Amendment). Most state courts also have protected internal whistleblowing. See, for example, *Appeal of Bio Energy Corporation*, 607 A.2d 606 (N.H. 1992). Additionally, the majority of state whistleblower protection laws explicitly protect, encourage, and/or require employees to report wrongdoing to their employers. See New Jersey Conscientious Employee Protection Act, N.J.S.A. 34:19. Contra, *Chandler v Dowell Schlumberger, Inc.*, 572 N.W.2d 210 (Mich. 1998).

27. Senate Report No. 848, 1978 U.S. Code Cong. & Admin. News at 7303; *Kansas Gas & Electric v Brock*, 780 F.2d 1505, 1511 (10th Cir. 1985). A lone court decision departed from the *Phillips* holding. See *Brown & Root, Inc. v Donovan*, 747 F.2d 1029, 1036 (5th Cir. 1984). This decision was rejected by other reviewing courts overturned by Congress in 1992. See, 42 U.S.C. § 5851(a) (1992). Due to the specific language in the SOX, the dispute over whether internal reporting of corporate securities fraud is protected has been rendered moot.

28. Accord., *Jones v TVA.*, 948 F.2d 258, 264 (6th Cir. 1991); *Willy v Coastal Corp.*, 85-CAA-1, D&O of SOL, at 13 (June 1, 1994); *Mandreger v Detroit Edison Co.*, 88-ERA-17, D&O of SOL, at 13-14 (March 30, 1994); *Crosier v Portland General Electric Co.*, 91-ERA-2, D&O of SOL, at 6-7 (January 5, 1994); *Pillow v Bechtel Construction*, 87-ERA-35, SOL D&O of Remand, at 11 (July 19, 1993); *Goldstein v EBASCO Constructors, Inc.*, 86-ERA-36, D&O of SOL, at 5-10 (April 7, 1992), *Rev'd EBASCO Construction, Inc. v Martin*, unpublished opinion of U.S. Court of Appeals for the Fifth Circuit, No. 92-4576 (February 19, 1993); *Nichols v Bechtel Construction, Inc.*, 87-ERA-44, D&O of SOL, at 9 (October 26, 1992); *Adams v Coastal Production Op., Inc.*, 89-ERA-3, D&O of SOL, at 8-9 (August 5, 1992); *Guttman v Passaic Valley Sewerage Commission*, 85-WPC-2, D&O of SOL, at 10-13 (March 13, 1992), aff'd 992 F.2d 474 (3rd Cir. 1993); *Johnson v Old Dominion Security*, 86-CAA-3/4/5, D&O of SOL, at 14 (May 29, 1991); *Chavez v EBASCO Services, Inc.*, 91-ERA-24, D&O of SOL, at 5 (November 16, 1992); *Dodd v Polysar Latex*, 88-SWD-4, D&O of SOL, at 6-7 (September 22, 1994).

29. *Saporito v FP&L*, 89-ERA-7/17, Order of SOL, at 6 (February 16, 1995).

30. *Sasse v Office of the U.S. Attorney*, 98-CAA-7, D&O of ARB, p. 11 (January 30, 2004).

31. *Mackowiak v University Nuclear Systems*, 735 F.2d 1159 (9th Cir. 1984) ("If the regulatory scheme is to function effectively, inspectors must be free from the threat of retaliatory discharge for identifying safety and quality problems."). See also *Jarvis v Battelle Pacific Northwest*, 97-ERA-15, D&O of ARB, at 8 (August 27, 1998); *Richter et al. v Baldwin Associates*, 84-ERA-9/10/11/12, D&O of Remand by SOL, at 11-12 (March 12, 1986).

32. *Jarvis v Battelle Pacific Northwest*, 97-ERA-15, D&O of ARB, at 8 (August 27, 1998).

33. *Mackowiak v University Nuclear Systems*, 735 F.2d 1159 (9th Cir. 1984); *Kansas Gas & Elec. Co. v Brock*, 780 F.2d 1505, 1507 (10th Cir. 1985).

34. *Leveille v New York Air National Guard*, 94-TSC-3/4, D&O of Remand by SOL, at 16-17 (December 11, 1995) (collecting cases).

35. *West v Systems Applications International*, 94-CAA-15, D&O of Remand by SOL, at 7 (April 19, 1995).

36. *Dutkiewicz v Clean Harbors Environmental Services*, 95-STA-34, D&O of ARB, at 7 (August 8, 1997), aff'd, *Clean Harbors Environmental Services v Herman*, 146 F.3d 12 (1st Cir. 1998). Contra., *Robbins v Jefferson County School District*, 186 F.3d 1253, 1260 (10th Cir. 1999) (upholding discipline against employee for "making inflammatory, insubordinate comments and disregarding chain of command").

37. *Saporito v Florida Power & Light Co.*, 89-ERA-7/17, SOL Remand Order, at 1 (June 3, 1994).

38. *Pillow v Bechtel*, 87-ERA-35, D&O of remand by SOL, at 11 (July 19, 1993).

39. *Nichols v Bechtel Construction, Inc.*, 87-ERA-44, D&O of SOL, at 9 (October 26, 1992).

40. *Nichols v Bechtel Construction, Inc.*, 87-ERA-44, D&O of SOL, at 9 (October 26, 1992); *McMahan v California Water Quality Control Bd.*, 90-WDC-1, D&O of SOL, at 4 (July 16, 1993); *Brockell v Norton*, 732 F.2d 664, 668 (8th Cir. 1984).

41. *Saporito v FP&L*, 89-ERA-7/17, Order of SOL, at 6 (February 16, 1995).

42. *Knox v U.S. Department of Interior*, 2001-CAA-3, D&O of ALJ, pp. 3, 43-44 (December 30, 2002).

43. *Lockert v Pullman Power Co.*, 867 F.2d 513, 518 (9th Cir. 1989); *Holtzclaw v Commonwealth of Kentucky*, 95-CAA-7, D&O of ARB, at 5-6 (February 13, 1997).

44. *Saporito v FP&L*, 89-ERA-7/17, Order of SOL, at 6 (February 16, 1995), D&O of ARB, at 8 (August 11, 1998) (internal quotations omitted) (citing cases).

45. *Pettway v American Cast Iron Pipe Co.*, 411 F.2d 998, 1006, n. 18 (5th Cir. 1969).

46. 18 U.S.C. § 1514A(a)(2).

47. 18 U.S.C. § 1514A(a).

48. *Sasse v Office of the U.S. Attorney*, 98-CAA-7, D&O of ARB, pp. 11-12 (January 30, 2004).

49. *U.S. v Glover*, 170 F.3d 411 (4th Cir. 1999).

50. *Merritt v Dillard Paper Co.*, 120 F.3d 1181, 1184 (11th Cir. 1997). In *Merritt* the court held that an employee who admitted, in testimony, to having participated in discriminatory conduct could not be discharged on the basis of the testimony alone. 120 F. 3d at 1188-1189.

51. *Kubicko v Ogden Logistics Services*, 181 F.3d 544 (4th Cir. 1999); *U.S. v Glover*, 170 F.3d 411 (4th Cir. 1999).

52. *Smith v ESICORP*, 93-ERA-16, D&O of Remand, at 7 (March 13, 1996); *Bryant v EBASCO Services, Inc.*, 88-ERA-31, D&O of SOL, at 4 (April 21, 1994).

53. *Thompson v TVA*, 89-ERA-14, D&O of SOL, at D&O of SOL, at 5 (July 19, 1993).

54. 18 U.S.C. § 1514A(a)(2).

55. *Macktal v DOL*, 171 F.3d 323 (5th Cir. 1999) (ERA); *Shallal v Catholic Social Services*, 566 N.W.2d 571 (Mich. 1997). Accord., *Mandreger v Detroit Edison Co.*, 88-ERA-17, D&O of SOL, at 14 (March 30, 1994) ("threat to report safety issues to the NRC also was a protected activity"). In *Helmstetter v Pacific Gas & Electric*, 86-SWD-

2, D&O of Remand by SOL, at 7 (citations and internal quotations omitted), the SOL explained the reasoning behind protecting such threats: "Concerning Complainant's alleged threat to report the spill to governmental authorities, it is well established that whistleblower provisions protect preliminary steps to commencing or participating in a proceeding when those steps could result in exposure of employer wrongdoing."

56. *Landers v Commonwealth-Lord Joint Venture*, 83-ERA-5, slip op. of SOL, at 1 (September 9, 1983). See also *Nunn v Duke Power Co.*, 84-ERA-27, D&O of Remand by Deputy SOL, at 12 (July 30, 1987); *Poulos v Ambassador Fuel Oil Co., Inc.*, 86-CAA-1, D&O of Remand by SOL, at 6-11 (April 27, 1987); *Hale v Baldwin Assoc.*, 85-ERA-37, recommended D&O of ALJ, at 17 (October 20, 1986); *Couty v Arkansas Power & Light Co.*, 87-ERA-10, recommended D&O of ALJ, at 9 (November 16, 1987), adopted by SOL (June 20, 1988), reversed on other grounds, 886 F.2d 147 (8th Cir. 1989); *Cram v Pullman-Higgins Co.*, 84-ERA-17, slip op. of SOL, at 1 (January 14, 1985); *Servaiva v Bechtel Power Corp.*, 84-ERA-24, slip op. of ALJ, at 7 (July 5, 1984).

57. *Landers v Commonwealth-Lord Joint Venture*, 83-ERA-5, slip op. of ALJ, at 3 (May 11, 1983), adopted by SOL (September 9, 1983), stay denied, *Commonwealth-Lord Joint Venture v Donovan*, 724 F.2d 67 (7th Cir. 1983). of ALJ, at 11. See also *Poulos v Ambassador Fuel Oil Co., Inc.*, 86-CAA-1, D&O of Remand by SOL, at 6-11 (April 27, 1987); *Ashcraft v Univ of Cincinnati*, 83-ERA-7, slip op. of SOL, at 10 (November 1, 1984).

58. *Poulos v Ambassador Fuel Oil Co., Inc.*, 86-CAA-1, D&O of Remand by SOL, at 6-11 (April 27, 1987). In *Francis v Bogan, Inc.*, 86-ERA-8, recommended decision of ALJ, slip op. at 13 (March 21, 1986), the administrative law judge held that the "about to commence" clause of the Energy Reorganization Act covers threats to report problems to the Nuclear Regulatory Commission, even if no actual complaint was filed. See also *Brown & Root, Inc. v Donovan*, 747 F.2d 1029, 1036 (5th Cir. 1984).

59. One-party surreptitious taping is conducted when one party to a conversation tapes the conversation without telling the other party that such taping is occurring. See, for example, *Heller v Champion Inter. Corp.*, 891 F.2d 432 (2nd Cir. 1989).

60. One-party taping is legal under federal law and most state laws. However, interception of a conversation without the consent of any party to that conversation is illegal under federal law (and most state laws). A small number of state laws are more restrictive than the federal wiretapping statute and prohibit one-party taping. A listing of state taping laws is set forth in footnote 6 of *Boehner v McDermott*, 191 F.3d 463 (D.C. Cir. 1999).

61. *Boddie v A.B.C.*, 731 F.2d 333, 338 (6th Cir. 1984) (citing authorities).

62. *U.S. v Phillips*, 540 F.2d 319, 325 (8th Cir. 1976). For an overview of federal law concerning one-party taping, see *Ali v Douglas Cable*, 929 F. Supp. 1362, 1376-1381 (D. Kan. 1996).

63. *Lopez v U.S.*, 373 U.S. 427, 442 (1963) (Chief Justice Warren concurring).

64. *Goggin Truck Line Co., Inc. v ARB,* 172 F.3d 872 (Table) (unpublished) (6th Cir. 1999); Accord., *U.S. v Wilkinson*, 53 F.3d 757, 761 (6th Cir. 1995).

65. 891 F.2d 432 (2nd Cir. 1989).

66. 891 F. 2d 432 (2nd Cir. 1989) at 436-37.

67. 891 F. 2d 432 (2nd Cir. 1989) (dissenting opinion of J. Van Graafeiland).

68. *Haney v North American Car Corp.*, 81-SWDA-1, R. D&O of ALJ (August 10, 1981), aff'd by SOL (June 30, 1982).

69. 91-ERA-1/11, D&O of Remand by SOL, at 13 (November 20, 1995). Accord., *Melendez v Exxon*, 93-ERA-6, D&O of ARB, at 12 (July 14, 2000)

70. *Goggin Truck Line Co., Inc. v ARB* 172 F.3d 872 (Table) (unpublished) (6th Cir. 1999).

71. *Gutierrez v Regents of the University of California*, 98-ERA-19, D&O of ARB, p. 6 (November 13, 2002).

72. *Donovan v R. D. Anderson Constr. Co.*, 552 F. Supp. 249, 253 (D. Kan. 1982).

73. *Carter v Electrical District No. 2*, 92-TSC-11, D&O of Remand by SOL, at 21 (July 26, 1995) (collecting cases) (holding that employer criticism of employee for "distributing false information" in the press did not justify adverse action). See also *Trimmer v LANL*, 93-CAA-93-ERA-55, D&O of ARB, at 2-3 (May 8, 1997). For a discussion of DOL cases protecting contacts with the news media, see *Phillips v Stanley Smith Security*, 96-ERA-30, D&O of ARB, pp. 17-18 (January 31, 2001) (dissenting opinion of Board Member Brown).

74. *Dunlop v Hanover Shoe Farms*, 441 F. Supp. 385, 388 (M.D. Pa. 1976) (complaint to attorney covered as hiring attorney constituted first step in the exercise of protected rights). Accord., *Harrison v Stone & Webster Group*, 93-ERA-44, D&O of SOL, at 12 (August 22, 1995).

75. 80-WPCA-1, slip op. of ALJ, at 10-11 (July 11, 1980), adopted by SOL (July 28, 1980).

76. *Donovan v R. D. Andersen Constr. Co.*, 552 F. Supp. 249 (D. Kan. 1982) (contact with the news media is protected activity under OSHA); *Nunn v Duke Power Co.*, 84-ERA-27, D&O of Remand by Deputy SOL, at 13 (July 30, 1987) (contact with citizen intervener protected).

77. *Crosby v Hughes Aircraft Co.*, 85-TSC-2, D&O of SOL, at 22-23 (August 17, 1993).

78. *Pillow v Bechtel*, 87-ERA-35, D&O of remand by SOL, at 11 (July 19, 1993); *Mandreger v Detroit Edison Co.*, 88-ERA-17, D&O of SOL, at 13 (March 30, 1994); *Simon v Simmons Industries, Inc.*, 87-TSC-2, D&O of SOL, at 4 (April 4, 1994), citing *Legutko v Local 816, International Brotherhood of Teamsters*, 606 F. Supp. 352, 358-359 (E.D. N.Y. 1985), aff'd (2nd Cir. 1988).

79. *Simon v Simmons Industries, Inc.*, 87-TSC-2, D&O of SOL, at 4 (April 4, 1994), citing *Legutko v Local 816, International Brotherhood of Teamsters*, 606 F. Supp. 352, 358-359 (E.D. N.Y. 1985), aff'd (2nd Cir. 1988).

80. *Diaz-Robainas v FP&L*, 92-ERA-10, D&O of Remand by SOL, at 14 (January 19, 1996).

81. *Hoffman v W. Max Bossert*, 94-CAA-4, D&O of Remand by SOL, at 8 (September 19, 1995).

82. *Dobreuenaski v Associated Universities, Inc.*, 96-ERA-44, D&O of ARB, at 9 (June 18, 1998).

83. *Simon v Simmons Industries, Inc.*, 87-TSC-2, D&O of SOL, at 4 (April 4, 1994), citing *Legutko v Local 816, International Brotherhood of Teamsters*, 606 F. Supp. 352, 358-359 (E.D. N.Y. 1985), aff'd (2nd Cir. 1988).

84. *Higgins v Pascack Valley Hosp.*, 730 A.2d 327 (N.J. 1999) (collecting state authorities).

85. *Harrison v Stone & Webster Group*, 93-ERA-44, D&O of SOL, at 12 (August 22, 1995); *Stone & Webster v Herman*, 115 F.3d 1568, 1574-1575 (11th Cir. 1997). Accord., *Donovan v Diplomat Envelope Corp.*, 587 F. Supp. 1417, 1424 (E.D. N.Y. 1984).

86. *Brock v Richardson*, 812 F.2d 121, 123-125 (3rd Cir. 1987); *Reich v Hoy Shoe, Inc.*, 32 F.3d 361, 368 (8th Cir. 1994); *Smith v ESICORP, Inc.*, 93-ERA-16, D&O of Remand by SOL, at 9-11 (March 13, 1996) (discussing circumstances behind management suspicion that employee engaged in protected activity).

87. *Willy v Coastal Corp.*, 85-CAA-1, SOL D&O, at 13-14 (June 1, 1994). Accord., *Ass't. Secretary v S&S Gravel, Inc.*, 92-STA-30, D&O of SOL, at 15 (February 5, 1993); *Brock v Richardson*, 812 F.2d 121, 123-125 (3rd Cir. 1987).

88. *Hochstadt v Worcester Foundation for Experimental Biology*, 545 F.2d 222 (1st Cir. 1976); *EEOC v Crown Zellerbach Corp.*, 720 F.2d 1008 (9th Cir. 1983); *Wrighten v Metropolitan Hospitals, Inc.*, 726 F.2d 1346 (9th Cir. 1984).

89. *Pettway v American Cast Iron Pipe Co.*, 411 F.2d 998 (5th Cir. 1969).

90. See *Linn v United Plant Guard, Workers of America*, 383 U.S. 53, 62 (1966); *Montefiore Hospital and Medical Center v NLRB*, 621 F.2d 510, 517 (2nd Cir. 1980).

91. *Linn*, at 62, quoting from *New York Times v Sullivan*, 376 U.S. 254 (1964).

92. *NLRB v Owners Maintenance Corp.*, 581 F.2d 44, 50 (2nd Cir. 1978).

93. *NLRB v A. Lasaponara Sons, Inc.*, 541 F.2d 992, 998 (2nd Cir. 1976).

94. *American Telephone & Telegraph Co. v NLRB*, 521 F.2d 1159, 1161 (2nd Cir. 1975).

95. *Kubicko v Ogden Logistics Services*, 181 F.3d 544 (4th Cir, 1999).

96. *Holtzclaw v SOL*, 172 F.3d 872 (Table), at 6 (unpublished, 6th Cir. 1999).

97. *American Nuclear Resources, Inc. v DOL*, 134 F.3d 1292, 1295 (6th Cir. 1998).

98. See *Linn v United Plant Guard, Workers of America*, 383 U.S. 53, 62 (1966); *NLRB v Washington Aluminum Co.*, 370 U.S. 9, 17 (1962); *Wrighten v Metropolitan Hosps., Inc.*, 726 F.2d 1346, 1355 (9th Cir. 1984); *Hochstadt v Worcester Found.*, 545 F.2d 222 (1st Cir. 1976).

99. *Parker v Baltimore and O.R. Co.*, 652 F.2d 1012, 1020 (D.C. Cir. 1981).

100. *Whatley v Met. Atlanta Rapid Transit*, 632 F.2d 1325, 1327 (5th Cir. 1980).

101. *Unt v Aerospace Corp.*, 765 F.2d 1440, 1446 (9th Cir. 1985).

102. *Hochstadt v Worcester Foundation, Etc.*, 545 F.2d 222, 228 (1st Cir. 1976).

103. *EEOC v Crown Zellerbach Corp.*, 720 F.2d 1008, 1014-15 (9th Cir. 1983).

104. *Keeneway v Matlack, Inc.*, 88-STA-20, D&O of SOL, at 6-7, 10-13 (June 15, 1989).

105. *Keeneway v Matlack, Inc.*, 88-STA-20, D&O of SOL, at 6-7, 10-13 (June 15, 1989).

106. *Kansas Gas & Elec. Co. v Brock*, 780 F.2d 1505, 1507 (10th Cir. 1985). See also *Mackowiak v University Nuclear Systems, Inc.*, 82-ERA-8, D&O of Remand by ALJ, at 7 (July 25, 1986).

107. *Timmons v Franklin Electric Cooperative*, 97-SWD-2, D&O of ARB, at 6 (December 1, 1998) (collecting cases).

108. *Passaic Valley Sewerage Commissioners v DOL*, 992 F.2d 474 (3rd Cir. 1993) (personality problem resulted from whistleblowing); *Mackowiak v University Nuclear Systems, Inc.*, 735 F.2d 1159 (9th Cir. 1984) (complaint about "bad attitude" arose from persistent protected activity); *Pogue v DOL*, 940 F.2d 1287, 1290 (9th Cir. 1991) (so-called insubordinate behavior resulted from whistleblowing). See *Dodd v*

Polysar Latex, 88-SWD-4, D&O of SOL, at 15-17 (September 22, 1994) (alleged "insubordinate and negative" behavior did not "upset the balance . . . between protected activity and shop discipline"); *Martin v Department of the Army*, 93-SDW-1, D&O of Remand by SOL, at 6-7 (July 13, 1995) (alleged unprofessional conduct was not "indefensible under the circumstances").

109. *Jarvis v Battle Pacific Northwest*, 97-ERA-15, D&O of ARB, at 9, n. 7 (August 27, 1998). Accord., *Carter v Electrical District No. 2*, 92-TSC-11, D&O of Remand by SOL, at 19-20 (July 26, 1995) (disruption caused by the method employee used to "deliver" his whistleblower speech, combined with the employee's "spontaneous" and "intemperate reactions" were not "indefensible under the circumstances" and remained protected).

110. *Carter v Electrical District No. 2*, 92-TSC-11, D&O of Remand by SOL, at 21 (July 26, 1995) (collecting cases) (holding that employer criticism of employee for "distributing false information" in the press did not justify adverse action).

111. 91-TSC-5, D&O of SOL, at 14 (October 6, 1992).

112. *Blake v Hatfield Electric Co.*, 87-ERA-4, D&O of SOL, at 9-10 (January 22, 1992).

113. 91-TSC-1, D&O of SOL, at 6-7 (January 13, 1993).

114. *Carter v Electrical District No. 2*, 92-TSC-11, D&O of Remand by SOL, at 21 (July 26, 1995) (collecting cases) (holding that employer criticism of employee for "distributing false information" in the press did not justify adverse action).

115. *Lockert v DOL*, 867 F.2d 513, 519 (9th Cir. 1989).

116. See *Laughlin v Metropolitan Washington Airports Authority*, 149 F.3d 253, 259 n. 3 (4th Cir. 1998) ("It is black letter law that illegal actions are not protected activity under Title VII.").

117. *O'Day v McDonnell Douglas*, 79 F.3d 756, 764 (9th Cir. 1996). Accord., *Laughlin v Metropolitan Washington Airports Authority*, 149 F.3d 253, 259 n. 3 (4th Cir. 1998) ("It is black letter law that illegal actions are not protected activity under Title VII.").

118. 132 F.3d 442, 445-446 (8th Cir. 1998).

119. 132 F.3d 442, 445-446 (8th Cir. 1998). See also *Grant v Hazelett Strip-Casting Corp.*, 880 F.2d 1564, 1570 (2nd Cir. 1989) (upholding jury verdict protecting employee who refused to return an incriminating document).

120. In *Whirlpool Corp. v Marshall*, 445 U.S. 1, 10-11 (1980), the U.S. Supreme Court upheld the legality of OSHA regulations that established a right to refuse work in limited situations where the risk of injury or death was reasonably perceived to be imminent. Accord., *Somerson v Yellow Freight System, Inc.*, 98-STA-9, D&O of ARB, at 12 n. 11 (February 18, 1999) (collecting cases concerning refusal to drive due to fatigue or illness); *Sutherland v Spray Systems*, 95-CAA-1, D&O of SOL, at 4 (February 26, 1996) (work refusal protected under Clean Air Act); *Eltzroth v Amersham Medi-Physics, Inc.*, 97-ERA-31, D&O of ARB, at 5-6 (April 15, 1999), and the dissenting opinion filed by ARB member Brown, at 12-13, 22-25 (work refusal under the ERA).

121. Examples of such cases are *Brock v Roadway Express, Inc.*, 481 U.S. 252, 255 (1987) (protecting employee under STAA for "refusing to operate a motor vehicle that does not comply with applicable state and federal safety regulations"); *LeBlanc v Fogelman Truck Lines, Inc.*, 89-STA-8, D&O of Remand by SOL, at 9 (December 20, 1989) (refusal to work based on commission of federal violation).

122. *Stockdill v Catalytic Industrial Maintenance*, 90-ERA-43, D&O of SOL, at 3 (1996) (collecting cases under ERA).

123. *Getman v. Southwest Securities*, 2003-SOX-8, D&O of ALJ, p. 11-15 (February 2, 2004).

124. *Getman v. Southwest Securities*, 2003-SOX-8, D&O of ALJ, p. 13 (February 2, 2004).

125. 92-ERA-10, D&O of Remand by SOL, at 8 (January 19, 1996).

126. 92-ERA-10, D&O of Remand by SOL, at 8 (January 19, 1996). ("While it might have been more prudent for Diaz-Robainas to comply with the order and then file his claim under the ERA, his assumption of the risk that he would be unable to prove discriminatory motivation in ordering the evaluation does not absolve Florida Power from wrongdoing in imposing the order in violation of the ERA.").

127. *Smith v. Western Sales & Testing*, 01-CAA-17, D&O of ARB, p. 9 (March 31, 2004). *Oliver v Hydro-Vac Services, Inc.*, 91-SWD-1, D&O of Remand by SOL, at 9 (November 1, 1995) (environmental whistleblower law); *Allum v Valley Bank of Nevada*, 970 P.2d 1062, 1068 (Nev 1998) (state public policy tort); *Yellow Freight System, Inc. v Martin*, 954 F.2d 353, 357 (6th Cir. 1992) (STA whistleblower law). But see *Ass't SOL v West Bank Containers*, 98-STA-30, D&O of ARB, at 10-14 (April 28, 2000) (holding that more than "categorical statements" demonstrating the existence of a real safety issue are necessary in order for an employee to prove a complaint was in fact safety related). For a discussion of this standard, see *Phillips v Stanley Smith Security*, 96-ERA-30, D&O of ARB, pp. 16-17 (January 31, 2001) (dissenting opinion of Board Member Brown).

128. 18 U.S.C. § 1514A(a)(1).

129. *Johnson v Oak Ridge Operations Office*, 95-CAA-20/21/22, D&O of ARB, at 8 (September 30, 1999) ("It is well settled that protected activities under the environmental whistleblower provisions are limited to those which are grounded in conditions constituting reasonably perceived violations of the environmental statutes.") (collecting cases); *Melendez v Exxon*, 93-ERA-6, D&O of ARB, at 12 (July 14, 2000); *Minard v Nerco*, 92-SWD-1, D&O of SOL at 7-16 (January 25, 1994).

130. *Welch v Cardinal Bankshares Corp.*, 2003-SOX-15, R.D&O of ALJ, p. 36 (January 28, 2004).

131. *Halloum v. Intel Corp.*, 2003-SOX-7, D&O of ALJ, p. 10 (March 4, 2004).

132. *Crosier v Westinghouse Hanford Co.*, 92-CAA-3, SOL D&O, at 6 (January 12, 1994) ("A complainant under an employee protection provision need not prove an actual violation of the underlying statute."); *Somerson v Yellow Freight System, Inc.*, 98-STA-9, D&O of ARB, at 12 n. 11 (February 18, 1999) (collecting cases concerning refusal to drive due to fatigue or illness), ("Protection is not dependent upon whether [the employee] was *actually* successful in proving a violation of a federal safety provision. The primary consideration is not the outcome of the underlying grievance hearing, but whether the proceeding is based upon possible safety violations.").

133. *McCafferty v Centerior Energy*, 96-ERA-6, Order Denying Stay by ARB, at 4 (October 16, 1996).

134. *Keene v EBASCO Constructors, Inc.*, 95-ERA-4, D&O of Remand by ARB, at 8 (February 19, 1997) ("An employee's reasonable belief that his employer is violating the ERA's requirements is sufficient, irrespective of after-the-fact determinations regarding the correctness of the employee's belief.").

135. *Pettway v American Cast Iron Pipe Co.*, 411 F.2d 998 (5th Cir. 1969).

136. 700 F.2d 281, 286 (6th Cir. 1983).

137. 405 U.S. 117, 122 (1972).

138. *DeFord v Secretary of Labor*, 700 F.2d 281, 286 (6th Cir. 1983). Cf. *NLRB v Mount Desert Island Hosp.*, 695 F.2d 634, 638 (5th Cir. 1984) (employer's action construed broadly to prevent intimidation of others in exercise of their rights); *John Hancock Mutual Life Ins. Co. v NLRB*, 191 F.2d 483, 485 (D.C. Cir. 1951) (broad construction necessary to prevent intimidation of prospective complainants and witnesses).

139. Senate Report No. 107-146, p. 19.

140. *Goldstein v EBASCO Constr., Inc.*, 86-ERA-36, recommended D&O of ALJ, at 11 (March 3, 1988); *Sartain v Bechtel Constr. Corp.*, 87-ERA-37, recommended D&O of ALJ, at 13 (January 14, 1988). See also *Wichita County v Hart*, 917 S.W.2d 779, 784-786 (Tex. 1996) (collecting cases and noting the lack of "consensus" on the issue of whistleblower motivation); *Melendez v Exxon*, 93-ERA-6, D&O of ARB, at 12 (July 14, 2000).

141. *Guttman v Passaic Valley Sewerage Commissioners*, 85-WPC-2, D&O of SOL (March 13, 1992), aff'd, 992 F.2d 474 (3rd Cir. 1993).

142. 85-WPC-2, D&O of SOL (March 13, 1992), aff'd, 992 F.2d 474 (3rd Cir. 1993).

143. 85-WPC-2, D&O of SOL (March 13, 1992), aff'd, 992 F.2d 474 (3rd Cir. 1993). The SOL has held that employees motivated by "self-gain" are protected and that "the purpose of the whistleblower statutes is to encourage employees to come forward with complaints of health hazards . . . and if such a course of action furthers the employee's own selfish agenda, so be it." *Oliver v Hydro-Vac Services, Inc.*, 91-SWD-1, D&O of Remand by SOL, at 9 (November 1, 1995) (environmental whistleblower law), at 14 (internal quotations and citations omitted). Accord., *Nichols v Gordon Trucking, Inc.*, 97-STA-2, D&O of ARB, at 1 (July 17, 1997) ("A complainant's motivation in making safety complaints has no bearing on whether the complaints are protected."); *Reid v Scientech, Inc.*, 99-ERA-20, at 1314 (January 28, 2000).

144. *Guttman v Passaic Valley Sewerage Commissioners*, 85-WPC-2 at 20.

145. 992 F.2d 474, 478 (3rd Cir. 1993).

146. 992 F.2d 474, 478 (3rd Cir. 1993).

147. *Crosby v Hughes Aircraft Co.*, 85-TSC-2, D&O of SOL, at 26 (August 17, 1993).

148. *Landers v Commonwealth-Lord Joint Venture*, 83-ERA-5, slip op. of ALJ, at 3 (May 11, 1983), adopted by SOL (September 9, 1983), stay denied, *Commonwealth-Lord Joint Venture v Donovan*, 724 F.2d 67 (7th Cir. 1983).

149. *Keene v EBASCO Constructors, Inc.*, 95-ERA-4, D&O of Remand by ARB, at 8 (February 19, 1997) ("An employee's reasonable belief that his employer is violating the ERA's requirements is sufficient, irrespective of after-the-fact determinations regarding the correctness of the employee's belief"). ("Most significantly, [the employer] did in fact commit the falsification exactly as alleged by [the whistleblower] and attempted to conceal this wrongdoing . . . all of which undermines the credibility of [the employer] and lends even more credence to [the whistleblower's] account.").

150. *Timmons v Mattingly Testing Services*, 95-ERA-40, D&O of Remand by ARB, p. 12 (June 21, 1996) (collecting cases).

151. *U.S. v Glover*, 170 F.3d 411, 413 (4th Cir. 1999).

152. *Learned v City of Bellevue*, 860 F.2d 928, 932 (9th Cir. 1988).

153. *U.S. v Glover*, 170 F.3d 411 (4th Cir. 1999), at 414, quoting *Robinson v Shell Oil Co.*, 519 U.S. 337 (1997).

154. *U.S. v Glover*, 170 F.3d 411 (4th Cir. 1999), at 414, quoting *Robinson v Shell Oil Co.*, 519 U.S. 337 (1997). Accord., *Merritt v Dillard Paper Co.*, 120 F.3d 1181 (11th Cir. 1997).

155. *Merritt v Dillard Paper Co.*, 120 F.3d 1181, 1184 (11th Cir. 1997). In *Merritt* the court held that an employee who admitted, in testimony, to having participated in discriminatory conduct could not be discharged on the basis of the testimony alone. 120 F. 3d at 1188-1189.

156. See *Clover v Total System Services, Inc.*, 176 F.3d 1346 (11th Cir. 1999) (Title VII retaliation claim dismissed due to lack of evidence of employer knowledge). In the context of environmental whistleblowing, the SOL has held that employer "knowledge" of the protected conduct is an "essential element of proof." *Miller v Thermalkem, Inc.*, 94-SWD-1, D&O of SOL, at 3 (November 9, 1995). Accord., *Ertel v Giroux Bros. Transp., Inc.*, 88-STA-24, D&O of SOL, at 25 n. 16 (February 16, 1989); *Hassel v Industrial Contractors, Inc.*, 86-CAA-7, D&O of SOL, at 2 (February 13, 1989); *Ledford v Baltimore Gas & Elec. Co.*, 83-ERA-9, slip op. of ALJ at 9-11, adopted by SOL; *Crider v Pullman Power Prods. Corp.*, 82-ERA-7, slip op. of ALJ, at 2 (October 5, 1982); *Flanagan v Bechtel Power Corp. et al.*, 81-ERA-7, D&O of SOL, slip op. of ALJ, at 11 (November 19, 1981).

157. *Crider v Pullman Power Prods. Corp.*, 82-ERA-7, slip op. of ALJ, at 2 (October 5, 1982).

158. *Merriweather v TVA*, 91-ERA-55, R. D&O of ALJ, at 4-5 (May 21, 1992), citing to *Bartlik v TVA*, 88-ERA-15, D&O of Remand by SOL, at 7 n. 7 (December 6, 1991). See also *Morris v The American Inspection Co.*, 92-ERA-5, D&O of SOL, at 6 (December 15, 1992); *Chavez v EBASCO*, 91-ERA-24, D&O of SOL, at 5 (November 16, 1992); *Young v Philadelphia Electric Co.*, 88-ERA-1, D&O of SOL, at 6, n. 3 (December 18,1992).

159. *NLRB v Instrument Corp. of America*, 714 F.2d 324, 328-329 (4th Cir. 1983); *Frazier v Merit Systems Protection Board*, 672 F.2d 150, 166 (D.C. Cir. 1982); *Larry v Detroit Edison Co.*, 86-ERA-32, slip op. of ALJ, at 6 (October 17, 1986); *Johnson v Transco Products., Inc.*, 85-ERA-7 slip op. of ALJ, at 4 (March 5, 1985); *Flenker v Williamette Industries, Inc.*, 68 F. Supp.2d 1261, 1266-1267 (D. Kan. 1999) (circumstantial evidence of knowledge).

160. *Reich v Hoy Shoe Co.*, 32 F.3d 361, 368 (8th Cir. 1994) (adverse action based on employer's suspicion of protected activities); *Smith v ESICORP, Inc.*, 93-ERA-16, D&O of Remand by SOL, at 9-11 (March 13, 1996) (discussing circumstances behind management suspicion that employee engaged in protected activity).

161. *Bartlik v TVA*, 88-ERA-15, D&O of Remand by SOL, at 7 n. 7 (December 6, 1991). Final D&O of SOL, at 4, n. 1 (April 7, 1993).

162. *Frazier v Merit Systems Protection Board*, 672 F.2d 150, 166 (D.C. Cir. 1982).

163. *Wagoner v Technical Products, Inc.*, 87-TSC-4, D&O of SOL, at 14 n. 8 (November 20, 1990).

164. *Larry v Detroit Edison Co.*, 86-ERA-32, slip op. of ALJ, at 6 (October 17, 1986).

165. *Bartlik v TVA*, 88-ERA-15, D&O of Remand by SOL, at 7 n. 7 (December 6, 1991): "[W]here managerial or supervisory authority is delegated, the official with ultimate responsibility who merely ratifies his subordinates' decisions cannot insulate a respondent from liability by claiming 'bureaucratic' 'ignorance.'"

166. *Ertel v Giroux Bros. Transp., Inc.*, 88-STA-24, D&O of SOL, at 25 n. 16 (February 16, 1989).

167. *Pillow v Bechtel Construction, Inc.*, 87-ERA-35, D&O of Remand by SOL (July 19, 1993).

168. *Thompson v TVA*, 89-ERA-14, D&O of SOL, at 5 (July 19, 1993).

169. *Jones v EG&G Defense Materials, Inc.*, 95-CAA-3, D&O of ARB, at 15 (September 29, 1998).

CHAPTER 9

1. 18 U.S.C. 1514A(a).

2. 29 C.F.R. 1980.102(b).

3. *Carter v Electrical District No. 2*, Case No. 92-TSC-11, Sec. Dec. (July 26, 1995), citing *DeFord v Secretary of Labor*, 700 F.2d 281, 283, 287 (6th Cir. 1983); *Jenkins v EPA*, Case No. 92-CAA-6, Sec. Dec., May 18, 1994, slip. op. at 14-16); *Varnadore v Oak Ridge National Laboratory*, Case No. 92-CAA-2/5, 93-CAA-1, 94-CAA-2/3, Final Consolidated Order of ARB, at 32-33 (June 14, 1996); *Earwood v Dart Container Corp.*, 93-STA-16, D&O of SOL (Dec. 7, 1994) (outlining "prophylactic rule" prohibiting negative references or comments about an employee even if it did not result in the loss of a job); *Leveille v New York Air National Guard*, Case No. 94-TSC-3/4, D&O of SOL (Dec. 11, 1995); *Marcus v EPA*, Case No. 96-CAA-3, RD&O of ALJ (Dec. 15, 1998).

4. *Jenkins v EPA*, 88-SWD-2, D&O of ARB, p. 20-21 (February 28, 2003).

5. *Earwood v Dart Container Corp.*, 93-STA-16, D&O of SOL (Dec. 7, 1994). Accord., *Leveille v New York Air National Guard*, Case No. 94-TSC-3/4, D&O of SOL (Dec. 11, 1995). The *Earwood* line of cases was applied to the United States EPA in the case of *Marcus v EPA*, Case No. 96-CAA-3, RD&O of ALJ (Dec. 15, 1998).

6. *Williams et al. v Mason & Hanger Corp.*, 97-ERA-14/18-22, D&O of ARB, p. 14. (November 13, 2002) affirmed in part, 2004 WL 1440554 (5th Cir.).

7. *Blake v Hatfield Elec. Co.*, 87-ERA-4, D&O of SOL, at 4 (January 22, 1992); *McCuistion v TVA*, 89-ERA-6, D&O of SOL, at 8 (November 13, 1991); *Nichols v Bechtel Constr. Inc.*, 87-ERA-44, D&O of SOL, at 11 (October 26, 1992).

8. *DeFord v Secretary of Labor*, 700 F.2d 281, 283 (6th Cir. 1983); *Fisher v Pharmacia & Upjohn*, 225 F.3d 915 (8th Cir. 2000); *Ellis Fischel State Cancer Hosp. v Marshall*, 629 F.2d 563, 566 (9th Cir. 1980); *Wells v Kansas Gas & Elec. Co.*, 83-ERA-12, slip op. of ALJ, at 18, adopted by SOL (June 14, 1984). Also see *van der Meer v Western Kentucky Univ*, 95-ERA-38, D&O of ARB (April 20, 1998) (denying academician the opportunity to teach and conduct research).

9. *Tracanna v Arctic Slope*, 97-WPC-1, D&O of ARB, pp. 14-15 (July 31, 2001); *Perez v Guthmiller Trucking Co., Inc.*, 87-STA-13, D&O of SOL, at 24-25 (December 7, 1988); *Talbert v Washington Public Power Supply System*, 93-ERA-35, D&O of ARB, at 10-11 (September 27, 1996); *Martin v Department of Army*, 93-SDW-1, D&O of ARB, at 7-9 (July 30, 1999) (discussing circuit split). The standard for finding a constructive discharge "is a higher one than for finding a hostile work environment," *Berkman v U.S. Coast Guard*, 97-CAA-2/9, D&O of ARB, at 22 (February 29, 2000).

10. *Egenrieder v Met. Edison Co.*, 85-ERA-23, D&O of Remand by SOL (April 20, 1987); *Simmons v Florida Power Corp.*, 89-ERA 28/29, R. D&O of ALJ (December 13,

1989); *Garn v Benchmark Tech.*, 88-ERA-21, D&O of SOL, at 9-11 (September 25, 1990); *Doyle v Hydro Nuclear Services*, 89-ERA-22, D&O of SOL (March 30, 1994); *Leidigh v Freightway Corp.*, 87-STA-12, D&O of ARB, at 3-4 (December 18, 1997). See also *Smith v TVA*, 90-ERA-12, D&O of SOL (April 30, 1992) (declining to find blacklisting and collecting cases).

11. *Jenkins v EPA*, 92-CAA-6, R. D&O of ALJ (December 14, 1992); D&O of SOL, at 14-15 (May 18, 1994); *Pogue v United States Dept. of the Navy*, 87-ERA-21 D&O of SOL, at 51 (May 10, 1990), Rev'd on other grounds sub nom. *Pogue v United States DOL*, 940 F.2d 1287 (9th Cir. 1991).

12. *Bassett v Niagara Mohawk Power Corp.*, 85-ERA-34, D&O of SOL, at 4 (September 28, 1993). See *Varnadore v Oak Ridge National Laboratory*, 92-CAA-2/5, 93-CAA-1, 94-CAA-2/3, Final Consolidated Order of ARB, at 32-33 (June 14, 1996) ("narrative contained in a performance appraisal may constitute adverse action") ("The most useful measure of whether a performance appraisal was given out of retaliatory motive is whether it is a fair and accurate description of an employee's job performance.") (collecting cases); *Shelton v Oak Ridge*, 95-CAA-19, D&O of ARB, pp. 6-9 (March 30, 2001) (evaluating whether a disciplinary letter constitutes adverse action). In *Calhoun v UPS*, 99-STA-7, D&O of ARB, p. 9 (November 27, 2002), the DOL held that a "supervisor's criticism of an employee, without more, does not constitute an adverse employment action."

13. *Diaz-Robainas v Florida Power & Light Co.*, 92-ERA-10, D&O of SOL (January 19, 1996) (finding referral to constitute illegal discrimination); *Mandreger v Detroit Edison*, 88-ERA-17, D&O of SOL (March 30, 1994) (upholding legality of referral). In fitness-for-duty referral cases, the DOL carefully examines the record to determine if "evidence" of "unusual or threatening behavior" existed sufficient to justify the referral. *Griffin v Consolidated Freightways*, 97-STA-10/19, at 7 (January 20, 1998).

14. *Diaz-Robainas v Florida Power & Light Co.*, 92-ERA-10, D&O of SOL.

15. *Thomas v APS*, 89-ERA-19, D&O of SOL, at 17 (September 17, 1993).

16. *Thomas v APS*, 89-ERA-19, D&O of SOL, at 17.

17. *Varnadore v SOL*, 141 F.3d 625, 631 (6th Cir. 1998).

18. *Varnadore v SOL*, 141 F.3d 625, 631.

19. *Nathaniel v Westinghouse Hanford Co.*, 91-SWD-2, D&O of SOL, at 13-14 (February 1, 1995).

20. *McMahan v California Water Quality Control Board*, 90-WPC-1, D&O of SOL, at 5 (July 16, 1993).

21. *Bryant v EBASCO Services, Inc.*, 88-ERA-31, D&O of SOL, at 8 (April 21, 1994). In *Earwood v Dart Container Corp.*, 93-STA-16, D&O of SOL (December 7, 1994) (internal citations and quotations omitted), the SOL outlined a "prophylactic rule prohibiting improper references," even if the reference did not result in the loss of a job:

> The fact that Complainant would not have lost an employment opportunity due to Dart's improper statement should not shield Dart from liability because its statement had a tendency to impede and interfere with Complainant's employment opportunities. I find that effective enforcement of the Act requires a prophylactic rule prohibiting improper references to an employee's protected activity whether or not the employee has suffered damages or loss of employment opportunities as a result.

22. *Hobby v Georgia Power Co.*, 90-ERA-30, D&O of Remand by SOL, at 27 (August 4, 1995).

23. *Leveille v New York Air National Guard*, 94-TSC-3/4, D&O of SOL (December 11, 1995) (adverse action in giving bad reference to a "reference checking company that the complainant had hired"); *Gaballa v The Atlantic Group, Inc.*, 94-ERA-9, D&O of SOL (January 18, 1996) (adverse action by informing a reference-checking company that employee had filed a discrimination complaint); *Marcus v EPA*, 96-CAA- 3 R. D&O of ALJ (Dec. 15, 1998). But see *Webb v CP&L*, 93-ERA-42, D&O of ARB, at 11 (August 26, 1997) (informal negative remark to a "colleague" and "friend," standing alone, did not constitute adverse action).

24. *Mandreger v Detroit Edison Co.*, 88-ERA- 17, D&O of SOL, at 14 (March 30, 1994). See also *House v TVA*, 91-ERA-42, D&O of SOL (January 13, 1993); *Crosier v Portland General Electric Corp.*, 91-ERA-2, D&O of SOL, at 8 (January 5, 1994). See, for example, *Helmstetter v Pacific Gas & Electric Co.*, 91-TSC-1, D&O of SOL (January 13, 1993).

25. *Flanagan v Bechtel Power Corp. et al.*, 81-ERA-7, D&O of SOL, at 6-7; *Samodurov v General Physics Corp.*, 89-ERA-20, D&O of SOL, at 9-10 (November 16, 1993); *Hasan v DOL*, 2002 WL 734775, p. 3 n. 2 (10th Cir. 2002).

26. *Simmons et al. v Fluor Constructors, Inc.*, 88-ERA-28/30, recommended D&O of ALJ, at 17 (February 8, 1989). See also *NLRB v News Syndicate Co.*, 279 F.2d 323 (2nd Cir.), aff'd, 365 U.S. 695 (1961).

27. *Nolan v AC Express*, 92-STA-37, D&O of remand by SOL, at 1 (January 17, 1995).

28. *Parkhurst v L. K. Comstock & Co., Inc.*, 85-ERA-41, recommended D&O of ALJ, at 10 (April 7, 1986).

29. *Hill et al. v TVA*, 87-ERA-23/24, D&O of Remand by SOL, at 9; *Artrip v EBASCO Services*, 89-ERA-23, D&O of SOL (March 21, 1995). Accord., *Sibley Memorial Hospital v Wilson*, 488 F.2d 1338, 1342-1343 (D.C. Cir. 1973).

30. *Artrip v EBASCO Services*, 89-ERA-23, D&O of SOL, at 6-7, 15. In *Artrip* the SOL, citing *Charlton v Paramus Board of Educ.*, 25 F.3d 194, 202 (3rd Cir. 1994), found that a "defendant's lack of direct authority" for the "ultimate adverse decision does not eliminate" potential liability. 89-ERA-23, at 7.

31. *Bassett v Niagara Mohawk Power Co.*, 86-ERA-2, order of remand by SOL, at 6 (July 9, 1985).

32. *Faragher v Boca Raton*, 524 U.S. 775, 118 S.Ct. 2275, 141 L.Ed.2d 662 (1998); *English v Whitfield*, 858 F.2d 957, 963 (4th Cir. 1988); *Smith v ESICORP, Inc.*, 93-ERA-16, D&O of Remand by SOL, at 23 (March 13, 1996); *Williams v ARB*, 2004 WL 1440554 (5th Cir.), 97-ERA-14/18-22, D&O of ARB (November 13, 2002).

33. *Delcore v W. J. Barney Corp.*, 89-ERA-38, D&O of SOL (April 19, 1995).

34. *Saporito v FP&L*, 89-ERA-7, D&O of ARB, p.8-9 (August 11, 1998). Accord., *NLRB v McCullough Environmental Services, Inc.*, 5 F.3d 923, 928 (5th Cir. 1993); *NLRB v Brookwood Furniture*, 701 F.2d 452, 460-462 (5th Cir. 1983).

35. *Griffith v Wackenhut Corp.*, 97-ERA-52, D&O of ARB, at 12 (noting that "concrete harm" may arise when employee conduct could have a chilling effect). Accord., *Hashimoto v Dalton*, 118 F.3d 671, 676 (9th Cir. 1997); *Morris v Lindau*, 196 F.3d 102, (2nd Cir. 1999) (employer policy may constitute prior restraint); *DeGuiseppe v Village of Bellwood*, 68 F.3d 187, 192 (7th Cir. 1995) ("potential for chilling employee speech").

36. *Ass't. Secretary v Carolina Freight Carrier*, 91-STA-25, D&O of SOL, at 7 (August 6, 1992) ("To permit an employer to rely on a facially-neutral policy to discipline an employee for engaging in statutorily-protected activity would permit the employer to accomplish what the law prohibits.") (collecting cases); *Assistant Secretary v Sysco Foods of Philadelphia*, 97-STA-30, D&O of ARB, at 8 (July 8, 1998); *Secretary of Labor v Mullins*, 888 F.2d 1448-1452 (D.C. Cir. 1989); *CL&P v SOL*, 85 F.3d 89, 95 (2nd Cir. 1996); *CL&P v SOL*, 85 F.3d 89, 95.

37. *Halloum v Intel Corp.*, 2003-SOX-7, D&O of ALJ, p. 10 and n. 18 (March 4, 2004). But see *White v Burlington Northern & Santa Fe Railway Co.*, 2004 Fed.App. 0101P (6th Cir. April 14, 2004); *Dolan v EMC Corp.*, 2004-SOX-1, D&O of ALJ (March 24, 2004) (negative performance evaluation not adverse action because it did not result in any tangible job detriment).

38. *Montandon v Farmland Industries*, 116 F.3d 355, 359 (8th Cir. 1997). See *Settle v Baltimore County*, 34 F. Supp.2d 969, 987-989 (D. Md. 1999) (collecting cases and discussing circuit split); *Webb v CP&L*, 93-ERA-42, D&O of ARB, at 11 (August 26, 1997) (requiring that a "substantial job detriment" be a "predictable and natural outcome" of defendant's alleged adverse action); *Griffith v Wackenhut Corp.*, 97-ERA-52, D&O of ARB, at 12 (February 29, 2000), quoting *Smart and Ball State University*, 89 F.3d 437, 441 (7th Cir. 1996); *Heno v Sprint/United Management Co.*, 208 F.3d 84 (10th Cir. 2000).

39. *Smyth v Johnson Controls*, 98-ERA-23, D&O of ARB (June 29, 2001).

40. *Wanamaker v Columbian Rope Co.*, 108 F.3d 462, 466 (2nd Cir. 1997).

CHAPTER 10

1. 15 U.S.C. § 1514A(b)(2)(A).

2. 49 U.S.C. § 42121(b)(3)(B).

3. Senate Report No. 107-146, p. 20.

4. *Nord v U.S. Steel Corp.*, 758 F.2d 1462, 1470-1471 (11th Cir. 1985) ("It is the duty of the district court, after a finding of discrimination, to place the injured party in the position he or she would have been absent the discriminatory actions."). Accord., *Getman v Southwest Securities*, 2003-SOX-8, D&O of ALJ, pp. 19–20 (February 2, 2004) ('The purpose of a back pay award is to make the employee whole, that is, to restore the employee to the same position she would have been in if not discriminated against.").

5. 422 U.S. 405, 418-420 (1975).

6. 422 U.S. 405, 418-419, quoting *Wicker v Hoppock*, 6 Wall. 94, 99 (1867).

7. *Reeves v Claiborne County*, 828 F.2d 1096, 1101 (5th Cir. 1987) ("Reinstatement" is "normally integral part of the remedy for a constitutionally impermissible employment action").

8. *Hobby v Georgia Power Co.*, 90-ERA-30, R. D&O of ALJ, at 48 (September 17, 1998). See also Penina Glazer and Myron Glazer, *The Whistleblowers: Exposing Corruption in Government and Industry* (New York: Basic Books, 1989).

9. See, for example, 42 U.S.C. § 5851(b).

10. *Reeves v Claiborne County Bd. of Ed.*, 828 F.2d 1096, 1101 (5th Cir. 1987).

11. *Allen v Autauga County Bd. of Ed.*, 685 F.2d 1302, 1306 (11th Cir. 1982). Accord., *Jackson v City of Albuquerque*, 890 F.2d 225, 234-235 (10th Cir. 1989); *Reeves*

v Claiborne County Bd. of Ed., at 1102. But see *McNight v General Motors Corp.*, 908 F.2d 104 (7th Cir. 1990) (discussing benefits of front pay in lieu of reinstatement).

12. *Hobby v Georgia Power Company*, 90-ERA-30, D&O on Damages by ARB, pp. 6-13 (February 9, 2001) (discussing rules related to reinstatement).

13. *Creekmore v ABB Power Systems*, 93-ERA-24, Supplemental Order of Deputy Sec. of Labor, at 3 (April 10, 1996).

14. *Sterzing v Fort Bend Ind. Sch. Dist.*, 496 F.2d 92, 93 (5th Cir. 1974). Accord., *Donnellon v Fruehauf Corp.*, 794 F.2d 598, 602 (11th Cir. 1986).

15. *Jackson v City of Albuquerque*, 890 F.2d 235.

16. *Tualatin Elec., Inc. v NLRB*, 84 F.3d 1202, 1205 (9th Cir. 1996).

17. *Tualatin Elec., Inc. v NLRB*, 84 F.3d 1205-1206.

18. *Tualatin Elec., Inc. v NLRB*, 84 F.3d 1206. Accord., *NLRB v Draper Corp.*, 159 F.2d 294, 297 (1st Cir. 1947); *NLRB v Jackson Farmers, Inc.*, 457 F.2d 516, 518 (10th Cir. 1972).

19. *Pecker v Heckler*, 801 F.2d 709, 712-713 (4th Cir. 1986).

20. *Hobby v Georgia Power Company*, 90-ERA-30, D&O on Damages by ARB, pp. 12-13 (February 9, 2001) and D&O of ALJ on Damages, pp. 54-57. Also see, for example, *Creekmore v ABB Power Systems* (June 20, 1996) (even after sale of a subsidiary the company that retained liability was obligated to reinstate the complainant to a substantially similar position); *DeFord v TVA*, 81-ERA-1 (Sec'y. August 16, 1984) (the SOL stated that, "[i]f [complainant's] former position no longer exists or there is no vacancy, TVA shall apply to the Administrative Law Judge for approval of the job in which it proposes to place DeFord with an explanation of the duties, functions, responsibilities, physical location and working conditions.").

21. *Kuepferle v Johnson Controls, Inc.*, 713 F. Supp. 171, 173 (M.D. N.C. 1988); *Sennello v Reserve Life Ins.*, 667 F. Supp. 1498, 1522 (S.D. Fla. 1987).

22. *NLRB v Taylor Mach. Products*, 136 F.2d 507, 516 (6th Cir. 1998).

23. *Firefighters v Stotts*, 467 U.S. 561, 579 (1983); *Walsdorf v Board of Commissioners*, 857 F.2d 1047, 1054 (5th Cir. 1988); *Hicks v Dothan City Bd. of Ed.*, 814 F. Supp. 1044, 1050 (M.D. Ala. 1993) (equitable power includes "authority to displace" an "incumbent employee").

24. *Walters v City of Atlanta*, 803 F.2d 1138, 1149 (11th Cir. 1986).

25. *Nolan v AC Express*, 92-STA-37, Remand Order of SOL, at 15-16 (January 17, 1995).

26. *Nolan v AC Express*, 92-STA-37, Remand Order of SOL, at 15-16.

27. *Pollard v E.I. du Pont*, 532 U.S. 843, 850 (2001).

28. *Blum v Witco Chem. Corp.*, 829 F.2d 367, 374 (3rd Cir. 1987).

29. *EEOC v Prudential Federal Sav.*, 763 F.2d 1166, 1172 (10th Cir. 1985).

30. *Clifton v U.P.S.*, 94-STA-16, D&O of ARB, at 2 (May 14, 1997). See also *Hobby v Georgia Power Co.*, 90-ERA-30, R. D&O of ALJ, at 54-57, for a discussion of when to order reinstatement or front pay.

31. *Wilson v A.M. General Corp.*, 979 F. Supp. 800, 802 (N.D. Ind. 1997).

32. *Johnson v Old Dominion*, 86-CAA-3/4/5, D&O of SOL, at 25 (May 29, 1991).

33. *NLRB v J. H. Rutter-Rex*, 396 U.S. 258, 263 (1969).

34. *Hobby v Georgia Power Co.*, 90-ERA-30, R. D&O of ALJ, at 57 (internal citations omitted), aff'd ARB and U.S. Court of Appeals for the 11th Circuit. Accord., *Clifton v U.P.S.*, 94-STA-16, D&O of SOL, at 2 (May 14, 1997) (under Surface Transportation whistleblower provision back pay "is not a matter of discretion but is mandated once it is determined" that the act was violated).

35. *Pettway v American Cast Iron Pipe Co.*, 494 F.2d 211, 260-261 (5th Cir. 1974); *Clay v Castle Coal & Oil Company*, 90-STA-37, D&O of SOL at 2 (June 3, 1994) (STA whistleblower case); *Lederhaus v Donald Paschen*, 91-ERA-13, D&O of SOL, at 9-10 (October 26, 1992) (nuclear whistleblower); *Hoffman v W. Max Bossert*, 94-CAA-4, D&O of SOL, at 2 (January 22, 1997) (environmental case). *Getman v Southwest Securities*, 2003-SOX-8, D&O of ALJ, p. 20 (February 2, 2004) (Sarbanes-Oxley whistleblower case).

36. *Ross v Buckeye Cellulose Corp.*, 764 F. Supp. 1543, 1547 (M.D. Ga. 1991) (citations omitted). Revsd on other grounds, 980 F.2d 648 (11th Cir. 1993). See also *IBT v U.S.*, 431 U.S. 324, 372 (1977).

37. *Ross v Buckeye Cellulose Corp.*, 764 F. Supp. 1543, 1547. Accord., *EEOC v Korn Industries, Inc.*, 622 F.2d 256, 263 (4th Cir. 1981).

38. *Cook v Guardian Lubricants*, 95-STA-43, D&O of remand by SOL, at 3 (May 30, 1997); *Creekmore v ABB Power Systems*, 93-ERA-24 D&O of ARB, at 4 (June 20, 1996).

39. *Assistant Secretary of Labor v T. O. Haas Tire Company*, 94-STA-2, D&O of SOL, at 9 (August 3, 1994).

40. *Dutile v Tighe Trucking, Inc.*, 93-STA-31, D&O of SOL, at 3-4 (October 31, 1994).

41. *Doyle v Hydro*, 89-ERA-22, Final D&O of ARB (May 17, 2000), reversed on other grounds (3rd Cir. 2002).

42. *Polgar v Florida Stage Lines*, 94-STA-46, modified D&O of SOL, at 3 (June 5, 1995).

43. *O'Brien v Stone & Webster Eng. Corp.*, 84-ERA-31, recommended D&O of ALJ, at 21 (February 28, 1985); *Landers v Commonwealth-Lord Joint Venture*, 83-ERA-5, slip op. of ALJ, at 16-17, adopted by SOL (1983); *Blackburn v Martin*, 982 F.2d 125 (4th Cir. 1992).

44. *Fischer v Town of Steilacoom*, 83-WPC-2, slip op. of ALJ, at 10 (1983); *Tritt v Fluor Constructors*, 88-ERA-29, D&O of remand by SOL, at 6 (March 16, 1995).

45. *Hufstetler v Roadway Express, Inc.*, 85-STA-8, D&O of SOL, at 58-59 (August 21, 1986). See, for example, *Donovan v Freeway Constr. Co.*, 551 P. Supp. 869, 880-881 (D. R.I. 1982).

46. *Donovan v Freeway Constr. Co.*, 551 P. Supp. 869, 880-881; *Blum v Witco Chemical Corp.*, 829 F.2d 367, 374 (3rd Cir. 1987).

47. *Blum v Witco Chemical Corp.*, 829 F.2d 367, 374 ; *Dutile v Tighe Trucking, Inc.*, 93-STA-31, D&O of SOL, at 3.

48. *Dutile v Tighe Trucking, Inc.*, 93-STA-31, D&O of SOL, at 3. Accord., *Sands v Runyon*, 28 F.3d 1323, 1329 (2nd Cir. 1994); *Bascom v APT Transportation*, 92-STA-32, D&O of ALJ, at 4 (September 14, 1992), aff'd by SOL (November 9, 1992).

49. *Chase v Buncombe County, N.C.*, 85-SWD-4, D&O of remand by SOL, at 6-7 (November 3, 1986).

50. *Bassett v Niagara Mohawk Power Co.*, 86-ERA-2, order of remand by SOL, at 4 (July 9, 1986).

51. *Crow v Noble Roman's Inc.*, 95-CAA-8, D&O of SOL, at 5 (February 26, 1996); *Blake v Hatfield Elec. Co.*, 87-ERA-4, recommended decision by ALJ, at 23-24 (August 13, 1987).

52. *Blake v Hatfield Elec. Co.*, 87-ERA-4, recommended decision by ALJ, at 23-24.

53. *Earwood v Dart Container*, 93-STA-16, D&O of SOL, at 6 (December 7, 1994).

54. *Cook v Guardian Lubricants*, 95-STA-43, D&O of remand by SOL, at 13.

55. *Edwards v Hodel*, 738 F. Supp. 426, 431 (D. Colo. 1990).

56. *Moyer v Yellow Freight*, 89-STA-7, D&O of SOL, at 17 (August 21, 1995).

57. *Clifton v U.P.S.*, 94-STA-16, D&O of ARB, at 3.

58. *Hoffman v W. Max Bossert*, 94-CAA-4, D&O of SOL, at 8 (January 22, 1997) (employer ordered to pay for schooling); *Studer v Flowers Baking Company*, 93-CAA-11, D&O of SOL, at 4 (June 19, 1995) (denial of training is adverse action).

59. *Creekmore v ABB Power*, 93-ERA-24, D&O of remand by SOL, at 26 (February 14, 1996); *Lansdale v Intermodal*, 94-STA-22, D&O of SOL, at 5 (July 26, 1995).

60. *Creekmore v ABB Power Systems*, 93-ERA-24 at 27.

61. *Dutile v Tighe Trucking, Inc.*, 93-STA-31, D&O of SOL, at 6-7.

62. *Creekmore v ABB Power Systems*, 93-ERA-24 at 21-22; *Hobby v Georgia Power Company*, 90-ERA-30, R. D&O of ALJ, at 64-65.

63. *Boytin v PP&L*, 94-ERA-32, D&O of remand by SOL, at 12 (October 20, 1995).

64. *Hobby v Georgia Power Company*, 90-ERA-30, D&O of ARB on Damages, pp. 36-42 (February 9, 2001), affirmed, Case No. 01-10916 (11th Cir. 2002).

65. *Phelps Dodge Corp. v NLRB*, 313 U.S. 188.

66. 15 U.S.C. 1514A(c)(2)(B). For a description of how the Department of Labor calculates interest, see *Hobby v Georgia Power Company*, 90-ERA-30, D&O of ARB on Damages, pp. 40-41 (February 9, 2001).

67. *Pogue v United States Dept. of the Navy*, 87-ERA-21, D&O on Remand by SOL, at 7 (April 14, 1994).

68. *Pogue v United States Dept. of the Navy*, 87-ERA-21, D&O on Remand by SOL, at 7.

69. 15 U.S.C. 1514A(c)(2)(C).

70. *Hammond v Northland Counseling Center*, 218 F.3d 886, 892-93 (8th Cir. 2000).

71. *Neal v Honeywell, Inc.*, 191 F.3d 827,832 (7th Cir. 1999).

72. *Smith v Atlas Off-Shore Boat Serv, Inc.*, 653 F.2d 1057, 1064 (5th Cir. 1981).

73. *English v Whitfield*, 868 F.2d 957 (4th Cir. 1988).

74. *Van der Meer v Western Kentucky University*, 95-ERA-38, D&O of ARB, at 8-9 (April 20, 1998); *Leveille v N.Y. Air National Guard*, 94-TSC-3/4, D&O of ARB (October 25, 1999).

75. *Neal v Honeywell, Inc.*, 995 F. Supp. 889, 895 (E.D. Ill. 1998).

76. *Neal v Honeywell, Inc.*, 995 F. Supp. 889, 895.

77. *Neal v Honeywell, Inc.*, 995 F. Supp. 889, 895.

78. *Creekmore v ABB Power*, 93-ERA-24, D&O of remand by SOL, at 26.

79. *Walters v City of Atlanta*, 803 F.2d 1135, 1146 (11th Cir. 1986).

80. *Muldrew v Anheuser-Busch, Inc.*, 728 F.2d 989, 992, n. 1 (8th Cir. 1984); *Wulf v City of Wichita*, 883 F.2d 842, 875 (10th Cir. 1989); *Assistant Secretary v Guaranteed Overnight Delivery*, 95-STA-37, D&O of ARB, at 2-3 (September 5, 1996).

81. 82-ERA-3, slip. op. of ALJ, at 7-8 (1982).

82. *Carey v Piphus*, 435 U.S. 264 n. 20; *Lederhaus v Donald Baschen*, 91-ERA-13, D&O of SOL, at 10.

83. *Hobby v Georgia Power Co.*, 90-ERA-30, R. D&O of ALJ, at 65-67, affirmed by the DOL ARB and U.S. Court of Appeals for the 11th Circuit.

84. *Hobby v Georgia Power Company*, 90-ERA-30, D&O of ARB on Damages, p. 20 (February 9, 2001), quoting from *Rasimas v Michigan Dep't of Mental Health*, 714 F.2d 614, 624 (6th Cir. 1983).

85. *Hobby v Georgia Power Company*, 90-ERA-30, D&O of ARB on Damages, p. 20 (February 9, 2001) (quoting from other cases). For additional cases on mitigation, see Kohn, *Concepts and Procedures in Whistleblower Law*, pp. 340–343.

CHAPTER 11

1. *Hammond v Northland Counseling Center*, 218 F.3d 886, 894 (8th Cir. 2000).

2. 18 U.S.C. § 1514A(c)(1) & (2)(C).

3. The Civil Rights Attorney's Fee Act, 42 U.S.C. § 1988, contains weaker language: "[T]he court, in its discretion, may allow the prevailing party, other than the United States, a reasonable attorney's fee as part of the cost."

4. *Olsovsky v Shell Western*, 96-CAA-1, D&O of ARB, at 3 (April 10, 1997). See also *Assistant Secretary v Florilli Corp.*, 91-STA-7, Order Denying Fee Application of SOL (October 22, 1992) (holding that employer is not entitled to fees under Equal Access to Justice Act).

5. *Abrams v Roadway Express, Inc.*, 84-STA-2, D&O of SOL (May 25, 1985). Employers may obtain a sanction "not exceeding $1,000.00" in attorney fees if the DOL were to hold that a complaint was "frivolous or was brought in bad faith," a small monetary sanction if a complaint was filed in "bad faith." 29 C.F.R. 1980.109(b).

6. *Ishmael v Calibur Systems*, 96-SWD-2, D&O of ARB, at 2 (October 17, 1997); *Berkman v U.S. Coast Guard Academy*, 97-CAA-2, D&O of Remand by ARB, at 33 (February 29, 2000).

7. *Goldstein v EBASCO Constr., Inc.*, 86-ERA-36, recommended supplemental D&O of ALJ, at 2 (May 17, 1988). D&O of SOL, at 26-27 (April 7, 1992); *Pittman v Goggin Truck Line*, 96-STA-25, ARB Order (July 30, 1999). *Blackburn v Reich*, 79 F.3d 1375 (4th Cir. 1996), Recommended D&O on remand by ALJ, at 7 (February 13, 1989); *Delcore v W. J. Barney Corp.*, 89-ERA-38, D&O of SOL, at 2 (June 9, 1995). Order of ARB (October 31, 1996). See also *Pittman v Goggin Truck Line*, 96-STA-25, ARB Order (July 30, 1999); *Mackowiak v University Nuclear Systems, Inc.*, 82-ERA-8, D& O on Remand by ALJ (July 28, 1986). But see *DeFord v Secretary of Labor*, 700 F.2d 281, 286.

8. 49 U.S.C. § 42121(b)(5) and (6), incorporated into the SOX through 15 U.S.C. § 1514A(b)(2)(A).

9. 885 F.2d 551, 558-559 (9th Cir. 1989).

10. See *Berkman v U.S. Coast Guard Academy*, 97-CAA-2, D&O of Remand by ARB, at 33 (February 29, 2000). (Citing case in which public relations work was compensable).

11. In enacting section 1988, Congress recognized the necessity of including attorney fees and costs as part of any recovery: "[i]f private citizens are to be able to assert their civil rights, and if those who violate the Nation's fundamental laws are not to proceed with impunity, then citizens must have the opportunity to recover what it costs them to vindicate these rights in court." S.Rep. 94-1011, at 3 (1976), reprinted in 1976 U.S.C.C.A.N. 5908, 5910. Since the passage of section 1988, the courts have "interpreted" the various fee-shifting statutes in a consistent manner. *Buckhannon Bd & Care Home, Inc. v West Virginia Dept. of Health & Human Services*, 532 U.S. 598, 603 n. 4 (2001).

12. *Hensley v Eckerhart*, 461 U.S. 424, 429 (1983), quoting, in part, H.R. Rep. 94-1558, at 1 (1976) (internal quotations omitted).

13. *Blum v Stenson*, 465 U.S. 886, 897 (1984). Accord., *Valley Disposal v Central Vermont Solid Waste*, 113 F.3d 357, 361 (2nd Cir. 1997); *Goos v National Association of Realtors*, 68 F.3d 1380, 1386 (D.C. Cir. 1995) (ability to obtain counsel who will provide "zealous representation").

14. *Hoffman v W. Max Bossert*, 94-CAA-4, D&O of ARB, at 5 (January 22, 1997).

15. *City of Riverside v Rivera*, 477 U.S. 561, 574 (1986) (J. Brennan, plurality).

16. 478 U.S. 546, 565 (1986).

17. 461 U.S. 424, 433-434 (1983). Accord., *Building Serv Local 47 Cleaning Contractors Pension Plan v Grandview Raceway*, 46 F.3d 1392 (6th Cir. 1995); *City of Burlington v Dague*, 505 U.S. 557 (1992); *Lederhaus v Paschen et al.*, 91-ERA-13, D&O of SOL (January 13, 1993).

18. 461 U.S. 424, 433-434 (1983).

19. *Hilton v Glas-Tec Corp.*, 84-STA-6, D&O awarding attorney fees by SOL, at 2-3 (July 15, 1986). See also *Pogue v U.S. Dept. of Navy*, 87-ERA-21 D&O of SOL, D&O awarding attorney fees by ALJ (March 24, 1988), vacated on other grounds by SOL (May 10, 1990).

20. *Pennsylvania v Delaware Valley Citizens Council for Clean Air*, 478 U.S. 546, 562 (1986); *Goldstein v EBASCO Constr., Inc.*, 86-ERA-36, recommended supplemental D&O of ALJ, at 2 (May 17, 1988).

21. *Thurman v Yellow Freight Systems*, 90 F.3d 1160, 1170 (6th Cir. 1996). In *Thurman*, the plaintiff only partially prevailed in his claims and was denied requests for reinstatement, compensatory and punitive damages, prejudgment interest, and front pay. *Thurman v Yellow Freight Systems*, 90 F. at 1164. In addition, the plaintiff was only successful on "two of his original six claims." *Thurman v Yellow Freight Systems*, 90 F. at 1169. Despite this limited success, the Court affirmed a reduction of only 5 percent of the requested fee. *Thurman v Yellow Freight Systems*, 90 F at 1170.

22. *Hensley v Eckerhart*, 461 U.S. 424, 436 (1983); *Scott v Roadway Express, Inc.*, 98-STA-8, D&O of ARB, at 17 (July 28, 1999).

23. The most "appropriate starting point for selecting the proper rate . . . is the community in which the court sits." *National Wildlife Federation v Hanson*, 859 F.2d 313, 317 (4th Cir. 1988). However, courts will also "entertain circumstances beyond the venue of the location" of the trial court in considering the most applicable markets. *Hoch v Clark County Health Dist.*, 98-CAA-12, Supplemental Order of ALJ, at 1 (March 15, 2000).

24. 488 F.2d 714, 718 (5th Cir. 1974).

25. *Blanchard v Bergeron*, 489 U.S. 87, 91-92 (1989).

26. See, for example, *Hamlin v Charter Township of Flint*, 165 F.3d 426, 437 (6th Cir. 1999).

27. If more than one attorney is involved, the possibility of duplication of effort along with the proper utilization of time should be scrutinized. It is appropriate to distinguish between legal work, in the strict sense, and investigation, clerical work, compilation of facts and statistics, and other work that can often be accomplished by nonlawyers.

28. See *Johnson v Georgia Highway Exp., Inc.*, 488 F.2d 714, 717-719 (5th Cir. 1974). The DOL has utilized this matrix and awarded premium rates to "experienced and skilled" attorneys for work on "complex and demanding" cases. *Hobby*

v *Georgia Power Company*, 90-ERA-30, Recommended D&O on Attorney Fees by ALJ, p. 3 (November 21, 2001).

29. *Farrar v Hobby*, 506 U.S. 103 (1992); 113 S.Ct. 566, 569 (1992).

30. *Covington v District of Columbia*, 57 F.3d 1101, 1111-1112 (D.C. Cir. 1995).

31. *Jenkins v U.S. E.P.A.*, 92-CAA-6, Final Decision of the Secretary of Labor, at 2 (December 7, 1994), citing *Hensley v Eckerhart*, 461 U.S. 424, 436 (1983). The Administrative Review Board has noted that use of the "lodestar method" of determining the "proper amount of attorney's fees" in "environmental whistleblower" claims is a "longstanding practice of the Department of Labor." *Van der Meer v Western Kentucky University*, 95-ERA-38, D&O of ARB, at 9. Accord., *Berkman v U.S. Coast Guard Academy*, 97-CAA-2, D&O of Remand by ARB, at 33 (February 29, 2000).

32. *Wieb van der Meer v Western Kentucky University*, 95-ERA-38, D&O of ARB, at 10.

33. *Blum v Stenson*, 465 U.S. 886, 894 (1984).

34. *Murry v Air Ride, Inc.*, 99-STA-34, D&O of ARB, p. 8 (December 29, 2000) (applying fee rates to private counsel in accordance with the *Laffey* matrix utilized by federal courts in the District of Columbia).

35. *Buckhannon Bd & Care Home, Inc. v West Virginia Dept. of Health & Human Services*, 532 U.S. 598, 603 n. 4 (2001).

36. 461 U.S. 424, 440 (1983).

37. *Gutierrez v Regents of the University of California*, 98-ERA-19, Order Awarding Attorney Fees by ARB, p. 3 (February 6, 2004).

38. *Blanchard v Bergeron*, 489 U.S. 87, 96 (1989). See, *Lederhaus v Paschen et al.*, 91-ERA-13, D&O of SOL (January 13, 1993). ("Respondents are liable only for reasonable attorney fees no matter what amount Complainant may have contracted to pay his attorney."). *Delcore v W. J. Barney Corp.*, 89-ERA-38, D&O of SOL, at 2 (June 9, 1995).

39. *Marek v Chesney*, 437 U.S. 1, 6-7 (1985).

40. *Washington v Philadelphia County*, 89 F.3d 1031, 1035 (3rd Cir. 1996).

41. The local market rate is usually based on rates applied in the geographic area where the trial court is located. However, "rates outside the forum may be used if local counsel was unavailable, either because they were unwilling or unable to perform or because they lack the degree of experience, expertise, or specialization required to handle the case." *Barjon v Dalton*, 132 F.3d 496, 500 (9th Cir. 1997). See, for example, *Casey v City of Cabool, Mo.*, 12 F.3d 799, 805 (3rd Cir. 1993) ("a market for a particular legal specialization may provide the appropriate market"); *Howes v Medical Components*, 761 F. Supp. 1193, 1195 (E.D. Pa. 1990) (rate paid at attorney's business location, if there is a "good reason"). *Ihler v Chisholm*, 995 P.2d 439 (Mont. 2000) (out-of-state rates if reasonable).

42. *Laffey v Northwest Airlines, Inc.*, 572 F. Supp. 354, 371-372 (D. D.C. 1983). Accord., *Blum v Stenson*, 465 U.S. 886, 896 n. 11 (1984); *Clay v Castle Coal*, 90-STA-37, D&O of SOL, at 7 (June 3, 1994).

43. *Hensley v Eckerhart*, 461 U.S. 424, 436 (1983).

44. 89 F.3d 1031, 1037-38 (3rd Cir. 1996).

45. *City of Burlington v Dague*, 505 U.S. 557 (1992). Accord., *Lederhaus v Paschen et al.*, 91-ERA-13, D&O of SOL (January 13, 1993). However, in some cases a fee enhancement above the loadstar rate may be available. *Guam Society of Obstetricians v Ada*, 100 F.3d 691, 697 (9th Cir. 1996).

46. *Howes v Medical Comp.*, 761 F. Supp. 1193, 1196 (E.D. Pa. 1990); *Drew v Alpine, Inc.*, 2001-STA-47, D&O of ARB adopting recommended findings of ALJ (June 30, 2003), RDO of ALJ on fees, p. 2 (April 22, 2002) (permitting out-of-state attorney to bill at higher rates than local attorney fee rates).

47. *Hardrick v Airway Freight Systems*, 2000 WL 263687 (N.D. Ill. 2000), citing *Blum v Stenson*, 465 U.S. 886 (1984), *Save Our Cumberland Mountains, Inc. v Hodel*, 857 F.2d 1516 (D.C. Cir. 1988) (en banc), and *Barrow v Falck*, 977 F.2d 1100, 1105 (7th Cir. 1992). Accord., *Goos v National Ass'n of Realtors*, 997 F.2d 1565, 1568 (D.C.Cir.1993) ("[A]ttorneys who quote a client a discounted rate to reflect non-economic goals may be compensated at prevailing market rates."); *Central States Pension Fund v Central States Cartage Co.*, 76 F.3d 114, 117 (7th Cir.1996) (Pension funds are entitled to fees on the basis of prevailing market rate, and not the rate paid to staff counsel, because "the court should make an award representing the cost the victorious litigant would have incurred to buy legal services in the market, no matter how the litigant acquired those services.")

48. 477 U.S. 561 (1986).

49. *Hoffman v W. Max Bossert*, 94-CAA-4, D&O of ARB, at 5 (January 22, 1997).

50. *Evans v Jeff D.*, 475 U.S. 717 (1986).

51. *Evans v Jeff D.*, 475 U.S 765 (J. Brennan, dissenting). Complainant's counsel may avoid the harshness of this waiver rule by having the client contractually agree not to waive the statutory fee. *Evans v Jeff D.*, 475 U.S. 766 (J. Brennan, dissenting).

52. *Missouri v Jenkins*, 491 U.S. 274, 284 (1989); *Barjon v Dalton*, 132 F.3d 496, 502 (9th Cir. 1997); *Covington v District of Columbia*, 839 F. Supp. 894, 902 (D. D.C. 1993); *Blackburn v Reich*, 79 F.3d 1375 (4th Cir. 1996), *Larry v Detroit Edison Co.*, 86-ERA-32, D&O on Costs by SOL, at 4 (May 19, 1992).

53. 491 U.S. at 283, n. 6 (1989).

54. *Hensley v Northwest Permanente P.C. Retirement Plan and Trust*, 1999 WL 1271576 (D. Or. 1999).

55. *Blackburn v Reich*, 79 F.3d 1375 (4th Cir. 1996); *Phelan v Bell*, 8 F.3d 369, 375 (6th Cir. 1993).

56. See, for example, *Hernandez v George*, 793 F.2d 264, 269 (10th Cir. 1986); *Schuenemeyer v United States*, 776 F.2d 329, 333 (Fed. Cir. 1985); *Tyler Business Servs., Inc. v NLRB*, 695 F.2d 73, 77 (4th Cir. 1982); *Larry v Detroit Edison Co.*, 86-ERA-32, D&O on Costs by SOL, at 4 (May 19, 1992). See also *Simmons v Florida Power Corp.*, 89-ERA-28/29, R. Supplement D&O, at 6-8 (April 11, 1990); *Clay v Castle Coal*, 90-STA-37, D&O of SOL, at 7 (June 3, 1994).

57. *Doyle v Hydro Nuclear Services*, 89-ERA-22, R. D&O of ALJ, at 2 (July 16, 1996), aff'd, ARB Final D&O, at 10 (September 6, 1996). See also *Public Interest Research Group v Windall*, 51 F.3d 1179, 1190 (3rd Cir. 1995).

58. 29 C.F.R. § 18.54(c); *Williams v TIW Fabrication*, 88-SWD-3, deferral of consideration of motion for attorney fees by ALJ (August 3, 1989).

59. *White v New Hampshire Dept. of Employment Security*, 455 U.S. 445 (1982).

60. This statutory language would appear to address concerns raised by the Supreme Court's decision in *Buckhannon Bd. & CareHome, Inc. v West Virginia Dept. of Health & Human Services*, 532 U.S. 598, 603 n.4 (2001), in which the Court had rejected the "catalyst theory" regarding fee awards under the Civil Rights Act.

61. *Laffey v Northwest Airlines, Inc.*, 572 F. Supp. 354, 371-372 (D. D.C. 1983). Accord., *Blum v Stenson*, 465 U.S. 886, 896 n. 11 (1984).

62. *Johnson v Bechtel Construction*, 95-ERA-11, Supplemental Order of SOL, at 2 (February 26, 1996).

63. *Laffey v Northwest Airlines, Inc.*, 572 F. Supp. 354, 371-372 (D. D.C. 1983). Accord., *Blum v Stenson*, 465 U.S. 886, 896 n. 11 (1984).

64. *Blum v Stenson*, 465 U.S. 886, 896 n. 11, at 382.

65. *Goldstein v EBASCO Constr., Inc.*, 86-ERA-36, recommended supplemental D&O of ALJ, at 2 (May 17, 1988). D&O of SOL, at 26-27 (April 7, 1992); *Johnson v Transco Prods. Inc.*, 85-ERA-7, supp. D&O of ALJ, at 2 (March 29, 1985).

66. *Missouri v Jenkins*, 491 U.S. 274 (1989).

67. *Ass't. Sec'y. v Consolidated Freightways*, 98-STA-26, D&O of ARB, at 8 (April 22, 1999).

68. See, for example, *Spanish Action Committee of Chicago v Chicago*, 811 F.2d 1129 (7th Cir. 1987); *Northcross v Board of Ed. of Memphis City Schools*, 611 F.2d 624, 632 (6th Cir. 1979) cert. denied, 447 U.S. 911; *Wheeler v Durham City Bd. of Education*, 585 F.2d 618, 623 (4th Cir. 1978); *Ramos v Lamm*, 632 F. Supp. 376 (D. Colo. 1986); *Population Servs. Intl. v Carey*, 476 F. Supp 4, 8 (S.D. N.Y 1979); *Larry v Detroit Edison Co.*, 86-ERA-32, D&O on Costs by SOL, at 4 (May 19, 1992).

69. *Tritt v Fluor Constructors*, 88-ERA-29, D&O of SOL, at 5 (March 16, 1995).

70. 499 U.S. 83 (1991).

71. 18 U.S.C. § 1514A(c)(2)(C).

CHAPTER 12

1. 29 C.F.R. § 1980.111(d)(1) (providing that OSHA must approve settlements entered into between the parties during the OSHA investigatory stage of the proceeding); 29 C.F.R. § 1980.111(d)(2) (requiring settlements entered into by the parties during the adjudicatory stage of the proceeding be approved by an Administrative Law Judge or the Administrative Review Board); 29 C.F.R. § 1980.108(a)(1) (granting authority to the Assistant Secretary of Labor for OSHA to file a petition for review related to the contents of a settlement agreement); 29 C.F.R. § 1980.108(a)(1); 29 C.F.R. § 1980.111(e) (settlements approved by the DOL constitute the "final order" of the DOL and may be enforced in federal court).

2. The Aviation Investment and Reform Act for the 21st Century (AIR 21), 49 U.S.C. § 42121(b)(3)(A), contained a mandatory settlement approval provision identical to that found within the Energy Reorganization Act. The case law under these laws unquestionably mandated DOL approval of settlement agreements. *Thompson v DOL*, 885 F.2d 551; *Macktal v SOL*, 923 F.2d 1150, 1153-54 (5th Cir. 1991); *Beliveau v DOL*, 170 F.3d 83 (1st Cir. 1999). The settlement-approval provision of AIR 21 was directly incorporated by reference into the SOX. 18 U.S.C. § 1514A(b)(2)(A). If, after the expiration of the 180 mandatory administrative review, an employee files a SOX claim in federal court, the controlling case law and regulations are not clear on the responsibility of either a federal court or the DOL to approve the agreement. In any event, if a case is settled without DOL approval, the employer is at risk of a collateral attack on the agreement by an employee. For example, under DOL case law, if the DOL finds an agreement void under public policy, the employee is permitted to keep the proceeds he or she obtained from the voided agreement, and the employee's discrimination case can

be reinstated. *Harris v TVA*, 97-ERA-26/50, Order Vacating Orders and Remanding Case by ARB, p. 11, n. 9 (November 29, 2000).

3. *Faust v Chemical Leaman Tank Lines*, 92-SWD-2/93-STA-15, D&O of ARB, at 3 (June 13, 1996); *Fuchko et al. v Georgia Power Co.*, 89-ERA-9/10, order to submit settlement agreement by SOL, at 2 (March 23, 1989); *Baena v Atlas Air, Inc.*, 02-AIR-4, Final Order Approving Settlement by ARB (January 10, 2003).

4. *McClure v Interstate Facilities, Inc.*, 92-WPC-2, D&O of SOL, at 3-4 (June 19, 1995); *Beliveau v Dept. of Labor*, 170 F.3d 83, 88 (1st Cir. 1999).

5. See U.S. Senate Subcommittee on Nuclear Regulation, *Hearings on Secret Settlement Agreements Restricting Testimony at Comanche Peak Nuclear Power Plant, etc.*, pp. 131–134, Senate hearing 101-190 (May 4, 1989) (hereinafter U.S. Senate Subcommittee hearings).

6. See Senate Hearing 101-90, Opening Statement of Sen. John Breaux, Chairman, at 2-3 (May 4, 1989).

7. See Senate Hearing 101-90, Opening Statement of Sen. John Breaux, Chairman, at 45 (May 4, 1989).

8. See *Khandelwal v Southern California Edison*, 97-ERA-6, Order of Remand by ARB (March 31, 1998).

9. See *Macktal v SOL*, 923 F. 2d. 1150 ; *Macktal v Brown & Root, Inc.*, 86-ERA-23, SOL Order Disapproving Settlement (October 13, 1993).

10. *CP&L v DOL*, 43 F.3d 912 (4th Cir. 1995).

11. See *Macktal v Brown & Root, Inc.*, Order of SOL (July 11, 1995) (finding DOL without authority to order employee to return settlement money).

12. See *Khandelwal v Southern California Edison*, 97-ERA-5. Accord., *Oubre v Entergy Op., Inc.*, 522 U.S. 422 (1998).

13. *Delcore v W. J. Barney Corp.*, 89-ERA-38, D&O of SOL (April 19, 1995).

14. See *Connecticut Light & Power v SOL*, 85 F.3d 95 n. 5.

15. See *Connecticut Light & Power v SOL*, 85 F.3d 97.

16. See *In re: JDS Uniphase Corp.*, 238 F.Supp.2d 1127, 1136 (N.D. Calf. 2002).

17. *Faust v Chemical Leaman Tank Lines*, 92-SWD-2/93-STA-15, D&O of ARB, at 2.

18. 29 C.F.R. § 18.9.

19. See, for example, *Marcus v EPA*, 96-CAA-3/7, Order of ARB (October 29, 1999).

20. 29 C.F.R. § 1980.111(d)(2) (requiring settlements entered into by the parties during the adjudicatory stage of the proceeding be approved by an Administrative Law Judge or the Administrative Review Board); 29 C.F.R. § 1980.108(a)(1).

21. 29 C.F.R. § 1980.111(d)(1) (providing that OSHA must approve settlements entered into between the parties during the OSHA investigatory stage of the proceeding).

22. *Rudd v Westinghouse Hanford Co.*, 88-ERA-33, at 11-12 (November 10, 1997), vacated on other grounds by DOL ARB.

23. See, for example, *McDowell v Doyon Drilling Services*, 96-TSC-8, Order of ARB (August 6, 1997).

24. *Biddy v Alyeska Pipeline*, 95-TSC-7, Final D&O of ARB, at 3 (December 3, 1996); *Pletcher v Horizon Air*, 2002-AIR-20, D&O of ALJ (March 11, 2003).

25. *Fuchko et al. v Georgia Power Co.*, 89-ERA-9/10, order to submit settlement agreement by SOL, at 2.

26. *Carter v Electrical District No. 2*, 92-TSC-11, Order of OAA, at 2-3 (April 24, 1996); *Debose v CP&L*, 92-ERA-14, Order of SOL (February 7, 1994); *McDowell v*

Doyon Drilling Services, 96-TSC-8, D&O of remand of ARB (May 19, 1997); *Goehring v Koppell Steel Corp.*, 97-ERA-11, Order of ARB (April 10, 1997); *Fuchko et al. v Georgia Power Co.*, 89-ERA-9/10, Order of SOL (June 13, 1994).

27. *McGlynn v Pulsair, Inc.*, 93-CAA-2, Order of SOL, at 2 (June 28, 1993).

28. *Stephenson v NASA*, 94-TSC-5, Order of SOL (June 19, 1995).

29. *McDowell v Doyon Drilling Services*, 96-TSC-8, Order of ARB (August 6, 1997)

30. *Thompson v DOL*, 885 F.2d 551, 556 (9th Cir. 1989).

31. *Hoffman v Fuel Economy Contracting et al.*, 87-ERA-33, order to submit settlement by SOL (August 10, 1988); *Fuchko et al. v Georgia Power Co.*, 89, order to submit settlement by SOL (March 23, 1989)-ERA-9/10.

32. *Tankersley v Triple Crown*, 92-STA-8, D&O of SOL, at 2 (October 17, 1994). See also *Trice v Bartlett Nuclear,* 97-ERA-40, Order of ARB, at 3 n. 2 (August 28, 1998) (parties bound by agreement even if one "subsequently believes the agreement is disadvantageous").

33. *O'Sullivan et al. v Northeast Nuclear Energy Co.*, 88-ERA-37/38, recommended D&O of ALJ, at 2-3; *Tankersley v Triple Crown*, 92-STA-8, D&O of SOL, at 2 (October 17, 1994); *Eash v Roadway Express,* 98-STA-28, D&O of remand by ARB (October 29, 1999) (rejecting oral agreement).

34. *Leidigh v Freightway Corp.*, 87-STA-12, Order of SOL, at 4 (January 22, 1995).

35. *Harris v TVA.*, 97-ERA-26/50, Order of ARB, pp. 10-11 (November 29, 2000).

36. *Aurich v Consolidated Edison Co.*, 86-CAA-2, order approving settlement by SOL (July 29, 1987); *Egenrieder v Metropolitan Edison Co.*, 85-ERA-23, order approving settlement (April 11, 1988); *Macktal v Brown & Root, Inc.*, 86-ERA-23, order rejecting in part by SOL, at 16-17 (November 14, 1989).

37. *Connecticut Light & Power v SOL*, 85 F.3d 89, 95 (2nd Cir. 1996).

38. *Rhyne v Brand Utilities*, 94-ERA-33/45, Order of SOL, at 2 (June 20, 1995).

39. *Rys v Spernak Airways, Inc.*, 2003-AIR-13, D&O of ARB (April 1, 2003); *Crider v Holston Defense Corp. et al.*, 88-CAA-1, order approving settlement by SOL, at 2 (March 1, 1989). See also *Cowan v Bechtel Constr., Inc.*, 87-ERA-29, D&O of remand by SOL, at 3 (August 9, 1989) ("Settlement of such a prior complaint does not . . . preclude litigation of an alleged separate and distinct act of discrimination after the settlement."); *Smyth v Regents*, 98-ERA-3, Order of ARB, at 2 (March 13, 1998).

40. *Macktal v Brown & Root, Inc.*, 86-ERA-23, order rejecting in part by SOL, at 14-16 (November 14, 1989) (vacated on other grounds).

41. *Rudd v Westinghouse Hanford Company*, 88-ERA-33, Order Approving Settlement by ARB (April 19, 2002).

42. *Rudd v Department of Labor*, 2003 WL 22417078 (9th Cir. 2003).

43. 29 C.F.R. §§ 1980.111(e) and 1980.113. Accord., *Williams v Metzler*, 132 F.3d 937 (3rd Cir. 1997) (enforcement of a settlement must be filed in federal court); *Rudd v Department of Labor*, 2003 WL 22417078 (9th Cir. 2003) (DOL decision whether to approve settlement is "distinct" from a civil action to enforce an agreement). See also *Pillow v Bechtel*, 87-ERA-35, Order of ARB, at 2-3 (September 11, 1997); *O'Sullivan et al. v Northeast Nuclear Energy Co.*, 88-ERA-37/38, recommended D&O of ALJ (potential new discrimination charge based on employer's postsettlement conduct); *Blanch v Northeast Nuclear*, 90-ERA-11, Order of SOL at 4

(May 11, 1994) (violation of settlement may constitute a separate, independent violation of the whistleblower law); *Cianfrani v Public Service Elec. & Gas Co.*, 95-ERA-33, Order of ARB, at 2 (September 19, 1996).

44. *Williams v Metzler*, 132 F.3d 937 (3rd Cir. 1997).

CHAPTER 13

1. 18 U.S.C. 1514A(d).
2. 18 U.S.C. 1514A(d).
3. 18 U.S.C. 1514A(d).
4. *English v General Electric Co.*, 496 U.S. 72 (1990).
5. Almost every state now protects whistleblowers under state law. Corporate whistleblowers may be protected in the majority of states that have adopted the public policy exception wrongful discharge tort. See Kohn, *Concepts and Procedures in Whistleblower Law*, pp. 21–77 (Greenwood Press, Westport Ct. 2000) for a comprehensive review of state whistleblower protections.
6. *Bowman v State Bank of Keysville*, 229 Va. 534 (1985); *Guy v Mutual of Omaha*, 79 S.W.3d 528 (Tenn. 2002). Accord., *Simas v First Citizens Federal Credit Union*, 63 F.Supp.2d 110 (D.Mass. 1999) (allegations about improper loan constituted protected whistleblowing).
7. For a complete overview of other DOL-administered corporate whistleblower laws, see Kohn, *Concepts and Procedures in Whistleblower Law*, pp. 79–117, 141–202, and 225–235.
8. Report of the Senate Judiciary Committee, "The Corporate and Criminal Fraud Accountability Act of 2002, Report No. 107-146," reprinted in 149 *Congressional Record* S7412 (July 26, 2002).
9. *EEOC v Waffle House, Inc.*, 534 U.S. 279 (2002) (arbitration agreement did not bar EEOC from pursuing victim-specific judicial relief on behalf of employee in federal court) ; *Reich v Sysco Corp.*, 870 F. Supp. 777 (S.D. Ohio 1994).
10. *Doyle v DOL*, 285 F.3d 243, 252 (3rd Cir. 2002) ("waiver" of right to file DOL whistleblower claim was "unenforceable").
11. *Ass't. Secretary of Labor v Greyhound Bus Lines*, 96-STA-23, D&O of ARB (June 12, 1998); *German v CalMat Company*, 99-STA-15, D&O of ARB, p. 4 (August 1, 2002) ("The decision to defer to the outcome of an arbitration must be made on a case-by-case basis and only where it is clear that the arbitration dealt adequately with all factual issues, that the proceedings were fair, regular and free of procedural infirmities, and that the outcome of the proceeding was not repugnant to the purpose and policy of the Act"); *Paynes v Gulf States*, 93-ERA-47, D&O of ARB, at 7 (the employee "had a right to file" his "contract claim in the arbitration process." However, "availing himself of separate forums and separate theories seeking redress" for "adverse actions" had no bearing "on ERA claim"); *Szpyrka v American Eagle Airlines*, 2002-AIR-9, Order of ALJ, p. 6 (July 8, 2002) ("deference" to private arbitration processes "unwarranted").
12. *Yellow Freight System, Inc. v Martin*, 983 F.2d 1195 (2nd Cir. 1993); *Calmat Co. v U.S. Department of Labor*, 364 F.3d 1117, 1125-26 (9th Cir. 2004) (setting forth identical standard under the Surface Transportation Act).

13. *Lassin v Michigan State University*, 93-ERA-31, D&O of SOL, at 6 (June 29, 1995) (recognizing the "strong federal polices" favoring arbitration); *Straub v APS/ANPP*, 94-ERA-37, D&O of SOL, at 4-5 (April 15, 1996) ("arbitration decisions must be considered during the adjudication of the whistleblower complaint; the probative weight to be accorded such decisions must be determined, based on the adequacy provided the employee's rights in such arbitral proceeding, on an *ad hoc* basis"); *McDonald v University of Missouri*, 90-ERA-59, D&O of SOL, at 10 (March 21, 1995) (decision of grievance committee "not binding," although it may be "persuasive"); *Smith v ESICORP, Inc.*, 93-ERA-16, D&O of SOL, at 22 n. 17 (March 13, 1996) ("terms of collective bargaining agreements do not diminish rights afforded to employees under the ERA").

14. Report of the Senate Judiciary Committee, "The Corporate and Criminal Fraud Accountability Act of 2002," Report No. 107-146-, p. 13, reprinted in 149 *Congressional Record* S7412 (July 26, 2002).

15. 18 U.S.C. 1514A(b)(2)(A), requiring DOL proceedings be conducted in accordance with AIR 21 procedures codified at 49 U.S.C. 42121(b).

16. *Szpyrka v American Eagle Airlines*, 2002-AIR-9, ALJ Order, p. 6 (July 8, 2002).

17. *Wright v Universal Maritime Service Corp.*, 525 U.S. 70, 76 (1998) (requirement to arbitrate a federal right contained in a collective bargaining agreement needed to be "clear" and "unmistakable." In addition to the terms of the arbitration agreement, at least one federal court held that the failure of an arbitration agreement to empower arbitrators to order a full "make whole" remedy, including reinstatement, rendered the arbitration agreement nonenforceable. *Terrell v Amsouth Investment Services*, 217 F.Supp. 1233 (M.D. Fla. 2002). The SOX provides for a full "make whole" remedy, including reinstatement. On the other hand, at least one court held that the SOX statute did not provide for a blanket exemption from the general requirement to arbitrate whistleblower disputes, once that dispute is filed in federal court. *Boss v Salomon Smith Barney, Inc.*, 263 F.Supp.2d 684, 2003 (S.D. N.Y. 2003).

18. *Nguyen v City of Cleveland*, 121 F.Supp.2d 642, 647 (N.D. 2000) (arbitration agreement nonenforceable due to its conflict with the purposes behind federal whistleblower law); *Duffield v Robertson Stephens & Co.*, 144 F.3d 1182 (9th Cir. 1998) (Civil Rights Act of 1991 precludes compulsory arbitration of civil rights claims); *Gibson v Neighborhood Health Clinics*, 121 F.3d 1126 (7th Cir. 1997) (arbitration agreement void due to a lack of consideration).

CHAPTER 14

1. H.R. Rep. No. 101-54(I), cited in *Simas v First Citizens' Federal Credit Union*, 170 F.3d 37, 43 (1st Cir. 1999).

2. *Haley v Retsinas*, 138 F.3d 1245, 1250 (8th Cir. 1998).

3. *Haley v Retsinas*, 138 F.3d 1245, 1250.

4. 12 U.S.C. § 1831j.

5. 12 U.S.C. § 1831j(e).

6. 12 U.S.C. § 1790b.

7. 31 U.S.C. § 5328.

8. *Rouse v Farmers State Bank of Jewell*, 866 F.Supp. 1191, 1208 (N.D. Iowa 1994) (finding *McDonnell Douglas v Green* Title VII formula for shifting burdens of production and proof "inapplicable" under the FIRREA).

9. *Frobose v American Savings and Loan*, 152 F.3d 602, 611-612 (7th Cir. 1998).

10. *Frobose v American Savings and Loan*, 152 F.3d 602, 611-612.

11. *Frobose v American Savings and Loan*, 152 F.3d at 613.

12. *Frobose v American Savings and Loan*, 152 F.3d at 613. (collecting cases).

13. 31 U.S.C. § 5328(b), 12 U.S.C. § 1970b(b), and 12 U.S.C. § 1831j(b).

14. *Haley v Retsinas*, 138 F.3d 1251.

15. 31 U.S.C. § 5328(a).

16. 12 U.S.C. § 1790b(a).

17. 12 U.S.C. § 1831j(a).

18. *Simas v First Citizens' Federal Credit Union*, 170 F.3d at 48.

19. *Hicks v RTC*, 767 F.Supp. 167, 172 (N.D. Ill. 1991).

20. *Hicks v RTC*, 767 F.Supp. 173.

21. 31 U.S.C. § 5328(c), 12 U.S.C. § 1970b(c), and 12 U.S.C. § 1831j(c).

22. *Oldroyd v Elmira Savings Bank*, 956 F.Supp. 393, 400-401 (W.D. N.Y. 1997), reversed on other grounds 134 F.3d 72 (2nd Cir. 1998).

23. *Haley v Retsinas*, 138 F.3d 1248.

CHAPTER 15

1. 13 U.S.C. § 7245.

2. "Appearing and practicing before the Commission" is defined as any attorney:

(i) Transacting any business with the Commission, including communications in any form; (ii) Representing an issuer in a Commission administrative proceeding or in connection with any Commission investigation, inquiry, information request, or subpoena; (iii) Providing advice in respect of the United States securities laws or the Commission's rules or regulations thereunder regarding any document that the attorney has notice will be filed with or submitted to, or incorporated into any document that will be filed with or submitted to, the Commission, including the provision of such advice in the context of preparing, or participating in the preparation of, any such document; or (iv) Advising an issuer as to whether information or a statement, opinion, or other writing is required under the United States securities laws or the Commission's rules or regulations thereunder to be filed with or submitted to, or incorporated into any document that will be filed with or submitted to, the Commission; but (2) Does not include an attorney who: (i) Conducts the activities in paragraphs (a)(1)(i) through (a)(1)(iv) of this section other than in the context of providing legal services to an issuer with whom the attorney has an attorney-client relationship; or (ii) Is a non-appearing foreign attorney.

17 C.F.R. § 205.2(a)(1).

3. 18 U.S.C. § 1514A.

4. 18 U.S.C. § 1514A (a).

5. 17 C.F.R. § 205.1.

6. "*Attorney*" is defined as "any person who is admitted, licensed, or otherwise qualified to practice law in any jurisdiction, domestic or foreign, or who

holds himself or herself out as admitted, licensed, or otherwise qualified to practice law." 17 C.F.R. § 205.2(c).

7. *"Report"* means "to make known to directly, either in person, by phone, by e-mail, electronically, or in writing." 17 C.F.R. § 205.2(n).

8. *"Evidence of a material violation"* is defined as "credible evidence, based upon which it would be unreasonable, under the circumstances, for a prudent and competent attorney not to conclude that it is reasonably likely that a material violation has occurred, is going, or is about to occur." 17 C.F.R. § 205.2(e).

"Material violation" is defined as "a material violation of an applicable United States federal or state securities law, a material breach of fiduciary duty arising under United States federal or state law, or a similar material violation of any United States federal or state law." 17 C.F.R. § 205(i).

9. *"Breach of fiduciary duty"* is defined as "any breach of fiduciary or similar duty to the issuer recognized under any applicable federal or state statute or at common law, including but not limited to misfeasance, nonfeasance, abdication of duty, abuse of trust, and approval of unlawful transactions." 17 C.F.R. § 205.2(d).

10. *"Issuer"* means "an issuer (as defined in section 3 of the Securities Exchange Act of 1934 (15 U.S.C. § 78c)), the securities of which are registered under section 12 of that Act (15 U.S.C. § 78l), or that is required to file reports under section 15(d) of that Act (15 U.S.C. § 78o(d)), or that files or has filed a registration statement that has not yet become effective under the Securities Act of 1933 (15 U.S.C. 77a et seq.), and that it has not withdrawn, but does not include a foreign government issuer. For purposes of paragraphs (a) and (g) of this section, the term "issuer" includes any person controlled by an issuer, where an attorney provides legal services to such person on behalf of, or at the behest, or for the benefit of the issuer, regardless of whether the attorney is employed or retained by the issuer." 17 C.F.R. § 205(h).

11. 17 C.F.R. § 205.5(a).

12. 17 C.F.R. § 205.5(b)-(c).

13. 17 C.F.R. § 205.5(c).

14. 17 C.F.R. § 205.2(n). The failure to document the report in writing could adversely affect the reporting attorney if a cover-up were to ensue and the reporting attorney is ultimately blamed for not reporting that which he or she did report orally.

15. 17 C.F.R. § 205.5(d).

16. 15 U.S.C. § 7245.

17. 17 C.F.R. § 205.4(a).

18. 17 C.F.R. § 205.5(a).

19. 17 C.F.R. § 205.4(b).

20. 17 C.F.R. § 205.4(b)-(c).

21. *"Qualified legal compliance committee"* is defined at 17 C.F.R. § 205.2(k).

22. 17 C.F.R. § 205.3(c)(1).

23. 17 C.F.R. § 205.3(b)(1).

24. 17 C.F.R. § 205.3(b)(4).

25. 17 C.F.R. § 205.3(b)(3).

26. 17 C.F.R. § 205.3(c)(1).

27. 17 C.F.R. § 205.3(b)(9).

28. *"Appropriate response"* means "a response to an attorney regarding reported evidence of a material violation as a result of which the attorney reason-

ably believes: (1) That no material violation, as defined in paragraph (i) of this section, has occurred, is ongoing, or is about to occur; (2) That the issuer has, as necessary, adopted appropriate remedial measures, including appropriate steps or sanctions to stop any material violations that are ongoing, to prevent any material violation that has yet to occur, and to remedy or otherwise appropriately address any material violation that has already occurred and to minimize the likelihood of its recurrence; or (3) That the issuer, with the consent of the issuer's board of directors, a committee thereof to whom a report could be made pursuant to § 205.3(b)(3), or a qualified legal compliance committee, has retained or directed an attorney to review the reported evidence of a material violation and either: (i) Has substantially implemented any remedial recommendations made by such attorney after a reasonable investigation and evaluation of the reported evidence; or (ii) Has been advised that such attorney may, consistent with his or her professional obligations, assert a colorable defense on behalf of the issuer (or the issuer's officer, director, employee, or agent, as the case may be) in any investigation or judicial or administrative proceeding relating to the reported evidence of a material violation." 17 C.F.R. §205.2(b).

29. 17 C.F.R. § 205.3(b)(8).

30. 17 C.F.R. § 205.3(b)(2); § 205.3(c)(2).

31. 17 C.F.R. § 205.3(b)(2).

32. 17 C.F.R. § 205.3(b)(2).

33. 17 C.F.R. § 205.3(b)(2).

34. 17 C.F.R. § 205.3(b)(2).

35. 17 C.F.R. § 205.3(b)(3).

36. 17 C.F.R. § 205(b)(3)(i)-(iii).

37. *"Reasonably believes"* is defined as "meaning that an attorney believes the matter in question and that the circumstances are such that the belief is not unreasonable." 17 C.F.R. § 205.2(m). *"Reasonable"* is defined as "conduct that would not be unreasonable for a prudent and competent attorney." 17 C.F.R. § 205.2(l).

38. 17 C.F.R. § 205(d)(2)(i).

39. 17 C.F.R. § 205(d)(2)(ii).

40. 17 C.F.R. § 205.3(d)(2)(iii).

41. 17 C.F.R. § 205.2(k)(4).

42. 17 C.F.R. § 205.2(k)(3); § 205.3(b)(4).

43. 17 C.F.R. § 205.2(k)(3).

44. 17 C.F.R. § 205.2(k)(3).

45. 17 C.F.R. § 205.2(k)(3).

46. 17 C.F.R. § 205.3(b)(7).

47. 17 C.F.R. § 205.2(k)(3).

48. 17 C.F.R. § 205.2(k)(4).

49. *Mackowiak v University Nuclear Systems*, 735 F.2d 1159, 1163 (9th Cir. 1984); *Kansas Gas & Elec. Co. v Brock*, 780 F.2d 1505 (10th Cir. 1985).

50. 17 C.F.R. § 205.3(b)(2).

51. 17 C.F.R. § 205.3(b)(2)

52. 17 C.F.R. § 205.3(c)(2)

53. 17 C.F.R. § 205.3(c)(2).

54. See SEC Proposed Rule on Implementation of Standards of Professional Conduct for Attorneys (January 29, 2003).

55. A definition of "Appearing and practicing before the Commission" can be found at 17 C.F.R. § 205.2(a)(1). As discussed later, lawyers who do not meet the "appearing and practicing" criteria may have a more limited ability to utilize confidential communications. See *Willy v The Coastal Corp.*, ARB No. 98-060, ALJ No. 1985-CAA-1 Final Decision and Dismissal Order (ARB Feb. 27, 2004), appeal docketed (5th Cir. 2004).

56. 15 U.S.C. § 7245.

57. U.S. Const., Art. IV, Cl. 2.

58. 17 C.F.R. § 205.1 ("These standards supplement applicable standards of any jurisdiction where an attorney is admitted or practices and . . . [w]here standards of a state or other United States jurisdiction where an attorney is admitted or practices conflict with this part, this part shall govern") and 17 C.F.R. §205.6(c)(any "attorney who complies in good faith with the provisions of this part shall not be subject to discipline or otherwise liable under inconsistent standards imposed by any state or other United States jurisdiction where the attorney is admitted to practice").

59. 17 C.F.R. § 205.3(d)(1).

60. ABA Model Rule 1.6(b)(3) (Aug. 2002) states:

> A lawyer may reveal information relating to the representation of a client to the extent the lawyer reasonably believes necessary . . . to establish a claim or defense on behalf of the lawyer in a controversy between the lawyer and the client, to establish a defense to a criminal charge or civil claim against the lawyer based upon conduct in which the client was involved, or to respond to allegations in any proceeding concerning the lawyer's representation of the client.

This language was first adopted by the ABA House of Delegates on August 2, 1983, and has appeared in the ABA's Model Rules since then. The ABA Model Rules were subsequently amended in 1987, 1989, 1990, 1991, 1992, 1993, 1994, 1995, 1997, 1998, 2000, 2002, and 2003. The 2002 amendments renumbered the subsections from b(2) to (b)(3), while the 2003 amendments renumbered the subsection to (b)(5). None of the amendments has altered the wording of the subsection.

61. Id.

62. ABA Formal Ethics Op. 01-424 (September 2001)(lawyers may bring "a retaliatory discharge or similar claim" against a client-employer and are free to use confidential information gained during the course of the representation as necessary).

63. *Willy v The Coastal Corp.*, ARB No. 98-060, ALJ No. 1985-CAA-1 Final Decision and Dismissal Order (ARB Feb. 27, 2004), appeal docketed (5th Cir. 2004).

64. Id. at p. 28.

65. Id. at p. 30 (quoting Fed. R. Evid. § 501).

66. *Supreme Court Standard 503(d)*, as reprinted in 56 F.R.D. 183, 236 (1972).

67. *Willy v The Coastal Corp.*, ARB No. 98-060, ALJ No. 1985-CAA-1 Final Decision and Dismissal Order at pp. 31-34 (ARB Feb. 27, 2004), appeal docketed (5th Cir. 2004).

68. Id. at p. 35.

69. *O'Brien v Stolt-Nielsen Trans. Group, Ltd.*, 1004 WL 304318 at p. 2 (Conn. 2004).

70. *Crews v Buckman Laboratories International, Inc.*, 78 S.W.3d 852 (Tenn. 2002)("we hereby expressly adopt a new provision in Disciplinary Rule 4-101(C) to

permit in-house counsel to reveal the confidences and secrets of a client when the lawyer reasonably believes that such information necessary to establish a claim or defense on behalf of the lawyer in a controversy between the lawyer and the client. This exception parallels the language of Model Rule of Processional Conduct.").

71. See, for example, *Spratley v State Farm Mutual Automobile Insurance Co.*, 78 P.3d 603 (Utah 2003)("the plain language in Rule 1.6 and the policy considerations outlined in other cases weigh in favor of allowing disclosure, in a limited fashion, of confidential client information in a suit by former in-house counsel for wrongful discharge"); *Crews v Buckman Laboratories International, Inc.*, 78 S.W.3d 852 (Tenn. 2002)("we hereby expressly adopt a new provision in Disciplinary Rule 4-101(C) to permit in-house counsel to reveal the confidences and secrets of a client when the lawyer reasonably believes that such information necessary to establish a claim or defense on behalf of the lawyer in a controversy between the lawyer and the client. This exception parallels the language of Model Rule of Processional Conduct"); *Burkhart v Semitool, Inc.*, 5 P.3d 1031, 1041 (Mont. 2000)("the plain language of Montana's Rules of Professional Conduct, Rule 1.6, contemplates that a lawyer may reveal confidential attorney-client information, to the extent the lawyer reasonably believes necessary, to establish an employment-related claim against an employer who is also a client"); *Parker v M & T Chemicals, Inc.*, 566 A.2d 215, 463 fn. 2. (N.J.Super. 1989)("a lawyer may use information to the extent the lawyer reasonably believes it necessary . . . to establish a claim or defense on behalf of the lawyer in a controversy between the lawyer and the client" under the New Jersey Rules of Professional Conduct).

72. *Willy v The Coastal Corp.*, ARB No. 98-060, ALJ No. 1985-CAA-1 Final Decision and Dismissal Order at p. 30 (quoting fed. R. Evid. § 501) (ARB Feb. 27, 2004), appeal docketed (5th Cir. 2004).

73. *Kachmar v Sungard Data Systems, Inc.*, 109 F.3d, 181 (3rd Cir. 1997).

74. Id. (quoting *Doe v A Corp.*, 709 F.2d, 1043, 1050 (5th Cir. 1983).

75. *Kachmar v Sungard Data Systems, Inc.*, 109 F.3d 173, 182 (3rd Cir. 1997). In *Kachmar* the court contemplated using equitable measures as a means to protect the release of any confidential information the lawyer may need to reveal in order to bring or maintain a claim. Yet, in *Willy*, the ARB cites to *Kachmar* for the proposition that "[e]videntiary use of confidential information outside the privilege could be protected through equitable measures. . . ." *Willy v The Coastal Corp.*, ARB No. 98-060, ALJ No. 1985-CAA-1 Final Decision and Dismissal Order, at p. 36 (ARB Feb. 27, 2004). The ARB's reliance on *Kachmar* may be misplaced.

CHAPTER 16

1. 15 U.S.C. 78(m)(4).
2. 15 U.S.C. 78(m)(4).
3. SOX Section 301 defines "Independent" as an audit committee member who does not receive, other than for service on the board of directors, any consulting, advisory, or other compensation from the company, and as not being an affiliated person of the company, or any subsidiary thereof.

4. See SEC Proposed Rule: Standards Relating to Listed Company Audit Committees (February 18, 2003).

5. 15 U.S.C. § 78u-4(b) (2000).

6. See, for example, *In re Cabletron Systems, Inc.,* 311 F.3d 11, 29 (1st Cir. 2002). But see, for example, *In re Silicon Graphics, Inc. Securities Litigation,* 183 F.3d 970 (9th Cir. 1999).

7. *Novak v Kasaks,* 216 F.3d 300, 314 (2nd Cir. 2000) (requiring securities fraud plaintiffs to name sources in their complaint would potentially discourage whistleblowing concerning corporate misconduct).

8. Todd Halvorson, "NASA management style shifts back to pre-Challenger days," *Florida Today* (October 2, 1996).

9. Ibid.

10. *Charles Hill et al. v Tennessee Valley Authority,* Case No. 87-ERA-23, RD&O of ALJ (July 24, 1991).

11. *Hill v TVA,* Case No. 87-ERA-23, RD&O of ALJ, p. 3 (July 24, 1991).

12. *Hill v TVA,* Case No. 87-ERA-23, RD&O of ALJ, p. 3 (July 24, 1991).

13. *Hill v TVA,* Case No. 87-ERA-23, RD&O of ALJ, p. 3 (July 24, 1991).

14. *Hill v TVA,* Case No. 87-ERA-23, RD&O of ALJ, p. 7 (July 24, 1991).

15. *Hill v TVA,* Case No. 87-ERA-23, RD&O of ALJ, p. 7 (July 24, 1991).

16. *Hill v TVA,* Case No. 87-ERA-23, RD&O of ALJ, p. 9 (July 24, 1991).

17. *Hill v TVA,* Case No. 87-ERA-23, RD&O of ALJ, p. 9 (July 24, 1991).

18. *Hill v TVA,* Case No. 87-ERA-23, RD&O of ALJ, p. 31 (July 24, 1991).

19. *Hill v TVA,* Case No. 87-ERA-23, RD&O of ALJ, p. 40 (July 24, 1991).

20. *Hill v TVA,* Case No. 87-ERA-23, RD&O of ALJ, p. 40 (July 24, 1991). Although the Department of Labor found that TVA illegally retaliated against the complainants, the case was dismissed as a result of the complainants' failure to meet the 30-day statute of limitations for filing the initial complaint.

21. *Linda Mitchell v Arizona Public Service Co. et al.,* Case No. 91-ERA-9, RD&O of ALJ, p. 9 (July 2, 1992).

22. *Mitchell v APS,* Case No. 91-ERA-9, RD&O of ALJ, p. 9 (July 2, 1992).

23. *Mitchell v APS,* Case No. 91-ERA-9, RD&O of ALJ, p. 9 (July 2, 1992).

24. *Mitchell v APS,* Case No. 91-ERA-9, RD&O of ALJ, p. 9 (July 2, 1992).

25. *Mitchell v APS,* Case No. 91-ERA-9, RD&O of ALJ, pp. 9-10 (July 2, 1992).

26. *Mitchell v APS,* Case No. 91-ERA-9, RD&O of ALJ, pp. 9-10 (July 2, 1992).

27. "NRC eases rules at Northeast's Millstone," *Reuters* (March 11, 1999).

28. Miles Moffeit, Diedtra Henderson, and David Migoya, "Critics: NASA stifles dissent," *Denver Post* (February 9, 2003).

29. Ibid.

30. Bureau of Land Management, News Release (March 25, 1997).

31. Bureau of Land Management, News Release (March 25, 1997).

32. See *Mackowiak v University Nuclear Systems,* 735 F.2d 1159 (9th Cir. 1984); *Kansas Gas & Electric v Brock,* 780 F.2d 1505 (10th Cir. 1985).

33. See, for example, 5 U.S.C. §1221(a)(2)(B).

34. See, *Mackowiak v University Nuclear Systems,* 735 F.2d 1159 (9th Cir. 1984); *Kansas Gas & Electric v Brock,* 780 F.2d 1505 (10th Cir. 1985).

35. 18 U.S.C. § 1514A(a)(1)(C).

36. *Mackowiak v University Nuclear Systems,* 735 F.2d 1159, 1163 (9th Cir. 1984).

CHAPTER 17

1. 18 U.S.C. § 1513(e).

2. 148 *Congressional Record*, p. H5464 (July 25, 2002) (Sensenbrenner).

3. 18 U.S.C. 1513(e) (PL 107-204, § 1107(a)).

4. 18 U.S.C. §1515(a)(4) ("As used in section 1513 of this title . . . the term 'law enforcement officer' means an officer or employee of the Federal Government, or a person authorized to act for or on behalf of the Federal Government or serving the Federal Government as an adviser or consultant B (A) authorized under law to engage in or supervise the prevention, detection, investigation, or prosecution of an offense; or (B) serving as a probation or pretrial services officer under this title.").

It appears that, in another context, courts have been willing to extend coverage to communication with state officials if the information would likely be transmitted to a federal authority. See *United States v Perry*, 335 F.3d 316, 321 fn. 7 (4th Cir. 2003)(citing *United States v Veal*, 153 F.3d 1233, 1251-52 (11th Cir. 1998)).

5. 18 U.S.C. §§ 1961-1968.

6. Pub.L. 91-452, 84 Stat. 922, 923.

7. Pub.L. 91-452, 84 Stat. 922, 923.

8. 18 U.S.C. §1964(c).

9. The state RICO laws do differ from the federal RICO statute on which they are based. These differentiations may provide dispositive based on the interpretations ultimately relied upon by the courts. For example, the Georgia state RICO statute offers standing to "[a]ny person who is injured by reason of any violation," whereas the federal RICO statute limits standing to any person injured in his "business or property." Compare Georgia Code Section 16- 14-4 and 18 U.S.C. § 1964(c). Whether the differentiations between the various state and federal RICO statutes will have any bearing on a case will ultimately depend on the interpretations given by the courts.

10. 18 U.S.C. § 1962(a)-(d).

11. An "enterprise" is defined as "any individual, partnership, corporation, association, or other legal entity, and any union or group of individuals associated in fact although not a legal entity." 18 U.S.C. §1961(4).

12. 18 U.S.C. § 1961(1).

13. *Beck v Prupis*, 592 U.S. 494, 120 S.Ct. 1608, 1617 (2000)("a person may not bring suit under § 1964(c). . . for injuries caused by an overt act that is not an act of racketeering or otherwise unlawful under the statute").

14. By way of example, a racketeering enterprise that swindled shareholders of a publicly traded company would permit the shareholders to bring a civil RICO action to recover their economic loss, whereas the whistleblower responsible for bringing the racketeering enterprise to light and who is terminated in the process could not bring a claim to recover the economic loss he or she suffered because that harm did not flow directly from one of the predicate acts of racketeering.

15. 18 U.S.C. § 1513. The amendments to this statute are set forth in the Sarbanes-Oxley Act at Pub.L. 107-204, § 1107(a) and at Pub.L. 107-273, § 3001(b). Both of these amendments add a new subsection (e). Consequently, there exist two separate subsection (e) provisions under 18 U.S.C. § 1513.

16. 18 U.S.C. § 1513(e) (PL 107-204, § 1107(a)). Note that a violation of 15 U.S.C. §1513 constitutes a predicate act of racketeering under 15 U.S.C. § 1961(1).

17. 18 U.S.C. § 1513(e) (PL 107-273, § 3001(b)).

18. See *Kramer v Bachan Aerospace Corp.*, 912 F.2d 151, 154-56 (6th cir. 1990)(Employee "whistleblower" could establish standing only if employee's discharge was direct result of employer's alleged RICO violations, but "allegations of obstruction of justice *might* satisfy standing requirement in certain cases involving dismissal of employees for reporting violations"(emphasis in original)); *Miranda v Ponce Federal Bank*, 948 F.2d 41 (1st Cir. 1991)("a claim for wrongful discharge cannot be successfully pursued under civil RICO when the injury itself is not the result of a predicate act"); *Hecht v Commerce Clearing House, Inc.*, 897 F.2d 21, 25 (2nd cir.1990)("Because the overt act of Hecht's discharge was not a section 1961(1) predicate act, his loss of employment does not confer civil standing."); *Reddy v Litton Industries, Inc.*, 912 F.2d 291, 294 (9th cir. 1990)("we hold that Reddy lacks standing to sue under § 1962(c) because the injury he suffered was the result of his alleged wrongful termination and was not caused by predicate RICO acts"); *Pujol v Shearson/Am. Express, Inc.*, 829 F.2d 1201 (1st Cir.1987) ("[t]he acts that injured Pujol . . . were not caused by the 'predicate acts'"); *Morast v Lance*, 807 F.2d 926, 933 (11th Cir. 1987)("Morast's injury, his discharge, did not flow directly from the predicate acts"); *Warren v Manufacturers Nat. Bank of Detroit*, 759 F.2d 542, 545 (6th Cir.1985) (holding that injury must be directly caused by the asserted RICO violations).

19. *Sedima, S.P.R.L. v Imrex Company, Inc.*, 473 U.S. 479, 489, 105 S.Ct. 3292 (1985).

20. *Radovich v National Football League*, 352 U.S. 445, 77 S.Ct. 390, 1 L.Ed.2d 456 (1957)(football player prevented from becoming a player-coach stated a cause of action under the antitrust laws); *Ashmore v Northeast Petroleum Div*, 843 F.Supp. 759, 760-70 (D.Me.1994) (employees discharged in retaliation for their failure to violate the antitrust laws sustained "antitrust injury" and had standing to sue); *Nichols v Spencer International Press, Inc.*, 371 F.2d 332, 334 (7th Cir. 1967)("the interest invaded by a wrongful act resulting in loss of employment is so closely akin to the interest invaded by impairment of one's business as to be indistinguishable in this context"); *Ostrofe v H. S. Crocker Co., Inc.*, 670 F.2d 1378, 1385 (9th Cir. 1982)(employee has standing to sue for damages incurred as a result of his discharge for his refusal to participate in effectuating an antitrust conspiracy); *Daily v Quality School Plan Inc.*, 380 F.2d 484 (5th Cir.1967) (loss of employment constitutes injury to business or property).

21. As defined in the RICO statute, a "'pattern of racketeering activity' requires at least two acts of racketeering activity, one of which occurred after the effective date of this chapter and the last of which occurred within 10 years (excluding any period of imprisonment) after the commission of a prior act of racketeering activity." 18 U.S.C. § 1961(5).

22. *Efron v Embassy Suites (Puerto Rico), Inc.*, 223 F.3d 12 C.A.1 (Puerto Rico), 2000. (Quoting *H.J. Inc. v Northwestern Bell Tel. Co.*, 492 U.S. 229, 239, 109 S.Ct. 2893, 106 L.Ed.2d 195 (1989)).

23. *H.J. Inc. v Northwestern Bell Tel. Co.*, 492 U.S. at 440.

24. *U.S. v Quintanilla*, 760 F.Supp. 687 (N.D.Ill.1991), affirmed 2 F.3d 1469.

25. *Kehr Packages, Inc. v Fidelcor, Inc.*, C.A.3 (Pa. 1991), 926 F.2d 1406, rehearing denied, certiorari denied 111 S.Ct. 2839, 501 U.S. 1222, 115 L.Ed.2d 1007.

26. *Foxy Lady, Inc. v City of Atlanta, Ga.*, 2003 WL 22351442 (11th Cir. 2003)(collateral estoppel available even if administrative agency does not have subpoena power).

27. *LaSalle Bank Lake View v Seguban*, 54 F.3d 387 (7th Cir. 1995) (motion for summary judgment granted solely on adverse inferences drawn from nonmovants' invocation of a Fifth Amendment privilege against self-incrimination)("The rule that adverse inferences may be drawn from Fifth Amendment silence in civil proceedings has been widely recognized by the circuit courts of appeals, including our own, in the two decades since *Baxter* [*v Palmigiano*, 425 U.S. 308, 96 S.Ct. 1551, 47 L.Ed.2d 810 (1976)] was decided. See, for example, *Daniels v Pipefitters' Ass'n Local Union No. 597*, 983 F.2d 800, 801-02 (7th Cir.1993); *National Acceptance*, 705 F.2d at 929-932; *Koester v American Republic Investments, Inc.*, 11 F.3d 818, 823-24 (8th Cir.1993); *RAD Services, Inc. v Aetna Casualty & Surety Co.*, 808 F.2d 271, 274-75, 277 (3d Cir.1986); *Brink's, Inc. v City of New York*, 717 F.2d 700 (2d Cir.1983); *Hoover v Knight*, 678 F.2d 578, 581-82 (5th Cir.1982); *United States v White*, 589 F.2d 1283, 1286-87 (5th Cir.1979).").

Resources

Attorney Referral Service
National Whistleblower Legal Defense and
Education Fund
PO Box 3768
Washington, DC 20027
Fax 202-342-1904
Phone 202-342-1902
http://www.whistleblowers.org/ars.htm

The National Whistleblower Legal Defense and Education Fund operates an Attorney Referral Service (ARS) to provide legal referrals to whistleblowers in search of competent counsel. The ARS is composed of attorneys from across the nation who are interested in whistleblowing cases. Those who have a legal question and/or are in need of a referral may download the intake form; attorneys wishing to become members of the ARS may download the membership form. The Fund also provides legal representation to whistleblowers.

Equal Employment Opportunity Commission (EEOC)
1801 L Street, NW
Washington, DC 20507
http://www.eeoc.gov/

The EEOC has jurisdiction over the antiretaliation laws governing traditional employment discrimination matters. The Web site catalogues laws prohibiting discrimination in employment, indicating those that the organization oversees. Guidance for employees is offered alongside information about how to file a charge. News stories and press releases, local field office contact information, and links to other sites are also available.

Ignet
Federal Inspectors General Web Page
http://www.ignet.gov/

This Web site contains a central point of contact for all 57 Offices of Inspector General and contact points for OIG oversight bodies. The OIGs are responsible for policing the conduct of federal regulatory agencies, many of whom have direct oversight duties for publicly traded corporations. Among the agencies that have OIGs are the following: Securities and Exchange Commission, Department of Labor, Department of Justice, for corporate conduct.

The National Whistleblower Center
3238 P Street, NW
Washington, DC 20007-2756
Fax 202-342-1904
Phone 202-342-1902
http://www.whistleblowers.org/

The National Whistleblower Center (NWC) is a nonprofit public interest organization devoted to the protection of whistleblowers. Founded in 1988, the NWC advocates on behalf of whistleblowers before Congress and in the Courts. The Center conducts educational programs and supports test case litigation. The Center's Web site provides additional information on legislative updates, publications, referrals, and employee rights.

Regulations.gov
http://www.regulations.gov/

Regulations.gov is a U.S. government Web site that publishes all proposed federal rules. On the site, members of the public can find, review, and submit comments on federal documents that are open for comment and published in the *Federal Register*. Most all federal whistleblower regulations are approved through the rule-making process. Additionally, many federal agencies seek public comment on issues directly related to whistleblowing and/or on issues that are of concern to whistleblowers.

Securities and Exchange Commission (SEC)
Center for Complaints and Enforcement Tips
450 Fifth Street, NW
Washington, DC 20549
Fax 202-942-9634
http://www.sec.gov/ divisions/enforce.shtml
Email address: enforcement@sec.gov

The SEC operates a Center for Complaints and Enforcement Tips, which offers information on filing complaints with the SEC and filing "tips" with the SEC regarding violations of securities law and provides "fast answers" to general questions regarding federal securities laws and investments. The SEC also operates a "bounty program" regarding tips provided by citizens concerning "insider trading." Information about the Complaints Center and the Bounty Program is posted on the SEC Web page.

Securities and Exchange Commission (SEC)
Consumer Information: 1-800-SEC-0330
Investor Information and Complaints: (202) 942-7040
Division of Enforcement: (202) 942-4500
Freedom of Information and Privacy: (202) 942-0090
http://www.sec.gov/

The main SEC Web page contains extensive information about the SEC, enforcement procedures related to potential violations of the securities laws, copies of all major securities laws (including the Securities and Exchange Act of 1934 and the Sarbanes-Oxley Act of 2002). The site is divided into the following general sections: information about the SEC, copies of forms filed with the SEC and various company filings, regulatory actions taken by the SEC, investor information, and information about securities litigation conducted by the SEC.

Stanford University School of Law
Securities Class Action Clearinghouse
http://www.securities.Stanford.edu

The Securities Clearinghouse Web site contains extensive information concerning litigation under the Private Securities Litigation Reform Act of 1995, including copies of court filings and legal documents related to the prosecution, defense, and settlement of securities fraud litigation.

U.S. Department of Justice
Freedom of Information Act Homepage
http://www.usdoj.gov/04foia/

The Department of Justice publishes a comprehensive Web page on the Freedom of Information Act (FOIA). It lists FOIA contact personnel at every federal agency and provides detailed information on filing FOIA requests. It contains links to various publications relevant to the FOIA, including the Department of Justice's comprehensive guide on FOIA law and procedures, an overview of the Privacy Act, and the Citizens Guide to the FOIA.

U.S. Department of Labor
Occupational Safety and Health Administration (OSHA)
200 Constitution Avenue, NW
Washington, DC 20210
http://www.osha.gov/

The worker's page of the OSHA Web site contains information regarding worker complaints; worker and employer rights and responsibilities; problems in the workplace; and worker resources. A list of laws administered by OSHA that protect whistleblowers and links to other government sites are also available. OSHA has investigatory authority over a number of federal whistleblower laws, including the environmental, nuclear, and transportation whistleblower laws. All Sarbanes-Oxley whistleblower complaints must be initially filed with OSHA.

U.S. Department of Labor
Office of Administrative Law Judges (OALJ)
800 K Street, NW, Suite 400N
Washington, DC 20210
http://www.oalj.dol.gov/

The OALJ conducts administrative adjudications under numerous federal whistleblower laws, including the corporate, airline, environmental, nuclear, and transportation whistleblower law. This site contains copies of most DOL rulings on whistleblower cases, copies of various administrative procedures, a periodic newsletter highlighting recent DOL whistleblower decisions, and various indexes and outlines of DOL whistleblower case law. It also contains links to other government whistleblower-related Web sites and law libraries. The OALJ conducts the administrative adjudication of SOX whistleblower cases. SOX decisions are published on the OALJ Web site.

U.S. Office of Special Counsel
1730 M Street, NW, Suite 201
Washington, DC 20036-4505
http://www.osc.gov/

The Web site for the Office of Special Counsel (OSC) offers information relevant to federal employee whistleblowers, including a description of prohibited personnel practices, an explanation of the federal Whistleblower Protection Act, and the process by which current and former government employees may make disclosures regarding alleged violations of law and/or abuses of authority. Additionally, the site contains the OSC Form 11, which is the required form federal employees must use to file discrimination claims with OSC under the Whistleblower Protection Act.

Table of Cases

FEDERAL AND STATE JUDICIAL DECISIONS

DEPARTMENT OF LABOR
WHISTLEBLOWER CASES

[DOL cases are not commercially published. They are available free of charge online and may be accessed from the following Web sites: www.whistleblowers.org/html/sarbanes-oxley.html or http:// OALJ.dol.gov/.]

Index

About the Authors

STEPHEN M. KOHN is a nationally recognized expert on whistle-blower law. A partner in the Washington, D.C., law firm of Kohn, Kohn & Colapinto, P.C., and a member of the Board of Directors of the National Whistleblower Center, he is the author of several books on whistleblowing, including *Concepts and Procedures in Whistleblower Law* (Quorum, 2000).

MICHAEL D. KOHN is a partner in Kohn, Kohn & Colapinto, P.C., and a member of the National Whistleblower Center. A specialist in whistleblowing law, he is co-author, with Stephen M. Kohn, of the *Labor Lawyer's Guide to the Rights and Responsibilities of Employee Whistleblowers* (Quorum, 1988).

DAVID K. COLAPINTO is a partner in Kohn, Kohn & Colapinto, P.C., and a member of the National Whistleblower Center. He has represented numerous whistleblowers before the U.S. Department of Labor and the U.S. Nuclear Regulatory Commission.